Cloud Computing Unlocked

Concepts, Architectures, and Real-World Applications

Mr. Nirav Shukla

Mr. Kunal Pandya

Title: *Cloud Computing Unlocked*
Subtitle: *Concepts, Architectures, and Real-World Applications*

Authors:
Mr. Nirav Sureshchandra Shukla
Mr. Kunal Dineshbhai Pandya

ISBN: 978-93-5525-289-0

About Author(s)

Nirav Sureshchandra Shukla is an academician and researcher with a strong focus on Cloud Computing and emerging computing paradigms. With extensive experience in teaching computer science and information technology subjects at the undergraduate level, he has consistently worked to bridge the gap between theoretical foundations and practical implementation. His academic interests include cloud computing architectures, distributed systems, virtualization, machine learning applications, and modern computing infrastructures. His teaching methodology emphasizes clarity, real-world examples, and hands-on learning, making advanced topics accessible to beginners. He regularly engages in academic workshops, faculty development programs, and technical training sessions to stay aligned with rapidly evolving cloud technologies. Through this book on Cloud Computing, the author aims to provide a structured, learner- centric resource that explains cloud concepts, service models, deployment strategies, security considerations and real-world applications in a simple and systematic manner. His goal is to empower students, educators and professionals with the knowledge required to understand, adopt and effectively utilize cloud computing in academic and industry environments.

Contact: +91 9328931250

Email: nirav2008@gmail.com

Kunal Pandya is a researcher, author, and Assistant Professor at Sardar Vallabhbhai Global University, specializing in Artificial Intelligence, Machine Learning, Deep Learning, and Digital Media Forensics. His academic and research work is deeply focused on DeepFake image and video detection, Vision Transformers (ViTs), and emerging quantum-inspired detection mechanisms for next-generation multimedia forensics. With strong expertise in Python development, Kunal actively designs and implements AI-driven frameworks using modern ML and DL architectures for multimedia authenticity verification. His work integrates computer vision, neural networks, and transformer-based models to address real-world challenges in digital media manipulation and integrity. He has contributed to multiple research studies, systematic literature reviews, and scholarly publications in the domain of DeepFake forensics, emphasizing robust, explainable, and ethical AI solutions.

Beyond research, Kunal Pandya is passionate about science communication, mentoring young scholars, and academic curriculum development. As an educator, he focuses on bridging theory with practical implementation, guiding students in Python programming, deep learning workflows, and responsible AI practices. His broader interests lie in AI ethics, media integrity, and the societal impact of intelligent systems, exploring how trustworthy AI can shape a more transparent and reliable digital world.

Contact:
Email: akkipandya2580@gmail.com
LinkedIn: linkedin.com/in/thekunalpandya
ORCID: 0009-0007-5859-6547

Table of Content

Abstract

This comprehensive technical series explores the paradigm shift from traditional localized computing to the global, elastic utility model of Cloud Computing. The narrative begins by grounding the cloud in the NIST framework, identifying its five essential characteristics, and tracing its lineage from 1960s mainframes through distributed grid systems. At its core, the series provides a rigorous deep dive into virtualization—the fundamental engine of the cloud—analyzing hypervisor taxonomy, CPU privilege rings, and memory management through the lens of both theory and industry-standard practices like VMware.

Moving up the stack, the series dissects the SPI (SaaS, PaaS, IaaS) delivery models and the shifting management boundaries within the Shared Responsibility Model. It further categorizes the deployment landscape into Public, Private, Hybrid, and Community clouds, while demystifying the physical engineering of hyper-scale data centers and the economic transition from CAPEX to OPEX. The study culminates in an analysis of the "Big Three" commercial platforms (AWS, Azure, GCP) and open-source ecosystems like Hadoop and OpenStack. Finally, the series addresses the "Road Ahead," evaluating the critical barriers of Zero Trust security and Data Sovereignty alongside the emerging frontiers of Serverless architectures, Edge Computing, and Quantum Cloud. Ultimately, this work frames the cloud not merely as a technology, but as the invisible, ubiquitous infrastructure of modern digital civilization.

Part – I

The Genesis of Cloud Computing

Chapter – 1

The Vision and Evolution of the Cloud

This chapter establishes the fundamental definition of cloud computing based on the NIST framework. It explores the transition from traditional on-premises computing to the "utility" model, emphasizing the five essential characteristics: on-demand self-service, broad network access, resource pooling, rapid elasticity, and measured service.

1. Defining the Cloud: NIST Definitions and Industry Perspectives

The concept of cloud computing is often shrouded in marketing terminology, yet at its core, it represents a fundamental shift in how computational power is generated and consumed. To establish a rigorous academic baseline, we look to the National Institute of Standards and Technology (NIST), which provides the definitive framework for what constitutes a "cloud" system. NIST defines cloud computing as a model for enabling ubiquitous, convenient, on-demand network access to a shared pool of configurable computing resources. These resources—which include networks, servers, storage, applications, and services—can be rapidly provisioned and released with minimal management effort or service provider interaction. This definition is not merely a description of technology but a set of criteria that distinguishes cloud computing from traditional hosting or simple outsourcing.

According to the NIST framework, five essential characteristics must be present for a service to be truly classified as "Cloud." The first is **On-demand Self-service**, which implies that a consumer can unilaterally provision computing capabilities, such as server time and network storage, as needed automatically without requiring human interaction with each service provider. This removes the traditional bottleneck of human-led procurement processes, transforming infrastructure into code. The second characteristic is **Broad Network Access**, ensuring that capabilities are available over the network and accessed through standard mechanisms that promote use by heterogeneous thin or thick client platforms, such as mobile phones, tablets, laptops, and workstations. This universal availability is what gives the cloud its "cloud-like" quality, where the physical location of the user and the hardware becomes irrelevant.

Furthermore, NIST emphasizes **Resource Pooling**. The provider's computing resources are pooled to serve multiple consumers using a multi-tenant model, with different physical and virtual resources dynamically assigned and reassigned according to consumer demand. There is a sense of location independence in that the customer generally has no control or knowledge over the exact location of the provided resources but may be able to specify location at a higher level of abstraction (e.g., country, state, or datacenter). This leads directly to the fourth characteristic: **Rapid Elasticity**. Capabilities can be elastically provisioned and released, in some cases automatically, to scale rapidly outward and inward commensurate with demand. To the consumer, the capabilities available for provisioning often appear to be unlimited and can be appropriated in any quantity at any time. Finally, the **Measured Service** characteristic ensures that cloud systems automatically control and optimize resource use by leveraging a metering capability at some level of abstraction appropriate to the type of service. Resource usage can be monitored, controlled, and reported, providing transparency for both the provider and consumer of the utilized service.

Beyond the technical rigor of NIST, industry perspectives provide a more pragmatic, value-oriented view of the cloud. From a business standpoint, the cloud is viewed primarily as a transition from Capital Expenditure (CapEx) to Operational Expenditure (OpEx). In the traditional IT model, a company had to forecast its peak demand years in advance and invest millions in hardware that would often sit idle during off-peak hours. The industry perspective of the cloud is one of "Economic Agility," where the cost of failure is lowered because resources can be decommissioned as quickly as they were hired. This "pay-as-you-go" or "utility" model is frequently compared to the electrical grid; just as we do not own power plants but pay for the kilowatts we consume, modern enterprises do not wish to own "server plants" but rather pay for the compute cycles they consume. This shift allows organizations to focus on their core competencies—developing software or selling products—rather than the "undifferentiated heavy lifting" of managing data centers.

2. The Historical Journey: From Mainframes to Distributed Systems

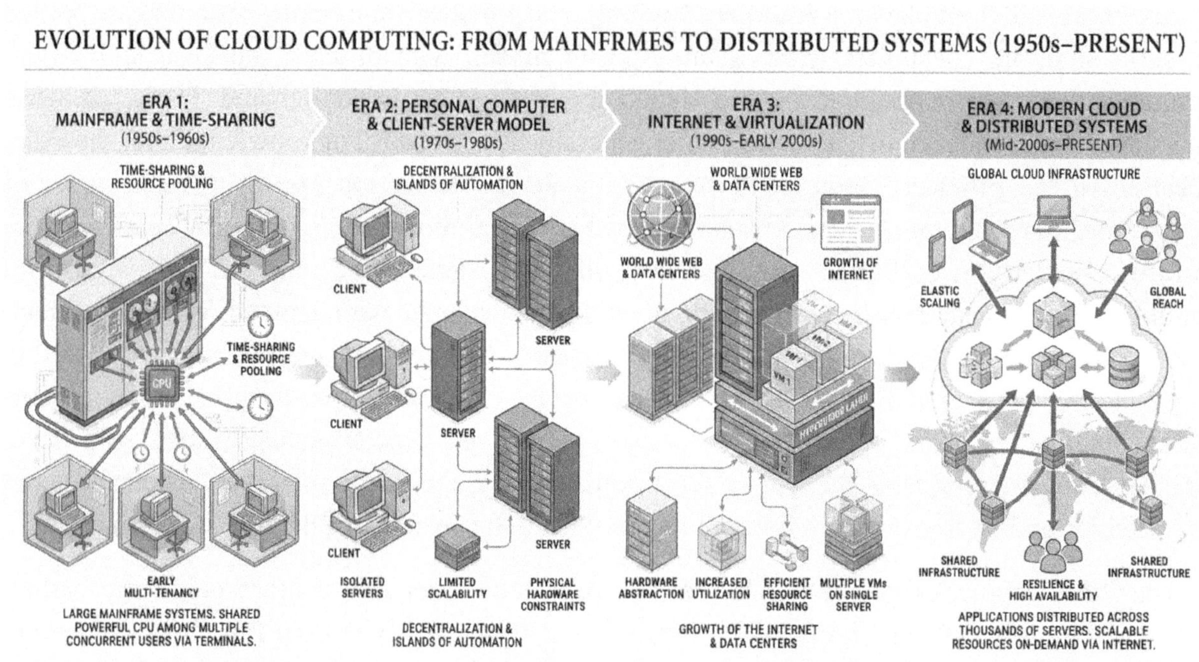

The evolution of cloud computing is not a story of a single invention, but rather a decades-long convergence of several distinct technological paths. To understand where we are, we must trace the lineage back to the 1950s and 60s, the era of the **Mainframe**. During this period, computers were massive, room-sized monoliths like the IBM 700/7000 series. Because these machines were prohibitively expensive, the concept of "Time-Sharing" was developed. Researchers realized that a single CPU was often faster than the human ability to interact with it. By allowing multiple users to connect to a single mainframe via "dumb terminals," the system could rotate through user requests so quickly that each user felt they had the machine's full attention. This was the first primitive ancestor of the cloud's "resource pooling" and "multi-tenancy" concepts.

As we moved into the 1970s and 80s, the paradigm shifted with the advent of the Personal Computer (PC). This era was characterized by a move toward decentralization. The "Client-Server" model emerged as the dominant architecture. In this setup, individual PCs (clients) performed some processing locally while requesting data or specialized services from more powerful central computers (servers). While this empowered individuals and small businesses, it created "islands of automation." Each server was a physical silo; if a company's web server reached its maximum capacity, the only solution was to physically purchase, ship, and install a new machine. This era highlighted the limitations of physical hardware—latency in procurement, lack of flexibility, and the high cost of maintenance.

The 1990s brought the "Inter-networking" revolution, which served as the essential plumbing for the future cloud. As the World Wide Web grew, the demand for high-speed connectivity and reliable hosting increased. This gave rise to Application Service Providers (ASPs), who attempted to host applications for businesses over the early internet. However, these attempts largely failed to scale because the underlying technology—Virtualization—was not yet mature. The breakthrough came in the late 90s and early 2000s when companies like VMware popularized the hypervisor. Virtualization allowed a single physical server to be partitioned into multiple "Virtual Machines" (VMs), each running its own operating system. This meant that hardware could finally be abstracted from software. A physical server that was only 10% utilized could now host ten different virtual servers, each serving a different purpose or client, vastly increasing efficiency and laying the groundwork for the modern data center.

The final leap toward the contemporary cloud occurred in the mid-2000s, driven by the needs of massive consumer web platforms. Companies like Amazon, Google, and Microsoft found themselves managing unprecedented scales of data and traffic. Amazon, in particular, realized that the internal infrastructure they built to handle the massive spikes of "Black Friday" shopping sat idle for most of the year. By developing a way to "rent out" this excess capacity to the public, Amazon Web Services (AWS) was born in 2006. This turned the historical journey full circle: we returned to the shared-resource model of the mainframe era, but with the global reach of the internet and the flexibility of virtualization. This "Distributed Systems" approach meant that a single application was no longer tied to a single machine; it lived across thousands of servers globally, providing a level of resilience and scale that was previously unimaginable.

3. The Role of Web 2.0 and the Shift Toward "Everything as a Service"

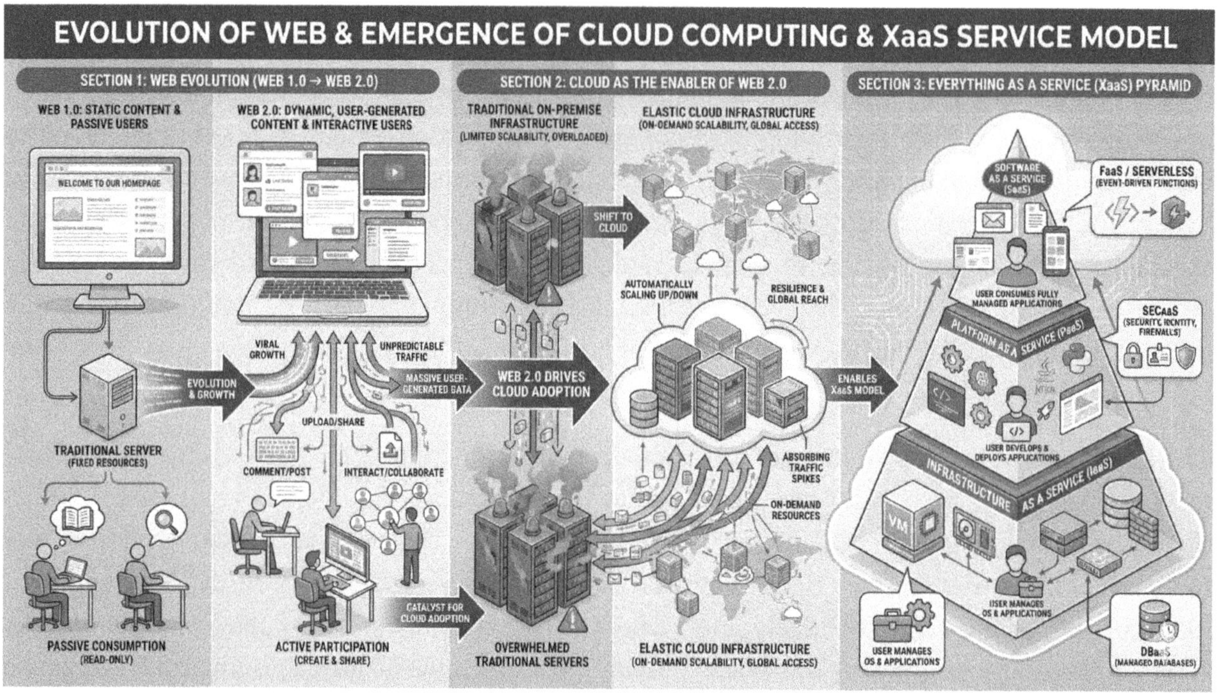

The transition from the early internet to the modern digital landscape is defined by the rise of Web 2.0. While Web 1.0 was primarily "read-only"—consisting of static pages where users were passive consumers of information—Web 2.0 transformed the internet into a "participatory" medium. This era was defined by social media, blogs, wikis, and video-sharing platforms where users became the primary creators of content. This explosion of user-generated data placed an enormous strain on traditional IT infrastructure. A platform like YouTube or Facebook could not predict how many millions of photos or videos would be uploaded in a single day. The static, siloed server models of the past simply could not handle this level of unpredictability and scale. Consequently, Web 2.0 acted as the primary catalyst for cloud adoption; the cloud provided the only infrastructure capable of supporting the "viral" growth patterns of the modern web.

As Web 2.0 matured, it fundamentally changed user expectations regarding software. Users no longer wanted to install bulky applications from physical discs or manage complex update cycles. They wanted "instant-on" access from any device. This demand led to the "Service-Oriented Architecture" (SOA), where software is built as a collection of modular services that communicate over a network. This modularity paved the way for the "Everything as a Service" (XaaS) revolution. XaaS is a collective term for the delivery of anything as a service. It recognizes that in a connected world, the "product" is no longer the asset itself, but the access to the asset's utility.

The XaaS model is traditionally categorized into three primary layers, often visualized as a pyramid. At the base is **Infrastructure as a Service (IaaS)**. In this model, the provider offers the fundamental building blocks of computing: virtual servers, storage, and networking. The customer does not manage the underlying physical hardware but is responsible for the operating system, middleware, and applications. This provides the highest level of control and flexibility, making it ideal for migrating existing legacy workloads to the cloud. IaaS allows a company to essentially "rent" a data center's capabilities without the burden of physical ownership.

The middle layer is **Platform as a Service (PaaS)**. Here, the provider offers a more managed environment that includes the operating system, runtime libraries, and development tools. The customer only manages the applications they build and the data they generate. PaaS is designed to accelerate the development cycle; developers can write code and deploy it instantly without worrying about configuring servers, patching operating systems, or managing load balancers. It represents a shift from "managing infrastructure" to "managing applications." This layer has become the breeding ground for the "Cloud Native" movement, where apps are designed specifically to take advantage of cloud elasticity.

At the top of the pyramid is **Software as a Service (SaaS)**. This is the most familiar model to the average user. In SaaS, the provider manages the entire stack, from the hardware up to the user interface. The consumer simply accesses the application through a web browser or mobile app. Examples like Gmail, Salesforce, and Microsoft 365 illustrate this model. SaaS eliminates the need for local installation, manual updates, and compatibility troubleshooting. It turns software into a continuous utility, where the provider is responsible for security, availability, and performance, while the user focuses solely on the utility the software provides.

The "Everything" in XaaS continues to expand into more specialized domains. We now see **Database as a Service (DBaaS)**, where the complexities of scaling and backing up a database are handled by the provider; **Security as a Service (SECaaS)**, where enterprise-grade firewalls and identity management are outsourced to cloud specialists; and even **Function as a Service (FaaS)**, also known as Serverless computing. In FaaS, the abstraction is taken to its logical extreme: the developer provides only a single piece of code (a function), and the cloud provider manages the execution, scaling, and billing for that specific function only when it is triggered. This "Everything as a Service" shift is more than just a delivery mechanism; it is a total reimagining of the digital economy. It enables a world where a two-person startup can have the same global reach and computational power as a Fortune 500 company, simply by "subscribing" to the necessary visions of the cloud.

4. The Vision: Convergence and the Future of Cloud Computing

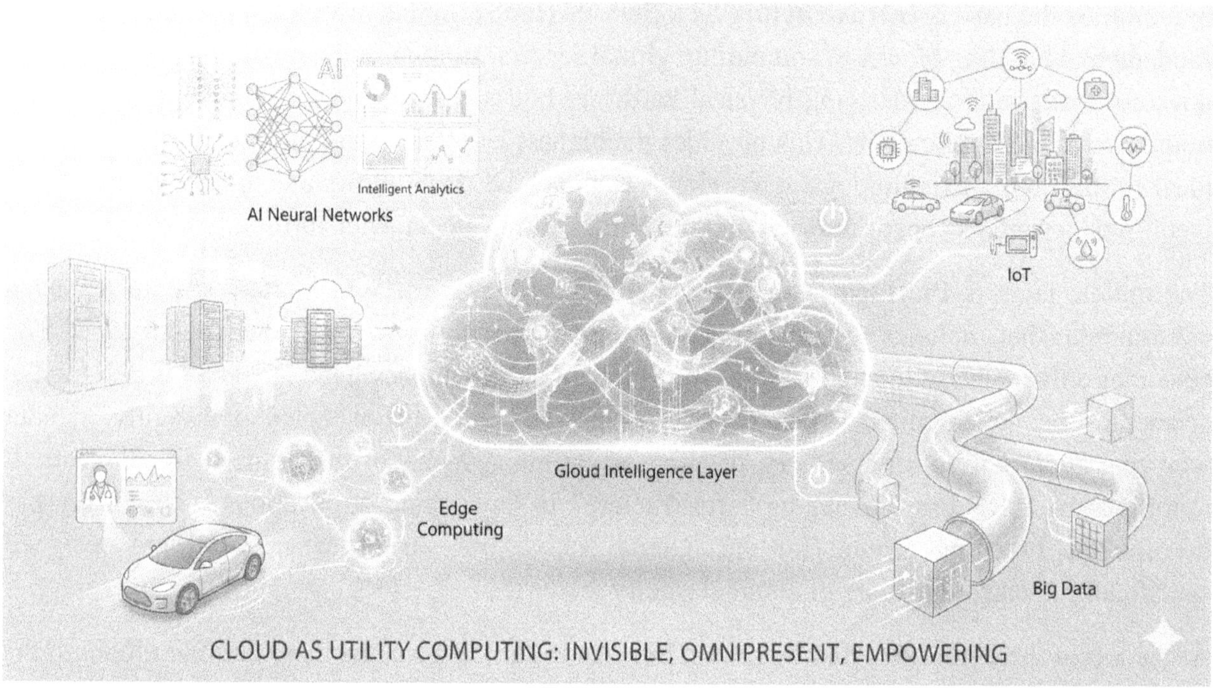

The ultimate vision of cloud computing is the realization of "Utility Computing"—a concept first proposed by John McCarthy in the 1960s, who suggested that "computation may someday be organized as a public utility." We are currently living in the fulfillment of that vision. The cloud has moved beyond being a mere storage locker for files to becoming the "nervous system" of the modern world. The convergence of Artificial Intelligence (AI), the Internet of Things (IoT), and Big Data is only possible because of the cloud's ability to process vast amounts of information in real-time.

In this visionary state, the cloud is no longer a destination users "go to"; it is an invisible layer that permeates every aspect of technology. The evolution continues with "Edge Computing," where the cloud's intelligence is pushed closer to the user to reduce latency for applications like autonomous vehicles or remote surgery. As we look back from the mainframe to the distributed systems of today, we see a clear trajectory toward the total abstraction of complexity. The future of the cloud lies in making technology so accessible, so elastic, and so pervasive that the underlying "evolution" becomes invisible, leaving only the "vision" of limitless human creativity supported by an infinite digital foundation.

In conclusion, Chapter 1 has illustrated that Cloud Computing is far more than a technical upgrade. It is a socio-economic revolution born from the necessity of Web 2.0, built upon the ruins of the mainframe era, and codified by the rigorous standards of NIST. It has transformed the IT industry from a hardware-centric discipline into a service-oriented economy. By understanding the Five Essential Characteristics, the Three Service Models, and the historical journey of distributed systems, one gains a comprehensive view of the most significant shift in the history of computing.

Chapter – 2

Foundations of Distributed and Parallel Computing

A historical exploration tracing the lineage of the cloud from 1960s mainframes to client-server architectures and grid computing. It analyzes how the convergence of high-speed networking and distributed algorithms made the modern cloud possible.

1. Eras of Computing: From Centralized to Decentralized

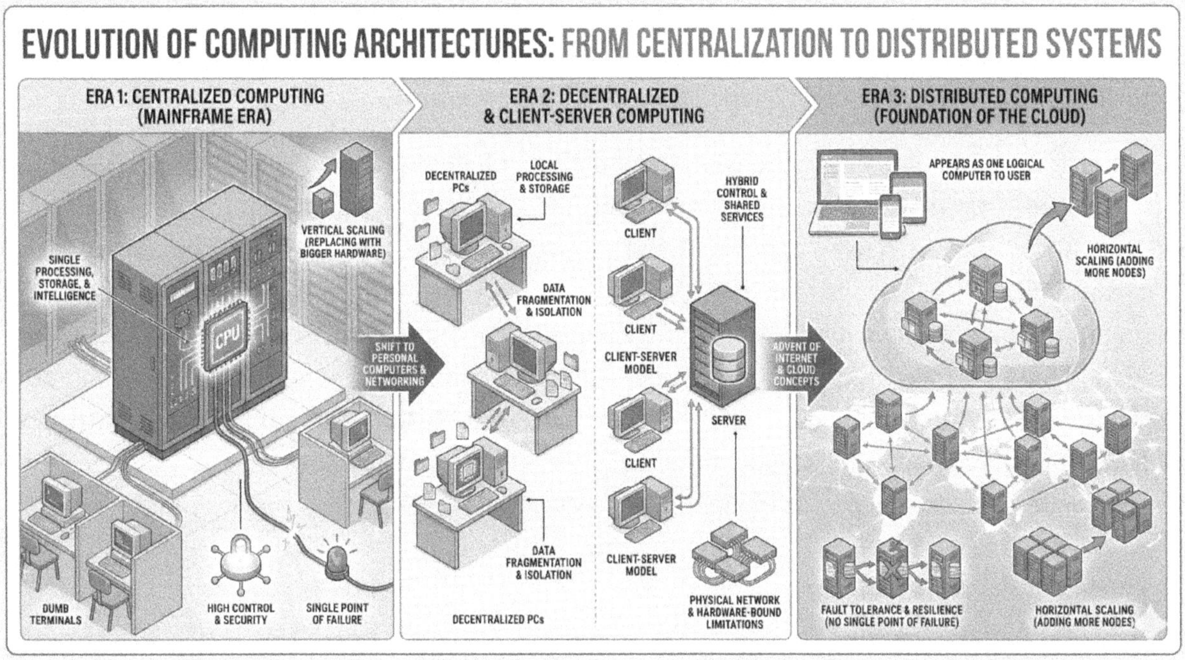

The history of computing is often characterized as a rhythmic oscillation between the poles of centralization and decentralization. To understand modern cloud architecture, one must first appreciate the foundational eras that dictated how data was processed and where control resided. The journey begins with the **Centralized Era**, dominated by the mainframe. In this period, all intelligence, storage, and processing power were contained within a single, massive physical unit. Users interacted with these behemoths through "dumb terminals," which possessed no local processing capability. This model was highly efficient in terms of control and security—since everything happened in one place—but it was plagued by single points of failure and immense costs. If the mainframe went offline, the entire organization's digital life ceased. Furthermore, scaling meant "scaling up" (vertical scaling), which involved replacing the entire machine with a larger, more expensive one, a process that was neither agile nor cost-effective.

As the limitations of the mainframe became apparent, the industry transitioned into the **Decentralized Era**, catalyzed by the invention of the microprocessor and the rise of the Personal Computer (PC). For the first time, computing power was distributed across the desks of individual employees. This era democratized technology but introduced a new set of challenges: fragmentation and management complexity. Data became trapped in local hard drives, leading to version control issues and security vulnerabilities. To bridge the gap between individual empowerment and collective coordination, the **Client-Server Era** emerged. This was a hybrid model where centralized servers handled heavy-duty tasks like database management and email, while decentralized clients (PCs) handled the user interface and local logic. While more flexible than the mainframe, the client-server model still relied on rigid, physical connections and specific hardware configurations that lacked the fluidity required for the modern age.

The current epoch is defined by the **Distributed Era**, which represents a sophisticated synthesis of its predecessors. In a distributed environment, the "computer" is no longer a single box but a vast network of interconnected nodes that work together to appear as a single coherent system to the end-user. This era leverages the best of both worlds: the centralized management and resource pooling of the mainframe with the local agility and geographic diversity of decentralized systems. Distributed computing allows for "horizontal scaling" (scaling out), where capacity is increased simply by adding more low-cost, commodity servers to a cluster. This architectural shift is the fundamental prerequisite for cloud computing, providing the resilience, fault tolerance, and massive scale necessary to power global digital services.

2. Parallel vs. Distributed: Understanding the Core Differences

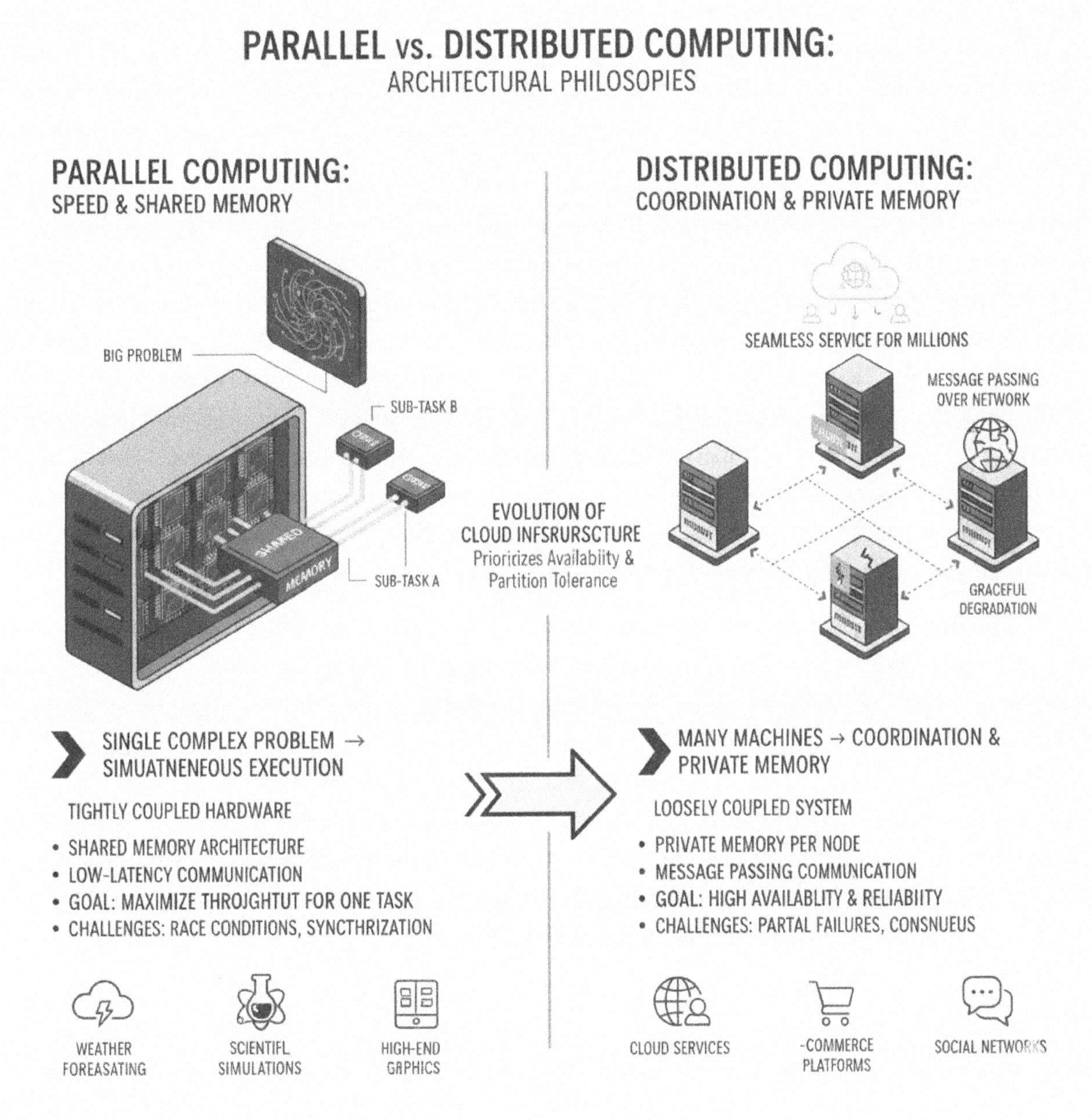

While "parallel" and "distributed" computing are terms often used interchangeably in casual conversation, they represent distinct architectural philosophies and technical implementations. Understanding the nuances between them is critical for any student of cloud infrastructure. **Parallel Computing** is primarily concerned with speed and the simultaneous execution of tasks to solve a single, complex problem. In a parallel system, a large task is broken down into smaller sub-tasks, which are then processed at the exact same time across multiple processors. The defining characteristic of a parallel system is **Shared Memory**. All processors typically reside within the same physical machine or are connected via a very high-speed backplane, allowing them to access a common memory space. This shared access enables extremely low-latency communication between processors, making parallel computing ideal for computationally intensive tasks like weather forecasting, scientific simulations, and high-end graphics rendering.

In contrast, **Distributed Computing** is focused on coordination, resource sharing, and reliability across geographically separated entities. In a distributed system, each processor (or node) has its own **Private Memory**. There is no global shared memory; instead, nodes communicate by passing messages over a network (LAN or WAN). Because these nodes are physically distinct, a distributed system is naturally "loosely coupled." This means that the failure of one node does not necessarily crash the entire system—a concept known as "graceful degradation." While parallel computing asks, "How fast can we solve this one big problem?", distributed computing asks, "How can we coordinate a thousand different machines to provide a seamless service to millions of users?" Distributed systems are the backbone of the cloud because they prioritize availability and partition tolerance over the raw, tightly-coupled speed of parallel clusters.

The distinction also extends to the software level. Parallel algorithms must be carefully designed to avoid "race conditions," where two processors attempt to update the same memory location simultaneously. This requires complex locking mechanisms and synchronization primitives. Distributed systems, however, must deal with "partial failures" and "network partitions." In a distributed environment, a message might be lost, or a node might become unreachable. Software built for distributed systems must incorporate "consensus algorithms" (like Paxos or Raft) to ensure that all nodes eventually agree on the state of the data despite these interruptions. Thus, while parallel computing pushes the limits of hardware physics, distributed computing pushes the limits of algorithmic coordination and network reliability.

3. Hardware Architectures for High-Performance Processing

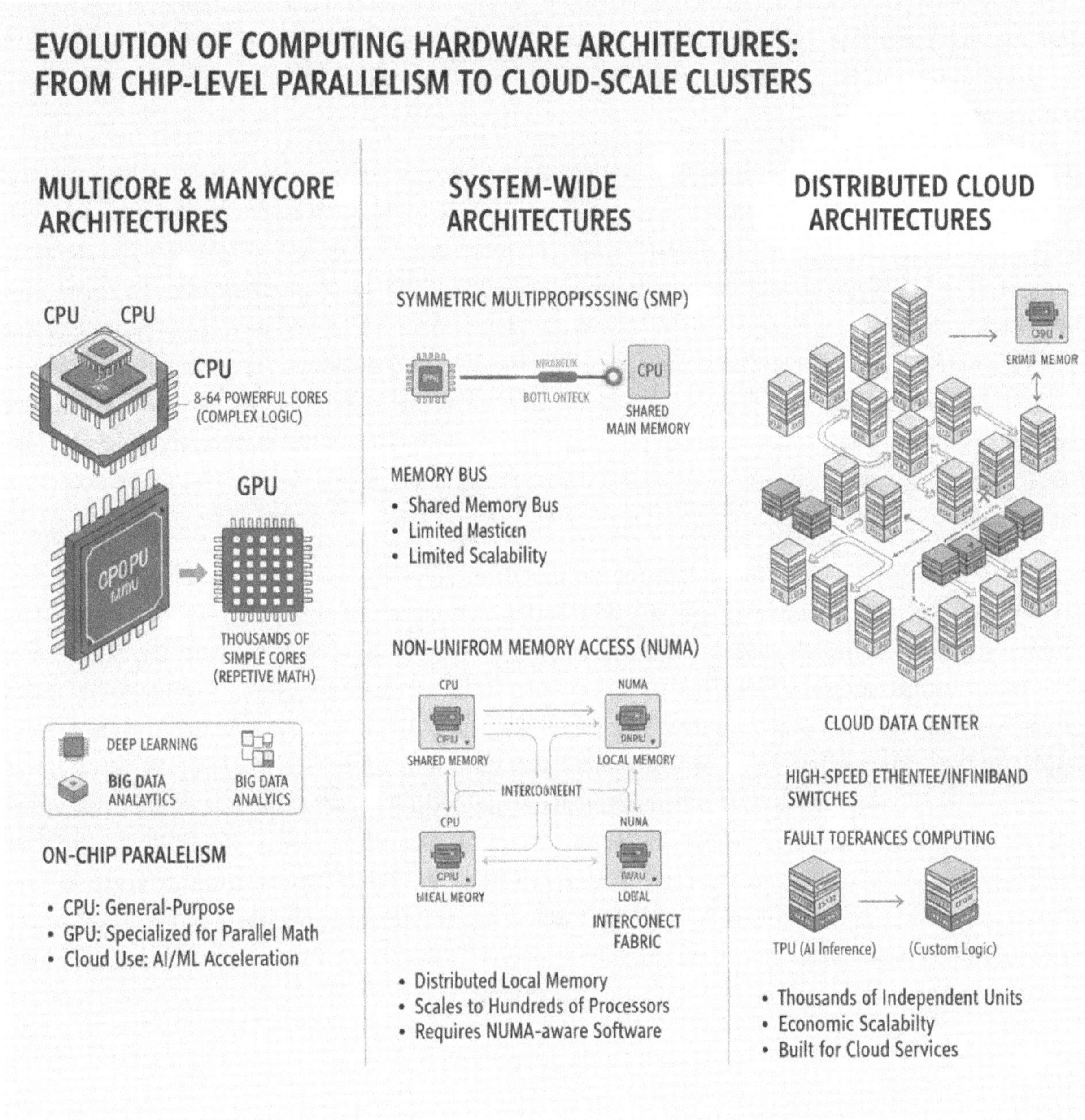

The physical foundation of both parallel and distributed systems lies in specialized hardware architectures designed to move data and execute instructions with maximum efficiency. At the most granular level, we look at **Multicore and Manycore Architectures**. Modern CPUs are no longer single-engine machines; they contain multiple "cores," each capable of executing its own instruction stream. This is a form of "on-chip parallelism." Taking this further, Graphics Processing Units (GPUs) represent a "Manycore" approach. While a standard CPU might have 8 to 64 powerful cores designed for complex logic, a GPU has thousands of smaller, simpler cores designed for repetitive mathematical operations. In the cloud, GPUs have been repurposed for Deep Learning and Big Data analytics, providing massive parallel processing power for matrix operations.

On a system-wide scale, we classify hardware based on how processors interact with memory. **Symmetric Multiprocessing (SMP)** involves multiple identical processors connected to a single, shared main memory. This is the classic parallel architecture. However, SMP faces a "bottleneck" as more processors are added; they all eventually fight for the same memory bus. To solve this, **Non-Uniform Memory Access (NUMA)** was developed. In a NUMA system, each processor has its own local memory but can still access the memory of other processors. Accessing local memory is very fast, while accessing "remote" memory across the interconnect is slower. NUMA allows parallel systems to scale to hundreds of processors by reducing the contention on a single memory bus, though it requires software to be "NUMA-aware" to ensure data is stored close to the processor that needs it.

For distributed systems and the cloud, the dominant architecture is the **Cluster of Commodity Servers**. Unlike the expensive, specialized "Supercomputers" of the past, modern cloud data centers are built using thousands of standard, off-the-shelf servers connected by high-speed Ethernet or InfiniBand switches. This is often referred to as a "Shared-Nothing Architecture." Each server is an independent unit with its own CPU, RAM, and Disk. The "intelligence" of the system resides in the software layer that orchestrates these thousands of units. This hardware strategy is preferred for the cloud because it is economically scalable; if a server fails, it is simply discarded and replaced, rather than requiring the repair of a multi-million dollar monolithic machine. Furthermore, the rise of **Tensor Processing Units (TPUs)** and **Field Programmable Gate Arrays (FPGAs)** in cloud environments represents a move toward "Heterogeneous Computing," where specialized hardware accelerators are mixed with general-purpose CPUs to handle specific cloud workloads like AI inference or real-time video encoding.

4. Inter-process Communication (IPC) and Service-Oriented Architecture (SOA)

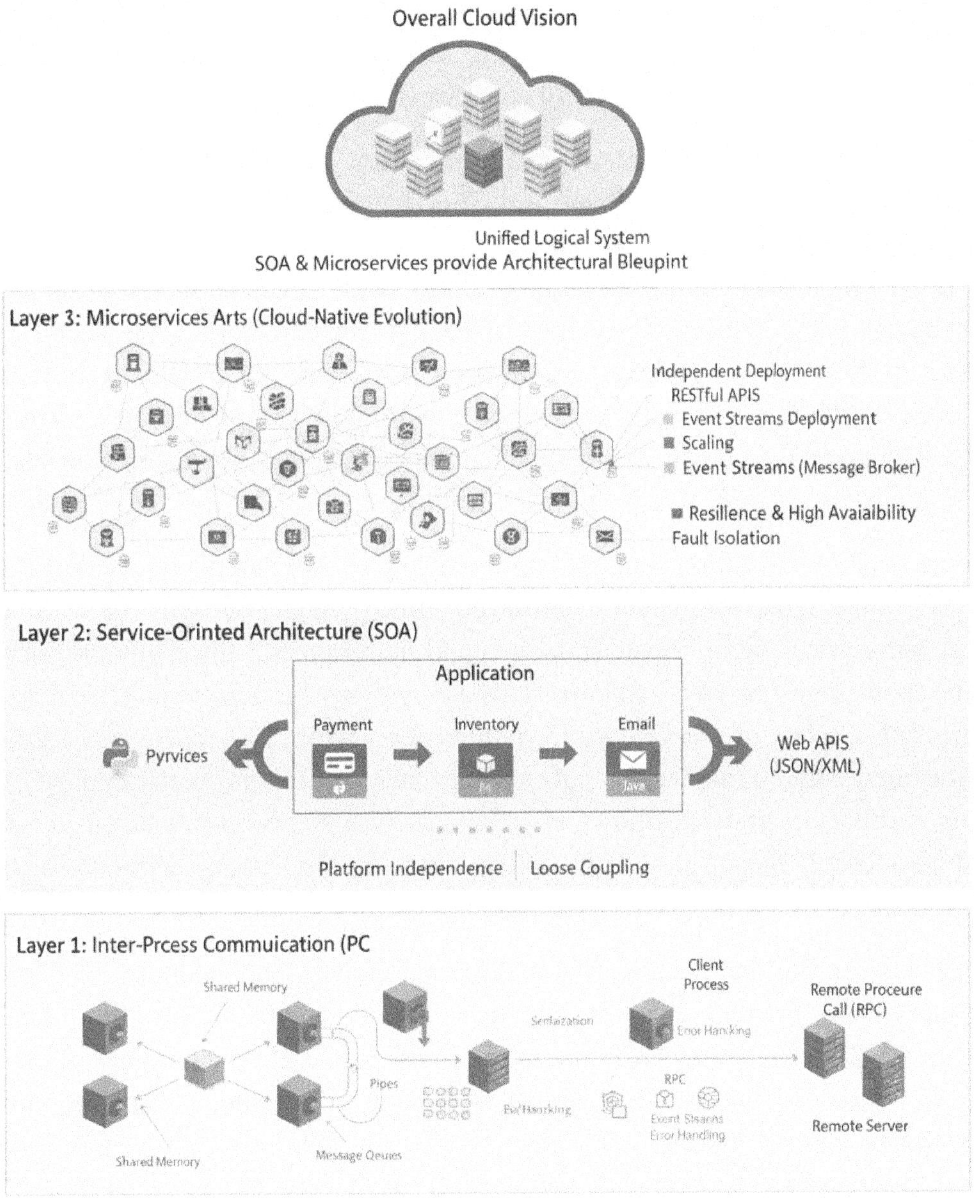

Layer 1: Inter-Prcess Commuication (PC)

For a distributed system to function as a unified whole, its constituent parts must have a reliable way to communicate and coordinate. This brings us to the dual concepts of low-level **Inter-**

process Communication (IPC) and high-level **Service-Oriented Architecture (SOA)**. IPC refers to the mechanisms provided by an operating system or a network protocol to allow different processes to exchange data. In a single-machine (parallel) environment, IPC can occur through "Shared Memory," "Pipes," or "Message Queues." However, in the distributed world of the cloud, the most critical form of IPC is the **Remote Procedure Call (RPC)**. RPC allows a program to execute a function on a different computer as if it were a local function call. The complexity of the network, data serialization (converting objects into a stream of bytes), and error handling is hidden from the developer, making it easier to build complex distributed applications.

As applications grew more complex, simple RPC was not enough to manage the thousands of different functions required by a global platform. This led to the development of **Service-Oriented Architecture (SOA)**. SOA is a design philosophy where an application is built as a collection of "services" that communicate with each other over a network. Each service represents a specific business function (e.g., "Process Payment," "Check Inventory," or "Send Email"). The key characteristic of SOA is that services are **Loosely Coupled** and **Platform Independent**. A payment service written in Java can communicate with an inventory service written in Python, provided they agree on a common communication protocol, usually based on web standards like XML or JSON.

The evolution of SOA in the cloud era has culminated in the **Microservices Architecture**. While traditional SOA often relied on a heavy, centralized "Enterprise Service Bus" (ESB) to coordinate messages, Microservices favor "smart endpoints and dumb pipes." Each microservice is a tiny, independent application that owns its own database and can be deployed, scaled, and updated without affecting the rest of the system. Communication typically happens via **RESTful APIs (Representational State Transfer)** or lightweight message brokers like RabbitMQ or Apache Kafka. This architecture is what allows cloud giants like Netflix or Amazon to update their software thousands of times a day. If the "Recommendations" microservice fails, the "Video Playback" service continues to function, ensuring a resilient user experience.

The synergy between IPC and SOA is what makes the "Cloud Vision" possible. IPC provides the technical "handshake" between machines, while SOA provides the architectural "blueprint" for organizing those handshakes into meaningful business value. Together, they allow a chaotic collection of thousands of distributed servers to behave like a single, elegant, and infinitely scalable computer.

5. Summary and Convergence

Chapter 2 has explored the foundational bedrock upon which cloud computing is built. We have seen how the computing world moved from the rigid centralization of mainframes to the resilient distribution of the modern era. We analyzed the critical trade-offs between the shared-memory speed of parallel computing and the private-memory reliability of distributed systems. We examined the hardware architectures, from NUMA to commodity clusters, that provide the raw power for these systems. Finally, we looked at how IPC and SOA provide the linguistic and structural frameworks that allow distributed components to collaborate.

Part – II

The Enabler – Virtualization

Chapter – 3

Virtualization Theory and Taxonomy

A deep dive into the "engine" of the cloud. This chapter covers the hypervisor's role in the Machine Reference Model, the mechanics of CPU privilege rings, memory management (EPT/NPT), and the taxonomy of Full, Para, and Hardware-Assisted virtualization.

1. Introduction to the Hypervisor and the Machine Reference Model

Virtualization Architecture & Cloud Computing Enabler: Hypervisor Abstraction Layer

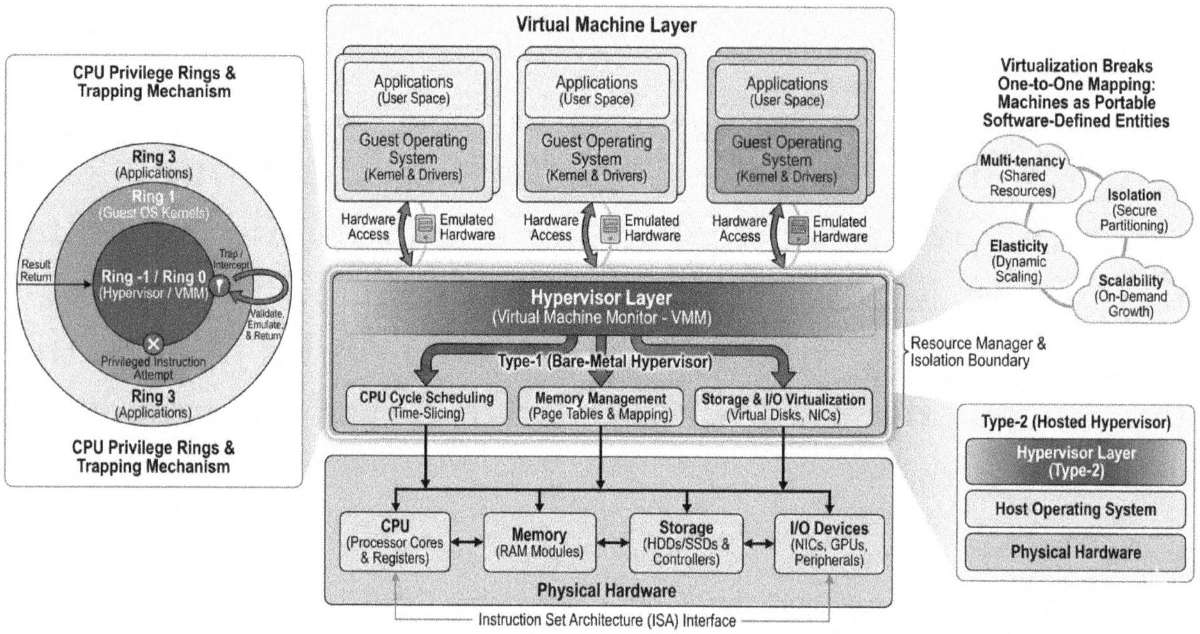

Virtualization is the fundamental technology that enables cloud computing by creating an abstraction layer between physical hardware and the software that runs upon it. This abstraction is not merely a technical convenience; it is the structural cornerstone that allows for the multi-tenancy, elasticity, and scalability that define the cloud era. At the heart of this abstraction lies the **Hypervisor**, also known as the Virtual Machine Monitor (VMM). The hypervisor is a specialized software layer that resides between the physical hardware and the operating systems of the virtual machines. Its primary responsibility is to manage the hardware's resources—such as the CPU, memory, and storage—and distribute them among multiple virtual machines (VMs) in a way that is transparent to the guest software. By doing so, it allows each VM to operate as if it has exclusive access to the underlying hardware, effectively "tricking" the guest operating system into believing it is the sole master of the silicon.

To understand how the hypervisor functions at a deep level, we must examine the **Machine Reference Model**. In a traditional, non-virtualized system, there is a direct and rigid mapping between the hardware, the operating system (OS), and the application. The hardware provides an interface known as the Instruction Set Architecture (ISA). In this legacy model, the OS communicates directly with the ISA, issuing "privileged instructions" to manage memory, handle interrupts, and control I/O devices. However, the introduction of a hypervisor disrupts this direct mapping by inserting a new interface layer. This model is visualized as a sophisticated stack: the physical hardware sits at the base, providing the raw compute cycles. The hypervisor sits directly on top of the hardware (in Type-1 or "bare-metal" virtualization) or on top of a host operating system (in Type-2 or "hosted" virtualization). The guest operating systems then sit on top of the hypervisor, separated from the hardware by a wall of software-defined abstraction.

The hypervisor acts as a "traffic cop" for the CPU. In the x86 architecture, there are four levels of privilege known as **Protection Rings**, ranging from Ring 0 (most privileged) to Ring 3 (least privileged). In a standard system, the OS kernel lives in Ring 0. When virtualizing, the hypervisor occupies Ring 0 (or a special "Ring -1" in hardware-assisted models), while the guest OS is pushed to a less privileged ring, such as Ring 1. Whenever the guest OS tries to execute a sensitive instruction—one that could potentially crash the system or affect other tenants—the hardware triggers a "trap" or "exception." The hypervisor intercepts this trap, validates the request, emulates the expected hardware response, and returns control to the guest. This architectural shift is revolutionary because it breaks the "one-to-one" relationship between software and hardware, turning the "machine" into a portable software definition consisting of configuration files and virtual disk images.

2. Characteristics of Virtualized Environments: Isolation, Consolidation, and Aggregation

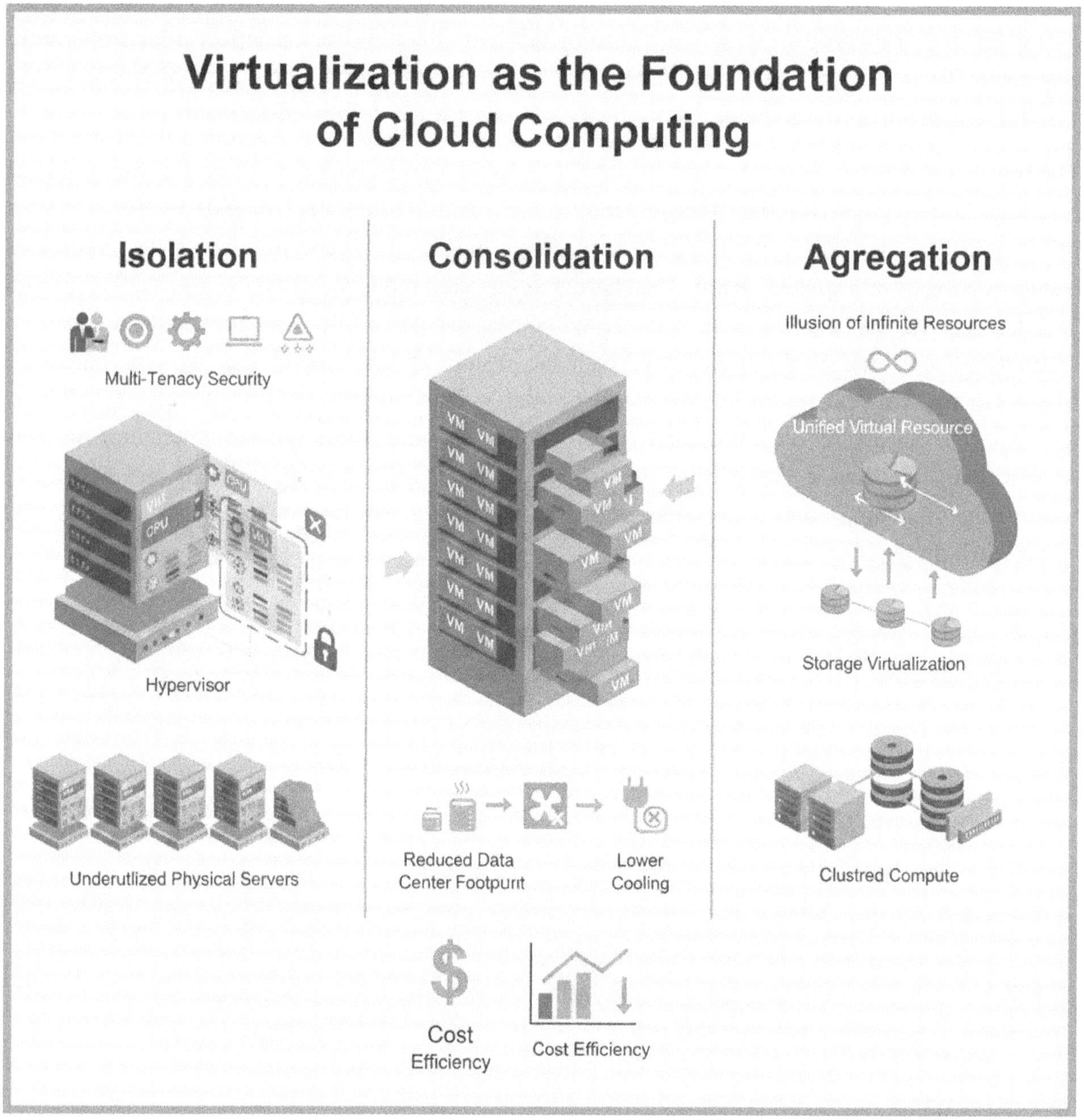

Virtualization is defined by three core characteristics that provide the operational efficiency and security required for cloud computing. These pillars—Isolation, Consolidation, and Aggregation—transform raw hardware into a dynamic, manageable utility.

Isolation is the most critical characteristic from a security and stability perspective. In a virtualized environment, each Virtual Machine is logically separated from every other VM running on the same physical host. Even though they share the same physical CPU and RAM, the hypervisor ensures that one VM cannot access the memory space, storage, or network data of another. This "sandboxing" effect is profound; if one guest operating system suffers a catastrophic failure, a kernel panic, or a malware infection, the other VMs on the same host remain completely unaffected. For cloud providers, this isolation is the prerequisite for multi-tenancy. It allows competitors, such as two rival banks or retail chains, to run their sensitive workloads on the same physical rack in a public cloud without the risk of data leakage. Isolation also extends to resource protection, preventing a "runaway process" in one VM from consuming all the physical CPU and starving the other tenants—a phenomenon often managed through strict resource quotas and scheduling algorithms.

Consolidation refers to the ability to run multiple virtual servers on a single physical server to increase resource utilization. Historically, in the era of physical servers, most machines operated at a staggering 5% to 15% of their total capacity. This was because IT administrators had to "over-provision" hardware to handle occasional peaks in traffic, resulting in massive amounts of wasted energy, floor space, and capital. Virtualization allows organizations to "bin-pack" these underutilized workloads. By hosting dozens or even hundreds of virtual servers on a single powerful physical host, utilization rates can be driven up to 70% or 80%. This consolidation leads to a significant reduction in the "data center footprint," resulting in fewer physical racks, reduced cooling requirements, and lower electricity bills. In the context of the cloud, consolidation is the primary driver of the "economies of scale." It is what allows a provider to offer a virtual server for pennies an hour, as the cost of the underlying hardware is amortized across many users.

Aggregation is the conceptual counter-point to consolidation. While consolidation puts many "small" virtual entities on one "large" physical entity, aggregation allows multiple physical resources to be combined and presented as a single, unified virtual resource. This is often seen in storage virtualization, where a single virtual disk might be backed by fragments of storage spread across ten different physical hard drives or even different storage arrays. Aggregation can also apply to memory and processing power, where high-performance computing (HPC) workloads utilize the combined resources of a cluster to function as a "Super-VM." This characteristic provides the "illusion of infinite resources" mentioned in the NIST definition of the cloud. From the user's perspective, they are interacting with a single, powerful, and seamless entity, while behind the scenes, the hypervisor and management software are aggregating disparate, fragmented physical components to meet that demand. This flexibility ensures that no single physical hardware limitation can prevent a virtual workload from growing.

3. Detailed Taxonomy of Virtualization: Full, Para, and Hardware-Assisted

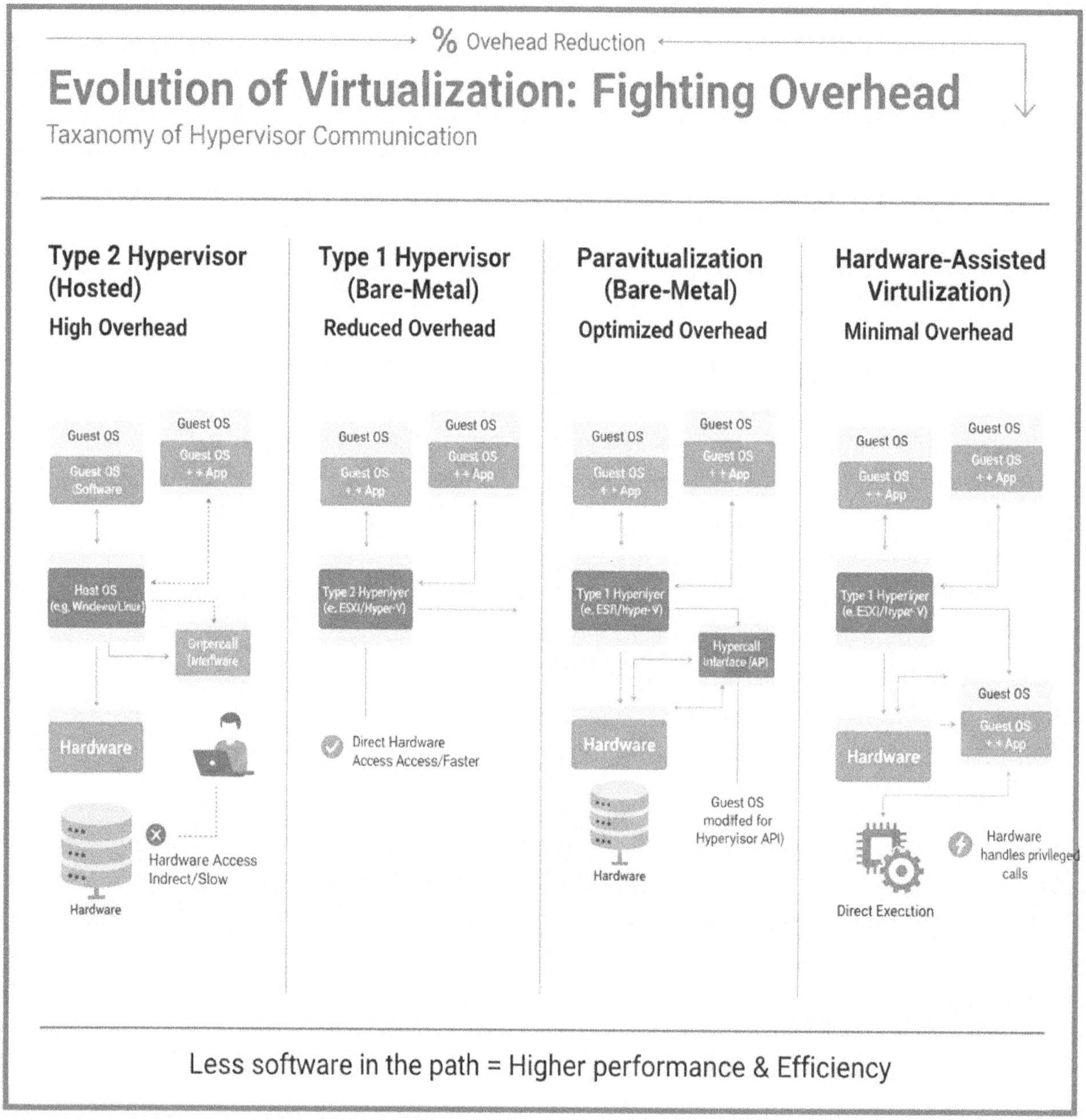

The evolution of virtualization has been a constant battle against "overhead"—the performance cost of having a software layer between the OS and the hardware. This has led to a taxonomy categorized by how the guest OS and hypervisor communicate.

3.1 Full Virtualization

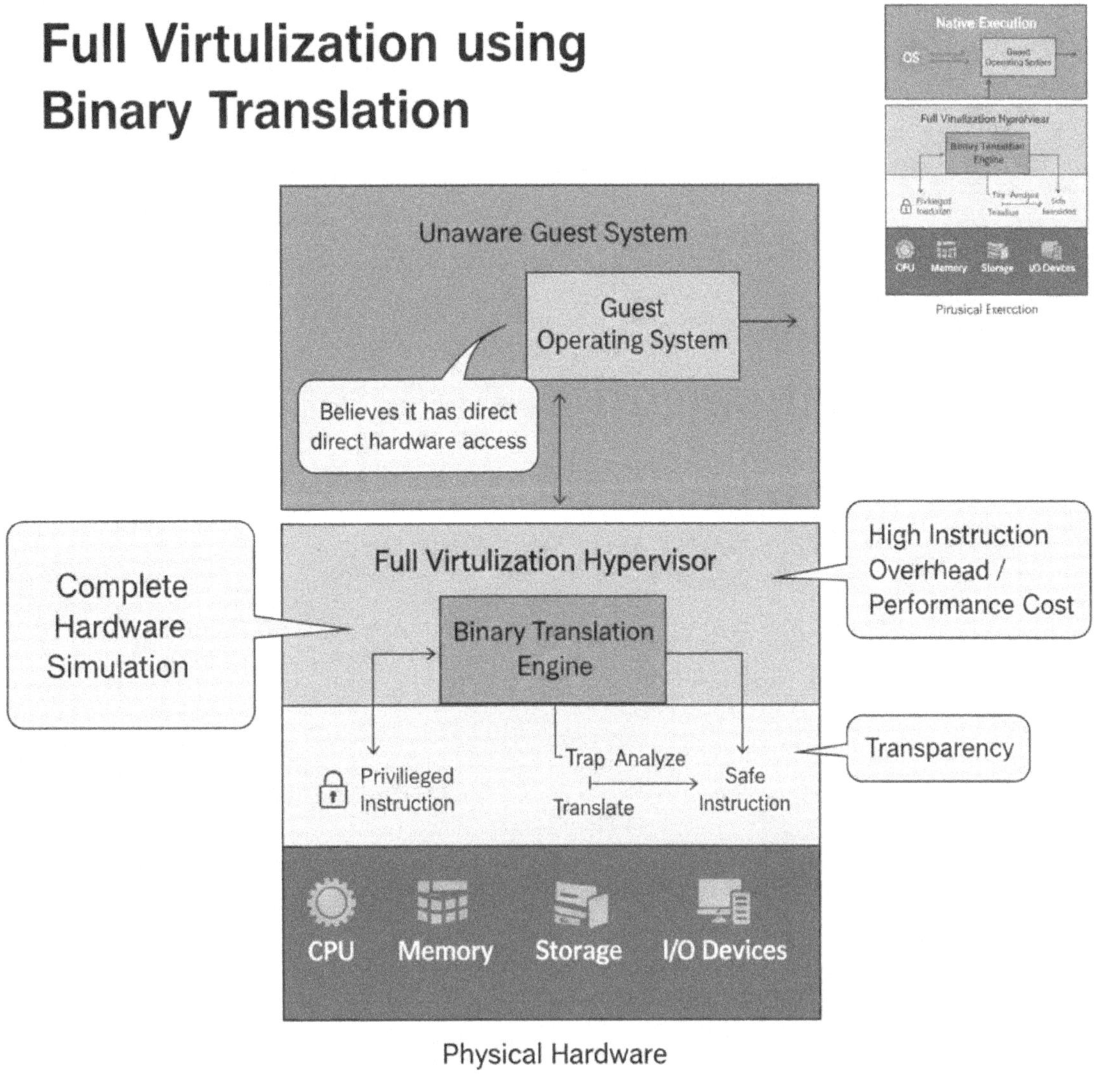

Full Virtualization is the most transparent form of virtualization. In this model, the hypervisor provides a complete and faithful simulation of the underlying hardware. The guest operating system is entirely unaware that it is running in a virtual environment; it believes it is interacting directly with the bare metal. To achieve this, early hypervisors used a technique called **Binary Translation**. When the guest OS issues a privileged instruction, the hypervisor intercepts the instruction in real-time, analyzes the binary code, translates it into a "safe" instruction that the hypervisor can execute, and then performs the action on the physical hardware.

The primary advantage of full virtualization is absolute compatibility. Since no modifications are required to the guest operating system, one can run legacy systems, proprietary software, or any OS for which source code is unavailable (like older versions of Windows). However, the performance cost is high. The constant "trap-and-emulate" cycle for every privileged instruction creates a significant computational tax, often making the system feel slower than a native installation.

3.2 Paravirtualization (PV)

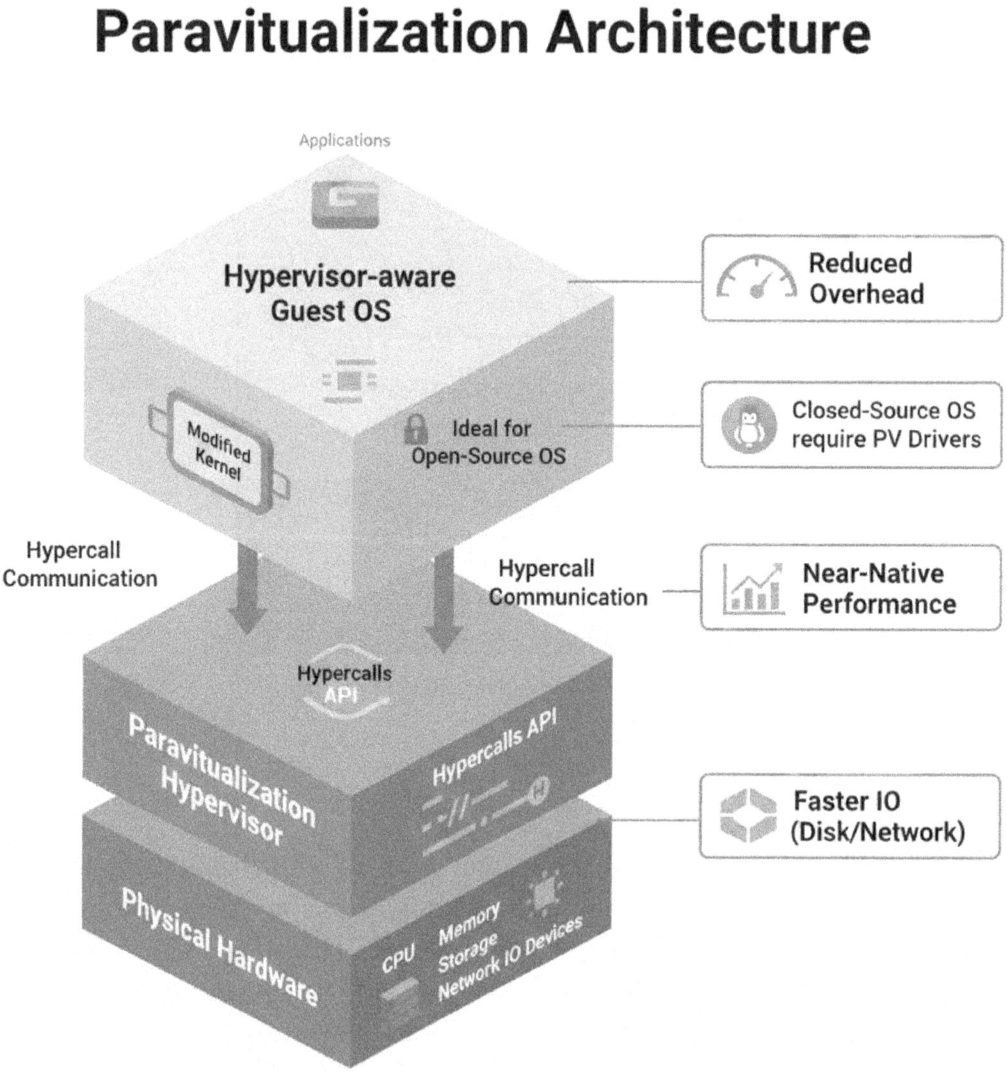

To solve the performance issues of full virtualization, Paravirtualization was developed. In this model, the guest operating system is "aware" that it is running on a hypervisor. The guest OS is modified (or "patched") so that it no longer attempts to execute privileged hardware instructions directly. Instead, it makes a **Hypercall**—a specialized API call that explicitly asks the hypervisor to perform a task on its behalf.

This cooperative model eliminates the need for expensive binary translation and the "trap-and-emulate" cycle. The guest OS essentially says, "I know I am a guest; please write this data to the disk for me." This results in performance that is very close to native speeds, particularly for network and disk I/O. The major downside is the requirement for a modified kernel. This means that open-source operating systems like Linux or BSD are easy to paravirtualize, but closed-source operating systems like Windows require the vendor to provide specialized "paravirtualized drivers" (PV drivers) to achieve similar benefits.

3.3 Hardware-Assisted Virtualization (HVM)

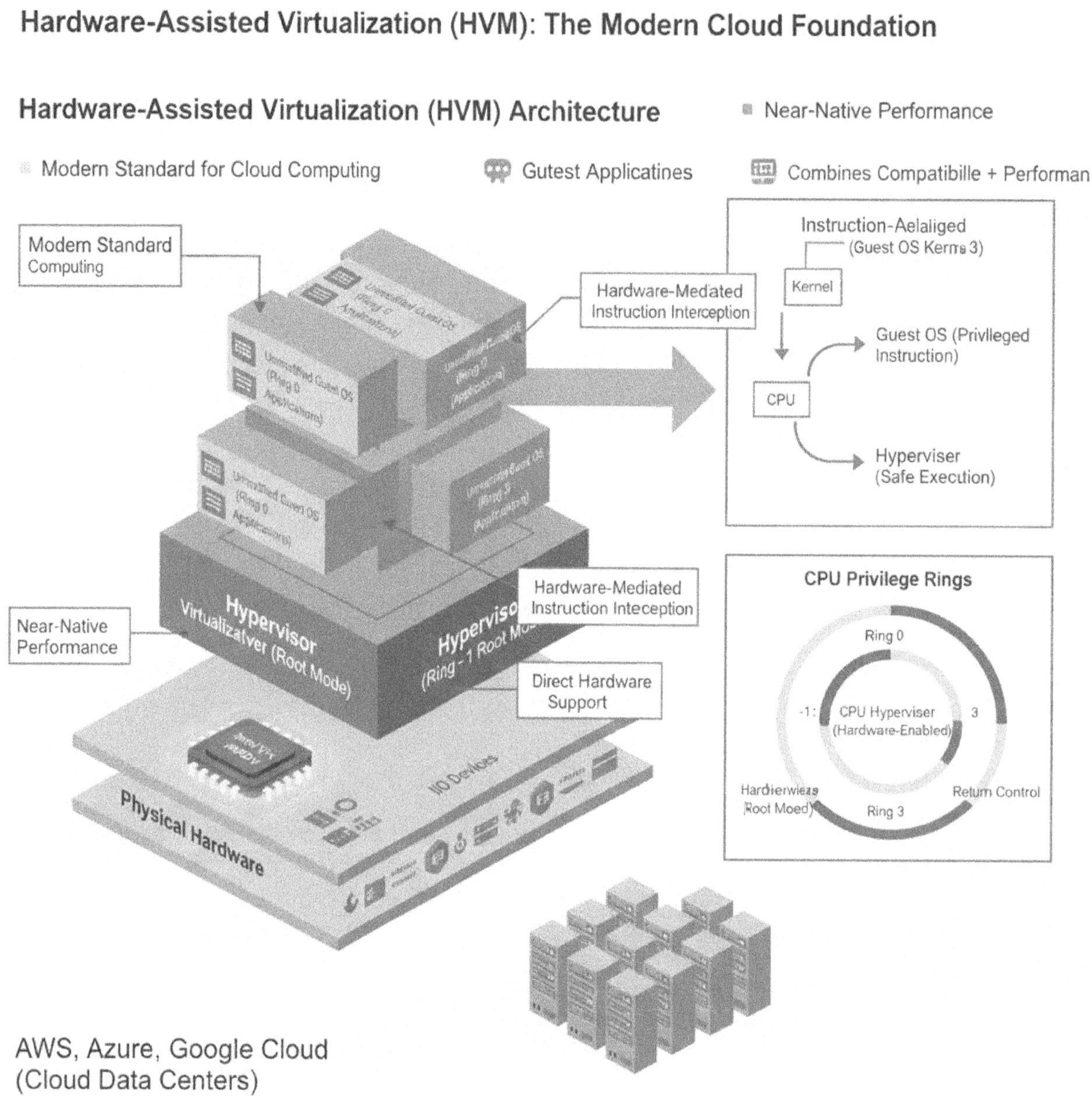

Hardware-Assisted Virtualization represents the modern gold standard. In the mid-2000s, Intel and AMD recognized that virtualization was the future and introduced specialized instructions directly into their silicon (Intel VT-x and AMD-V). These extensions created a new, higher privilege level for the hypervisor, effectively creating a **Ring -1** (often called "Root Mode").

With HVM, the hardware itself takes over the task of intercepting privileged instructions from the guest OS and handing them to the hypervisor. This removes the software overhead of binary translation while allowing unmodified guest operating systems to run at near-native speeds. Modern cloud providers (AWS, Azure, Google Cloud) almost exclusively use hardware-assisted virtualization. It provides the perfect balance: the compatibility of full virtualization with the performance of paravirtualization.

4. Advanced Resource Management: CPU, Memory, and I/O

Virtualization is more than just a CPU trick; it requires the total abstraction of every hardware subsystem.

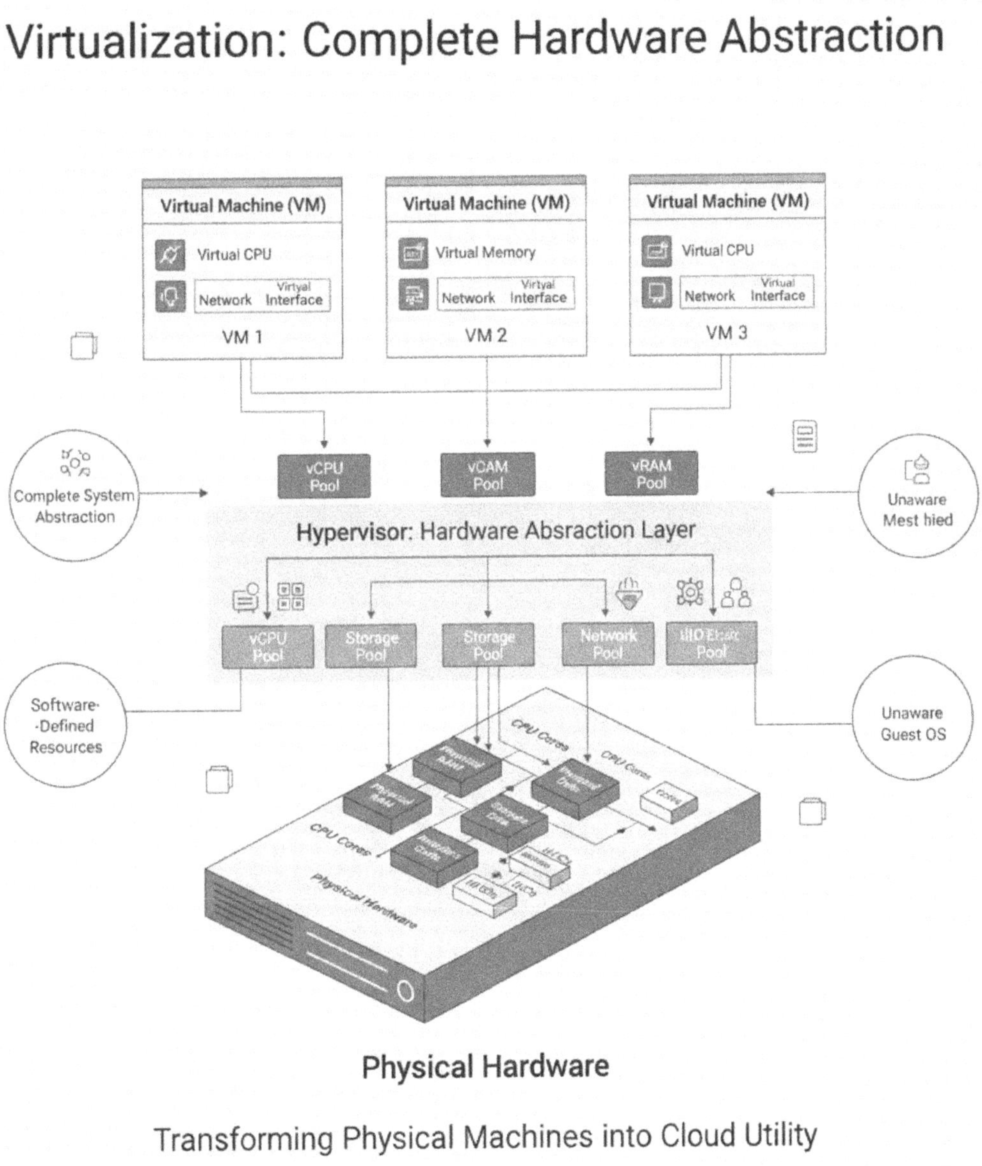

4.1 CPU Scheduling and Overcommitment

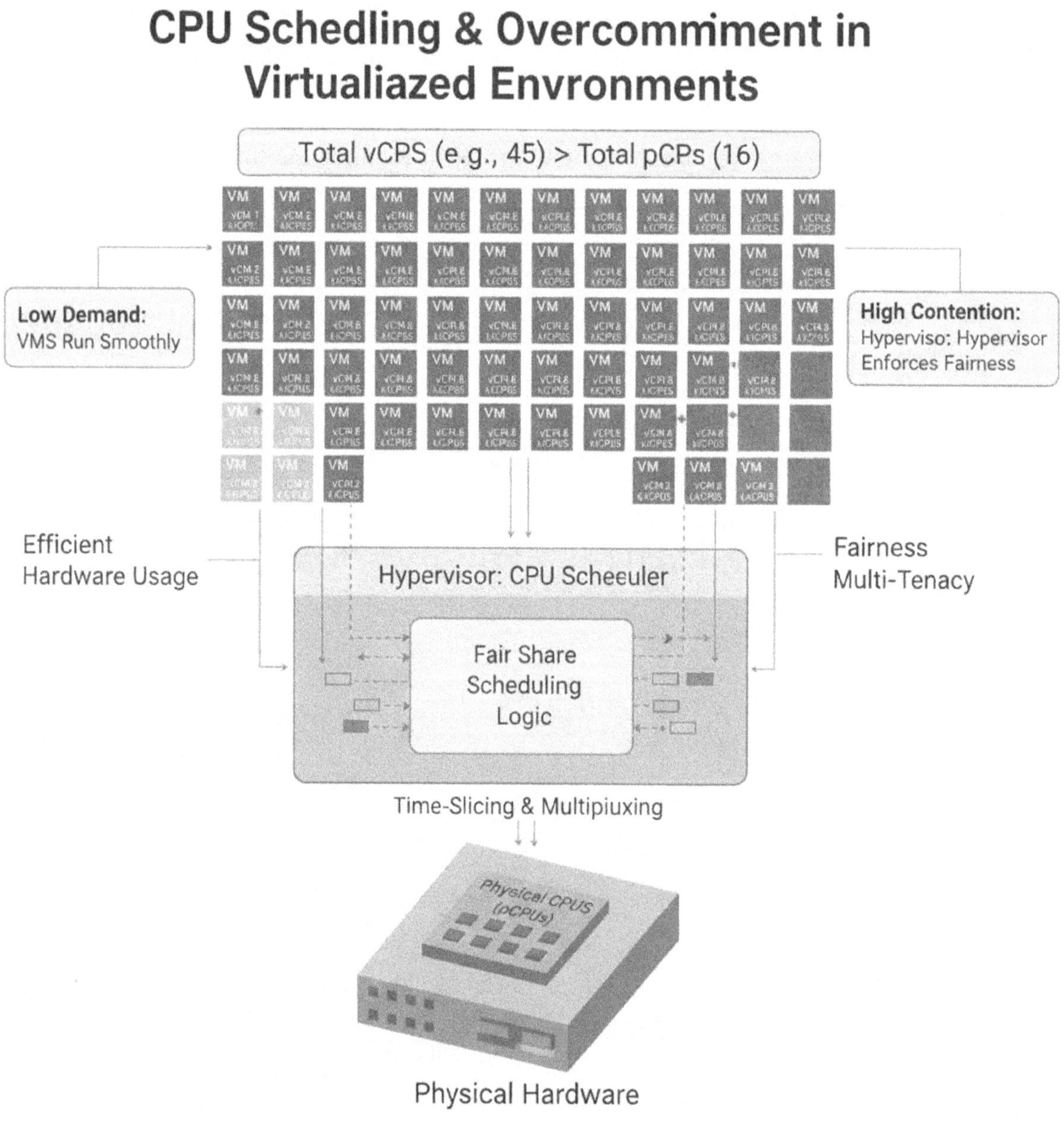

In a virtualized environment, the hypervisor acts as a scheduler, deciding which VM gets to use the physical CPU cores at any given millisecond. This allows for **CPU Overcommitment**, where a host with 16 physical cores might host 50 virtual machines, each with 2 virtual CPUs (vCPUs). As long as all 50 VMs are not requesting 100% CPU power at the exact same moment, the hypervisor can multiplex the physical cores effectively. If contention occurs, the hypervisor uses algorithms like "Fair Share Scheduling" to ensure no single tenant monopolizes the host.

4.2 Memory Virtualization and Shadow Page Tables

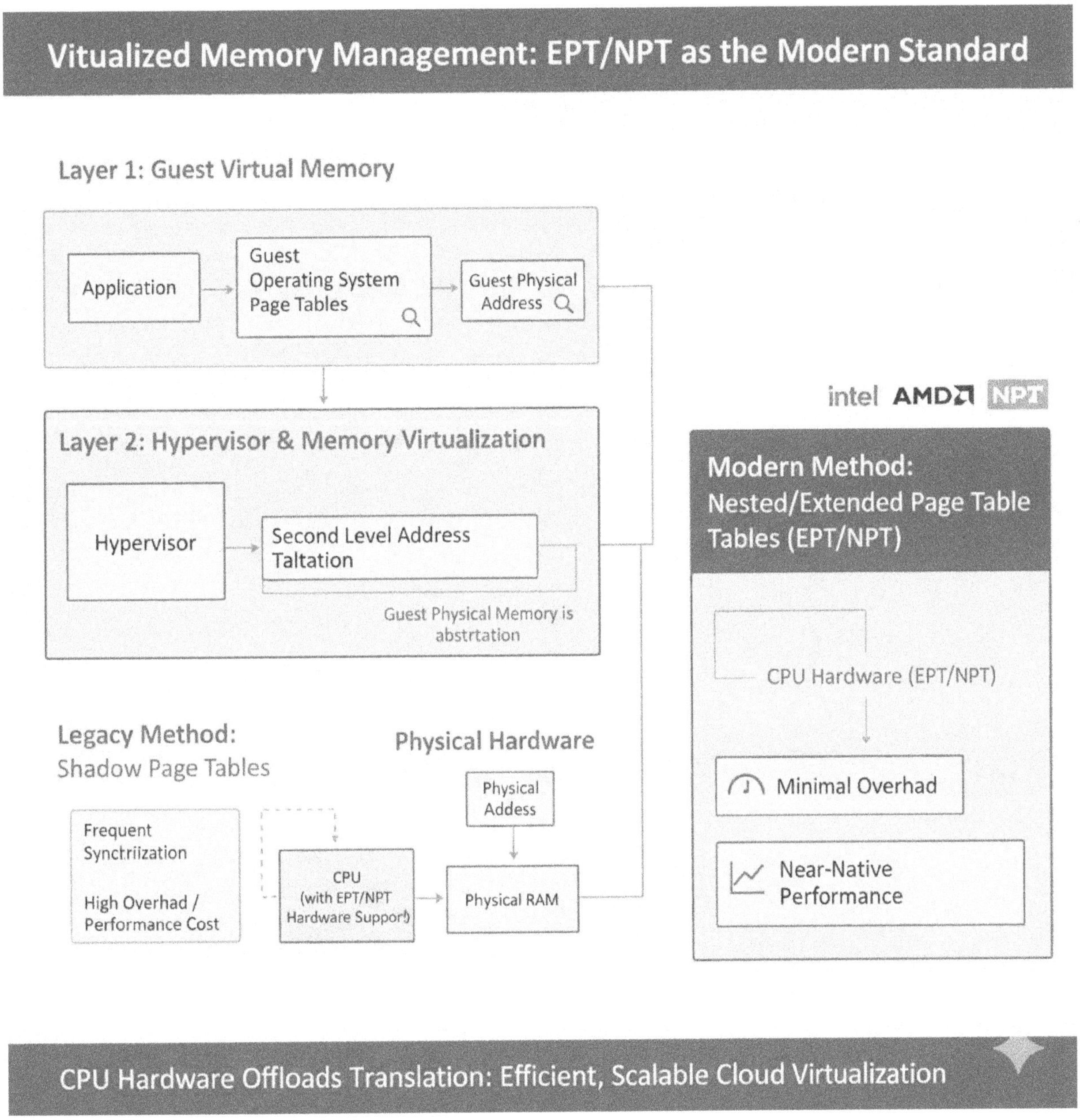

Memory management is perhaps the most complex part of virtualization. Each guest OS manages its own "Virtual Memory" and "Physical Memory." However, what the guest thinks is "Physical Memory" is actually "Guest Physical Memory," which must be mapped to the "Host Physical Memory" (the actual RAM sticks).

Early hypervisors used **Shadow Page Tables**. The hypervisor would maintain a secret copy of the guest's memory map and update it whenever the guest made a change. This was incredibly slow.

Modern CPUs now include **Nested Page Tables (NPT)** or **Extended Page Tables (EPT)**, which allow the hardware to perform this double-translation (Guest Virtual -> Guest Physical -> Host Physical) in a single step, virtually eliminating the memory overhead of virtualization.

4.3 I/O and Network Virtualization

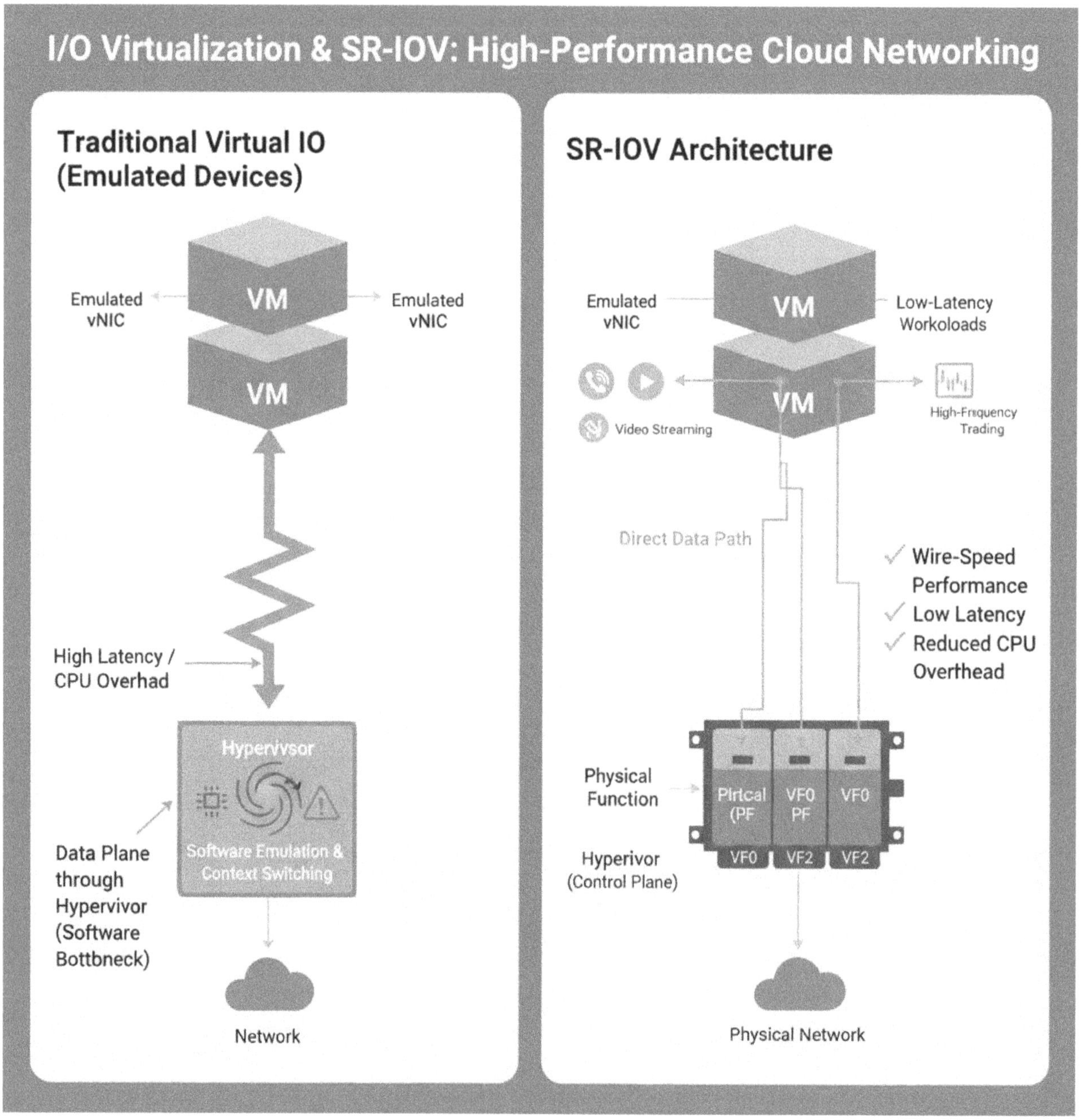

I/O devices like hard drives and network cards are typically the biggest bottlenecks. In a standard setup, the hypervisor must emulate a virtual NIC for every VM, which involves significant software overhead for every packet sent or received. To bypass this, techniques like **SR-IOV (Single Root I/O Virtualization)** were developed. SR-IOV allows a single physical network card to present itself as hundreds of "Virtual Functions" (VFs). Each VM can be directly mapped to a VF, allowing data to bypass the hypervisor entirely and move at "wire speed." This is essential for low-latency cloud applications like VOIP, video streaming, and high-frequency trading.

5. Storage Virtualization: From Blocks to Objects

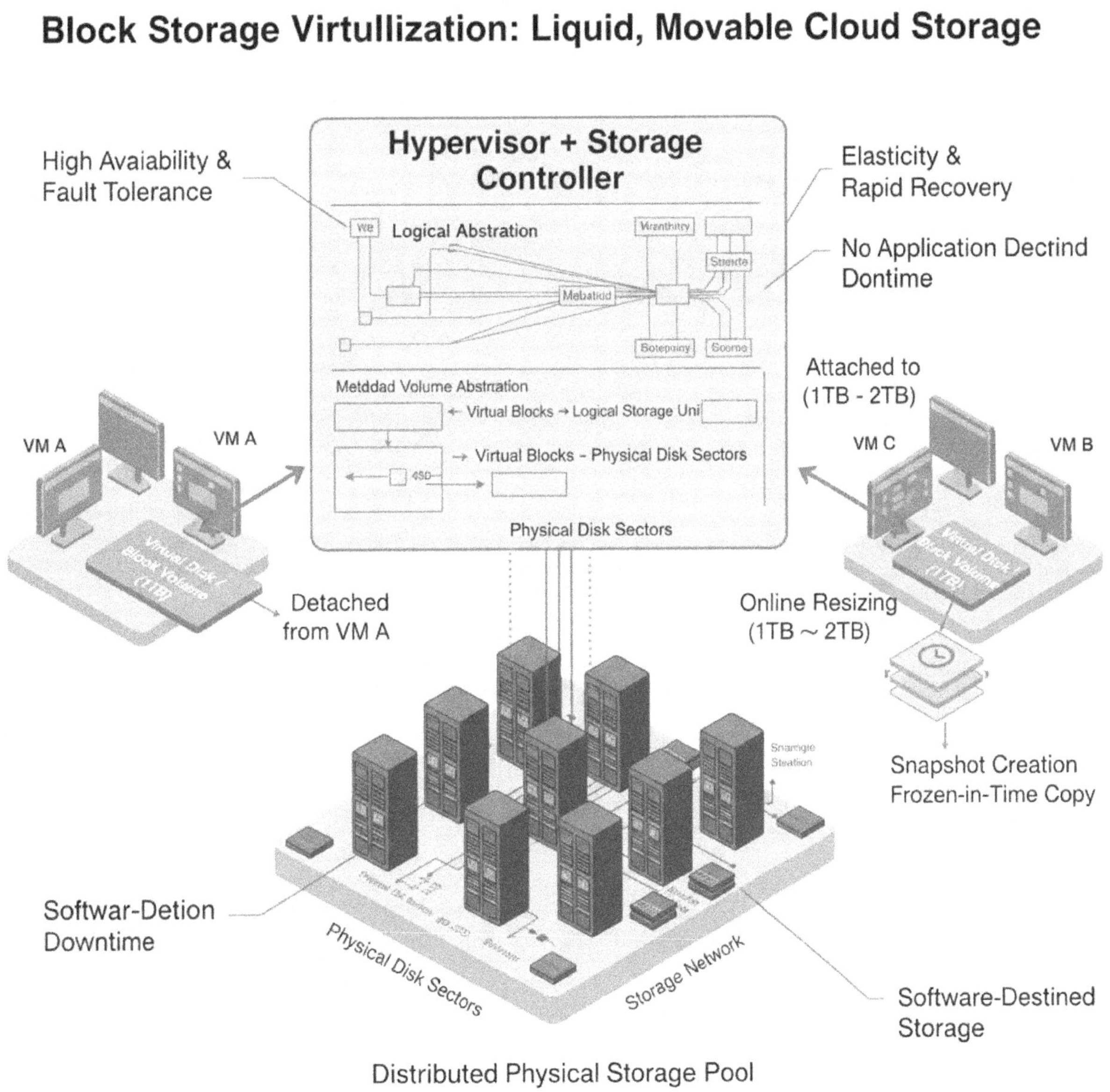

The cloud has transformed storage from a physical disk into a liquid resource. **Block Storage Virtualization** (like Amazon EBS) allows a virtual disk to be detached from one VM and reattached to another, or even resized while the system is running. Behind the scenes, the hypervisor and the storage controller manage a complex mapping of virtual blocks to physical sectors across a distributed storage network. This abstraction is what enables "snapshots" and "backups," where the state of a massive database can be frozen in time in a matter of seconds without interrupting the application.

6. Security Implications and the "Noisy Neighbor" Problem

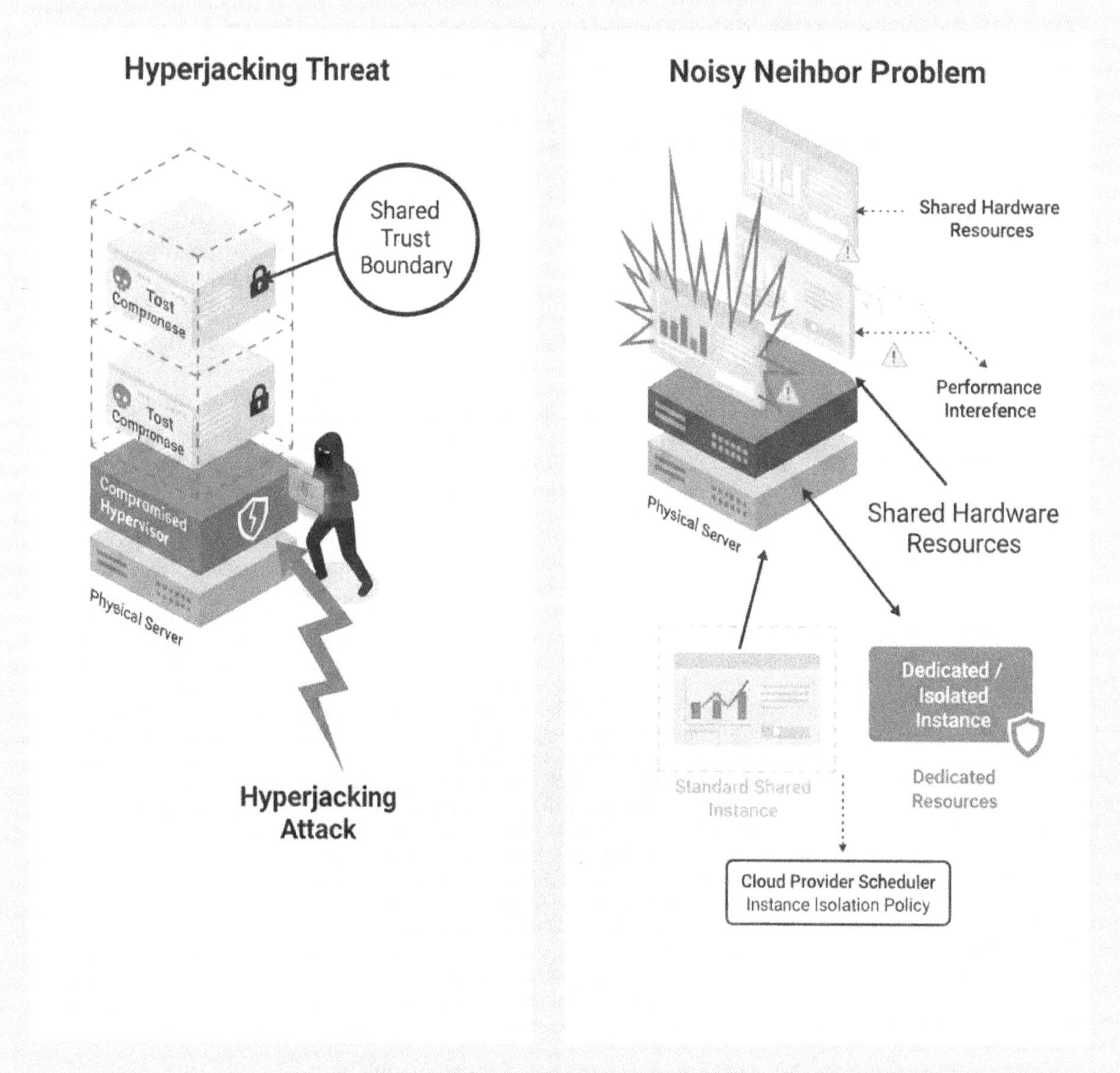

Why Cloud Providers Offer Dedicated Instances at Higher Cost.

While virtualization provides isolation, it also introduces new risks. **Hyperjacking** is a theoretical attack where a hacker takes control of the hypervisor itself; if the hypervisor is compromised, every VM on that host is compromised. Furthermore, the **"Noisy Neighbor"** problem occurs when one VM performs a task that stresses a non-isolated resource (like the CPU cache or the memory bus), causing performance degradation for other VMs on the same host. Cloud providers mitigate this through "instance types"—charging more for dedicated resources that ensure a "Quiet Neighbor" experience.

7. Summary and Evolutionary Impact

Chapter 3 has dissected the internal mechanics and theoretical frameworks that make the cloud possible. We have moved from the broad "vision" of the cloud in Chapter 1 to the "foundational distribution" in Chapter 2, and now into the "virtualization engine" in Chapter 3. We have seen how the hypervisor acts as the gatekeeper of the Machine Reference Model and how the core pillars of isolation, consolidation, and aggregation provide the efficiency and security necessary for modern IT.

Chapter – 4

Virtualization in Practice

Moves from theory to implementation, focusing on industry leaders like VMware and the practicalities of Virtual Desktop Infrastructure (VDI). It analyzes the performance "tax" of virtualization versus the benefits of live migration (vMotion) and snapshotting.

1. Industry Solutions: A Deep Dive into VMware and Desktop Virtualization

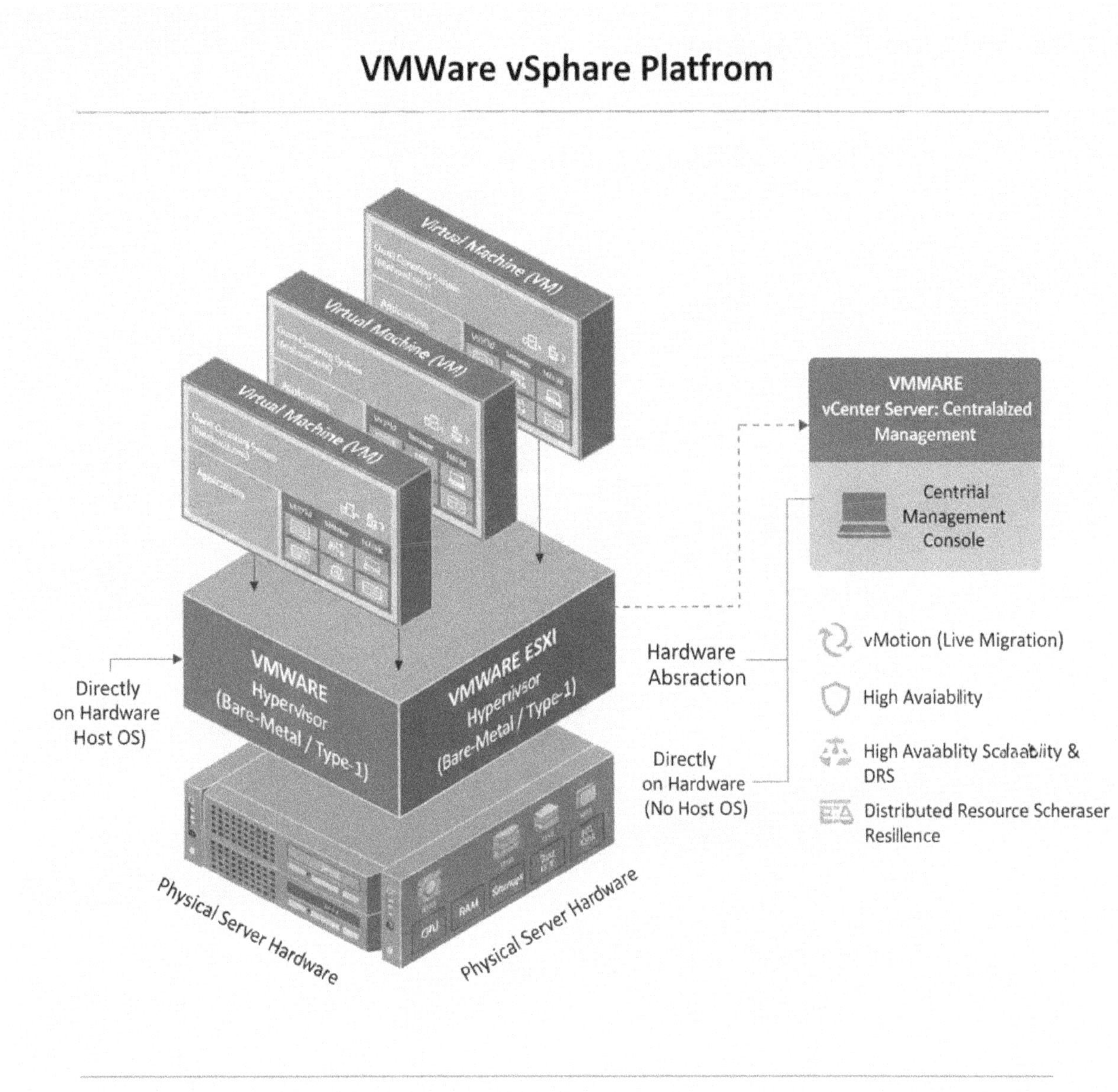

Operationalizing Abstraction, Isolation, & Resource Pooling for Cloud-Scale Virtualization

While the theoretical concepts of hypervisors and abstraction layers provide the "blueprints," industry solutions like VMware represent the actual "construction" of the virtual world. VMware is widely credited with bringing x86 virtualization to the mainstream, transforming it from a niche academic interest into the backbone of global enterprise IT. To understand virtualization in practice, one must examine the architecture of VMware vSphere and its flagship hypervisor, ESXi.

1.1 The VMware ESXi Architecture

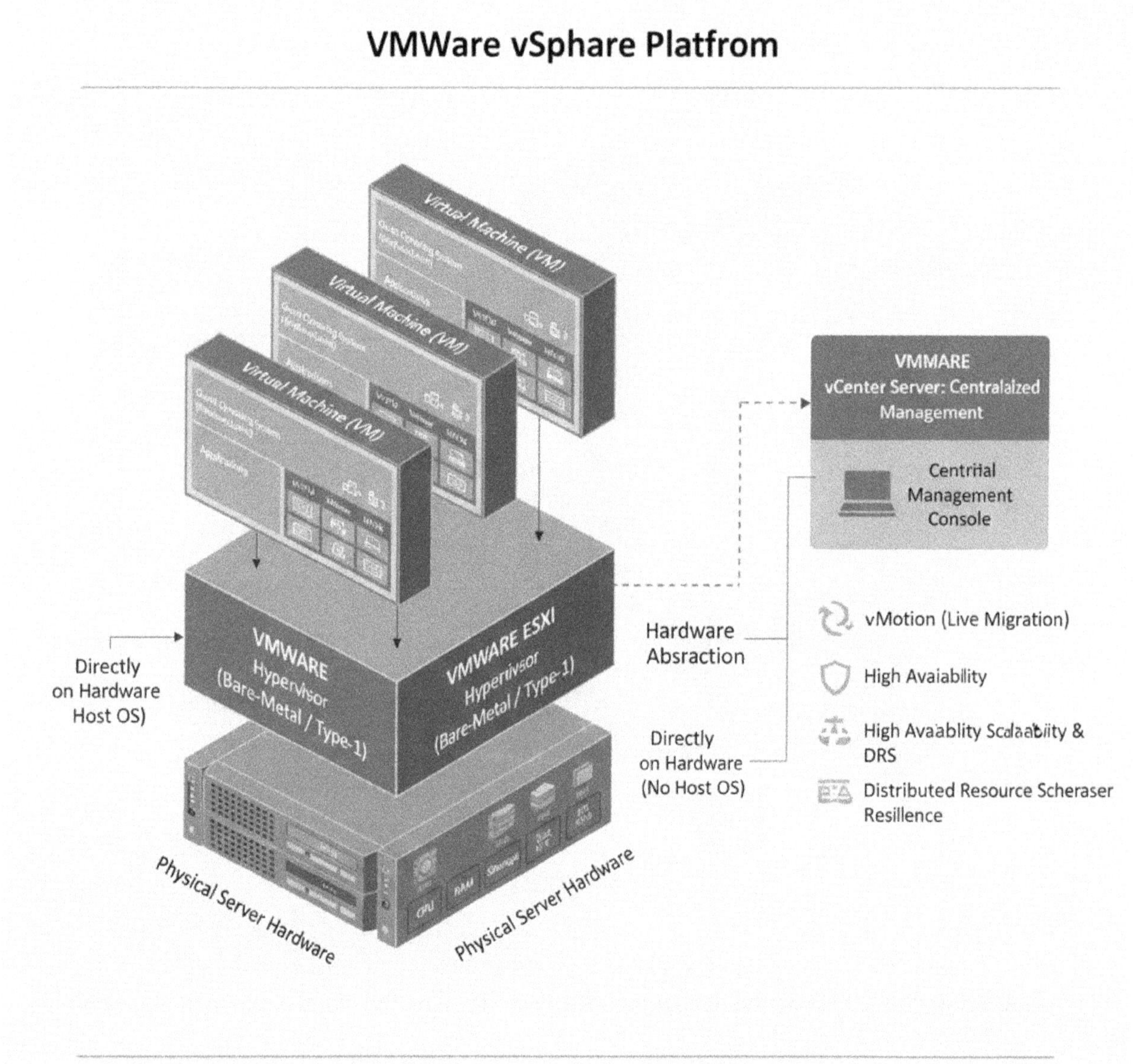

Operationalizing Abstraction, Isolation, & Resource Pooling for Cloud-Scale Virtualization

VMware ESXi is a Type-1, or "bare-metal," hypervisor. Unlike hosted virtualization solutions that run as an application on top of an operating system (like Windows or Linux), ESXi installs directly onto the physical hardware. This is a critical distinction in practice because it eliminates the overhead of a middleman operating system. ESXi is a "thin" hypervisor, meaning it has an extremely small footprint—often less than 150 MB. This small size is intentional; it reduces the "attack surface" for hackers and ensures that nearly 100% of the physical hardware's power is dedicated to running virtual machines rather than maintaining the hypervisor itself.

In a practical data center environment, ESXi does not operate in isolation. It is managed by **vCenter Server**, a centralized management console that allows administrators to treat a cluster of hundreds of physical servers as a single pool of resources. This management layer enables features that are synonymous with modern cloud reliability, such as **vMotion**. vMotion allows for the live migration of a running virtual machine from one physical host to another without any interruption to the user. From a practical standpoint, this means an administrator can perform hardware maintenance—like replacing a faulty RAM stick or upgrading a CPU—during business hours by simply "sliding" the active VMs over to a different server.

1.2 Desktop Virtualization and VDI

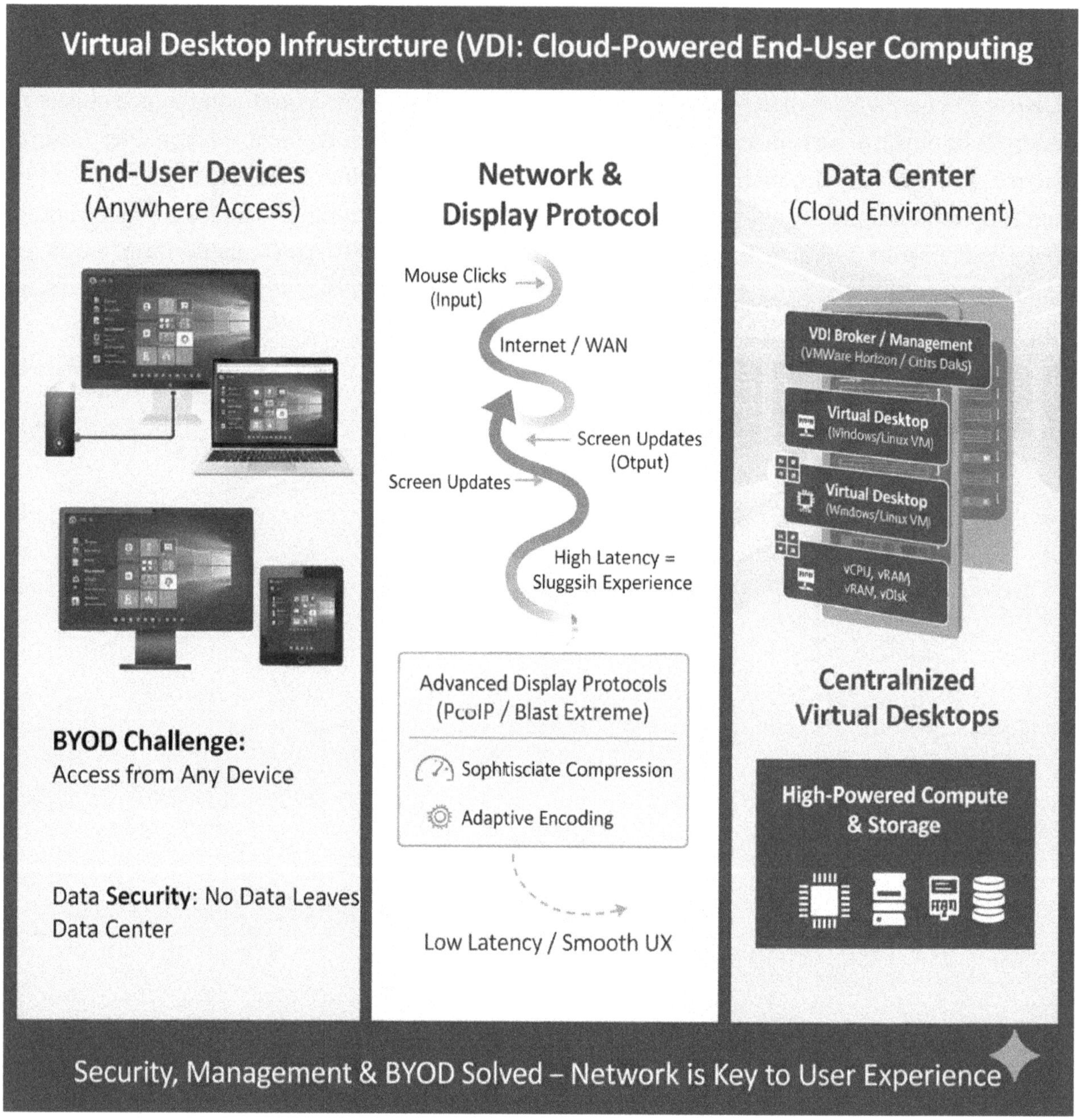

While server-side virtualization drives the cloud, **Virtual Desktop Infrastructure (VDI)** brings virtualization to the end-user. Solutions like VMware Horizon or Citrix Virtual Apps and Desktops allow companies to host a user's entire desktop environment (Windows or Linux) on a central server in the data center. The user accesses their desktop via a "thin client" or even a web browser.

In practice, VDI offers immense security and management benefits. Because the actual data and processing never leave the data center, a lost or stolen laptop does not result in a data breach. Furthermore, it solves the "Bring Your Own Device" (BYOD) challenge; an employee can access a high-powered, secure corporate desktop from a personal iPad or an old home PC. However, the practical challenge of VDI lies in the network. Since every mouse click and screen refresh must travel over the network, high latency can make the virtual desktop feel "sluggish." To combat this, industry solutions use advanced display protocols (like PCoIP or Blast Extreme) that use sophisticated compression and adaptive encoding to ensure a smooth user experience even over low-bandwidth connections.

2. Pros and Cons: Performance Overhead vs. Resource Flexibility

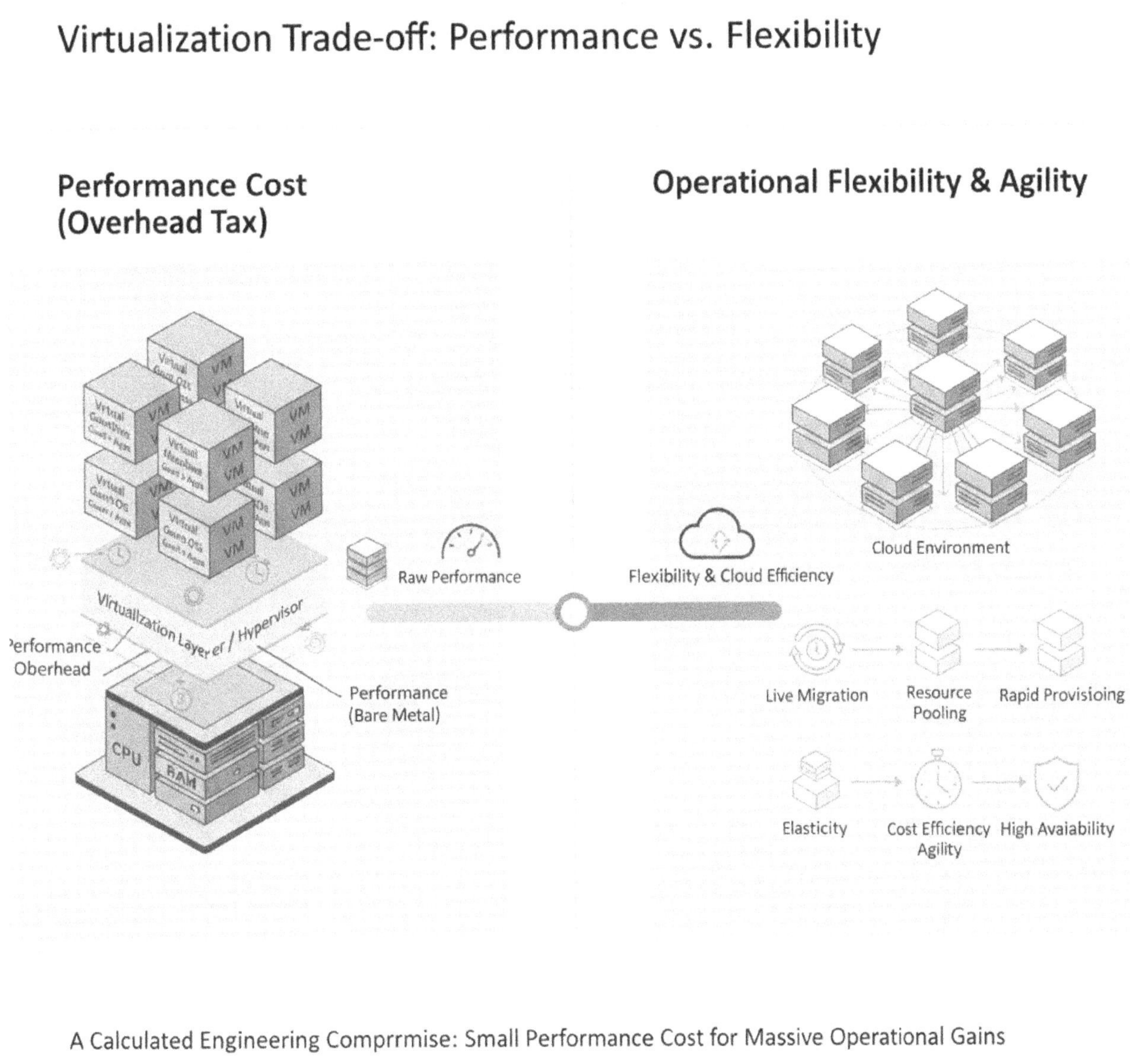

The adoption of virtualization in practice is always a balancing act. No matter how efficient a hypervisor is, it is still a layer of software that sits between the application and the hardware. This introduces a "tax" on performance, which must be weighed against the immense flexibility that virtualization provides.

2.1 The Performance Overhead (The Cons)

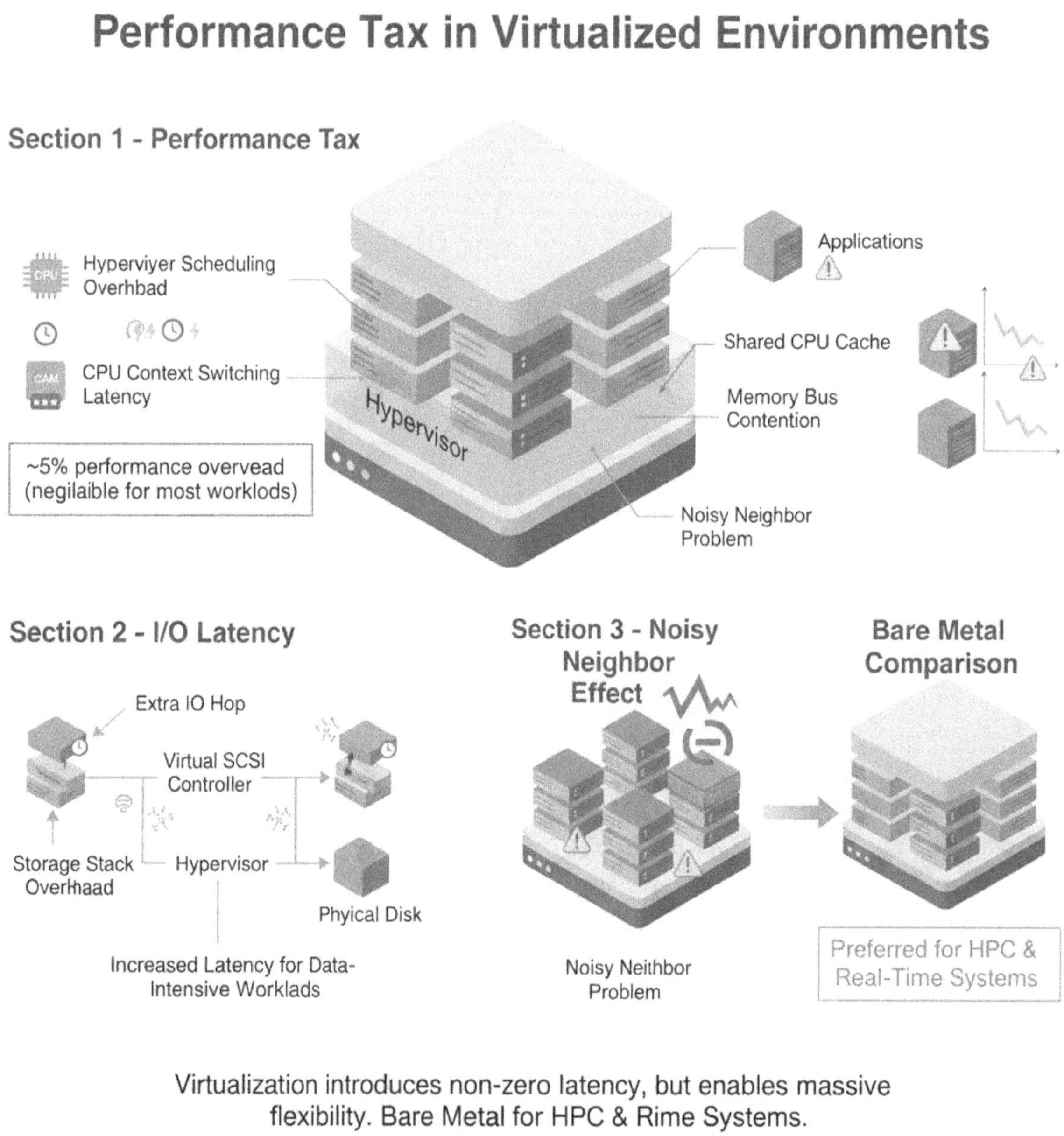

The primary "con" of virtualization is the **Performance Tax**. Even with hardware-assisted virtualization (Intel VT-x/AMD-V), there is a non-zero latency involved in the hypervisor's management of CPU cycles and memory mapping. For most general-purpose applications, like web servers or database systems, this overhead is negligible (often less than 5%). However, for "High-Performance Computing" (HPC) tasks or real-time signal processing, that 5% can be a deal-breaker.

Another practical disadvantage is **I/O Latency**. When a VM wants to write data to a disk, that request must pass through the virtual SCSI controller, through the hypervisor's storage stack, and finally to the physical storage controller. This "extra hop" can create bottlenecks in data-heavy environments. Furthermore, we must consider the **"Noisy Neighbor" effect**. In a multi-tenant cloud, you have no control over what other users are doing on the same physical host. If a "neighbor" VM suddenly starts a massive data-mining operation, it can saturate the CPU cache or the memory bus, causing your application's performance to jitter or drop. This unpredictability is why some companies still prefer "Bare Metal" servers for their most mission-critical, performance-sensitive workloads.

2.2 Resource Flexibility and Agility (The Pros)

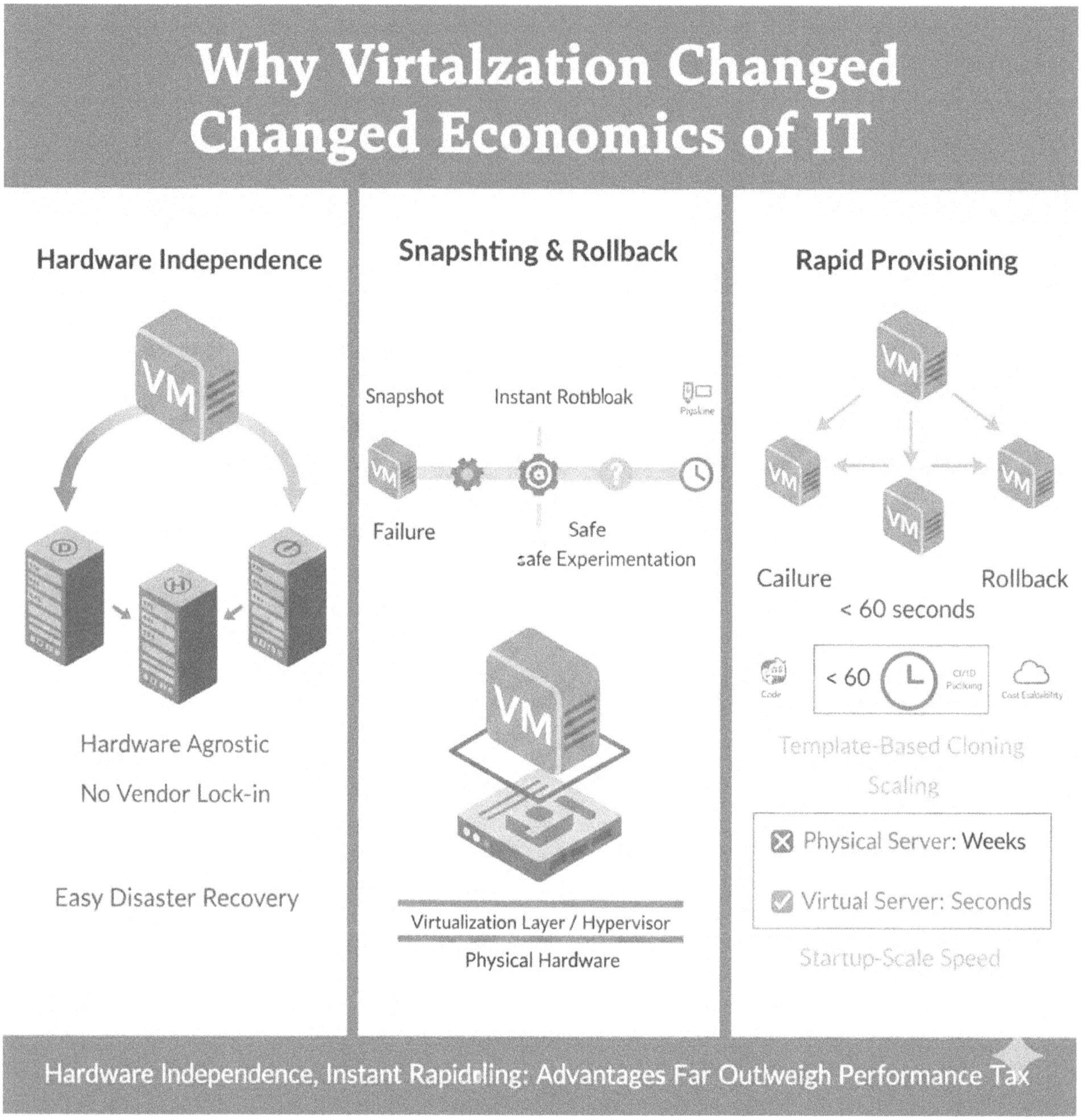

The "pros" of virtualization, however, are so overwhelming that they have fundamentally changed the economics of IT. The first major pro is **Hardware Independence**. Because a VM is abstracted from the hardware, it doesn't care if it's running on a Dell, HP, or Cisco server. This eliminates "vendor lock-in" at the hardware level and makes disaster recovery significantly easier. You can restore a backup of a server onto completely different hardware in a matter of minutes.

The second major pro is **Snapshotting and Encapsulation**. In a physical world, if a software update fails and corrupts the OS, you might spend hours rebuilding the server. In a virtual world, you simply take a "Snapshot" before the update. If things go wrong, you "Roll Back" to the previous state in seconds. This capability alone has increased the speed of software development and deployment (DevOps) by orders of magnitude.

Finally, there is the benefit of **Rapid Provisioning**. In the physical era, getting a new server meant raising a purchase order, waiting for shipping, racking, cabling, and installing the OS. This took weeks. In a virtualized environment, a new server can be cloned from a template and be online in less than sixty seconds. This speed is the "oxygen" that allows modern startups to scale at a global level.

3. The Symbiotic Relationship Between Virtualization and Cloud Scaling

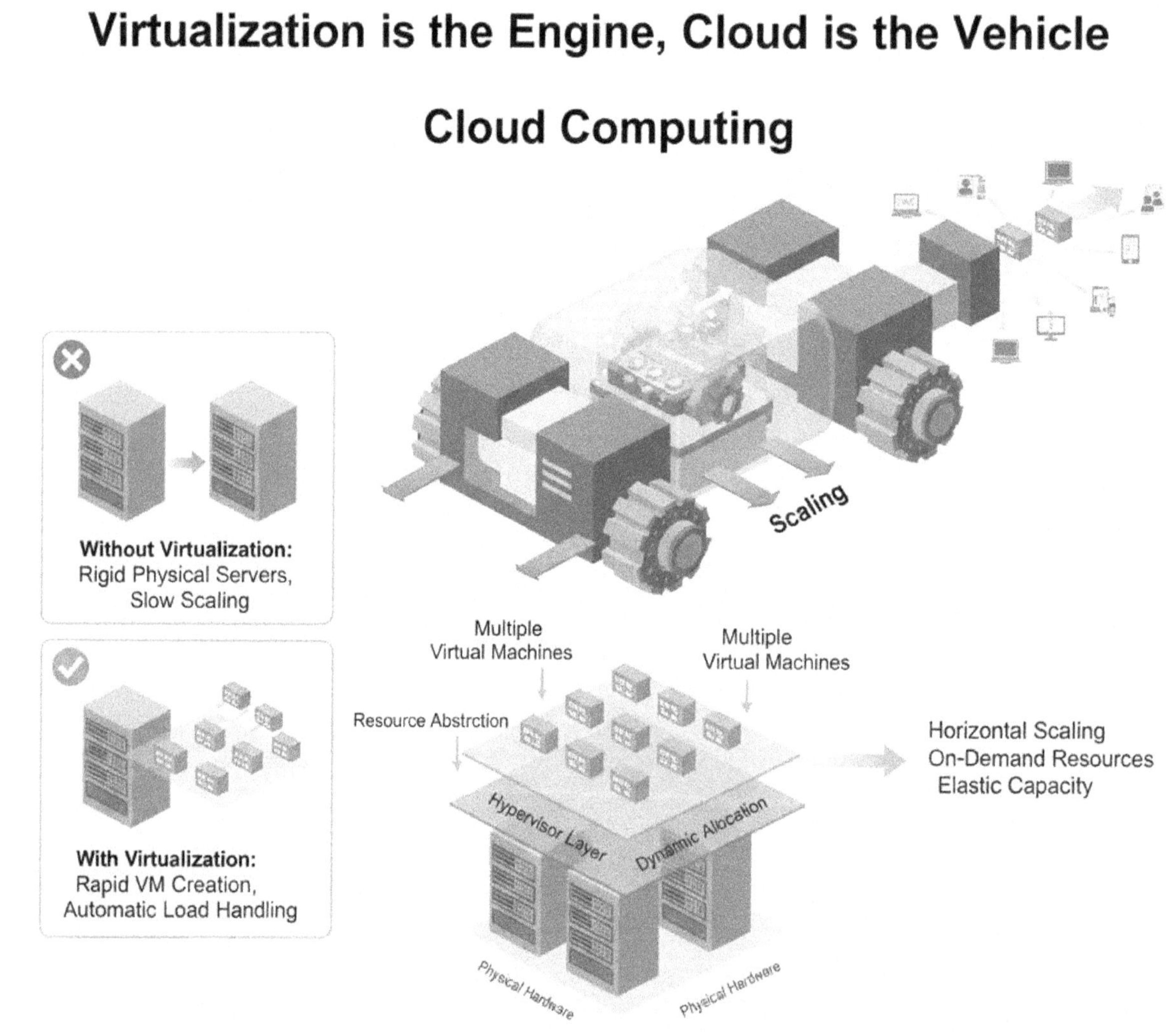

Virtualization enables Cloud capabilties through Hardware Hardware Absraction, VM Elasticity, and Resource Pooling

Cloud computing and virtualization are often confused, but it is more accurate to say that virtualization is the *engine* and the cloud is the *vehicle*. Scaling—the ability to handle more users by adding resources—is the defining feature of the cloud, and it is made possible entirely through the mechanisms of virtualization.

3.1 Vertical Scaling (Scaling Up)

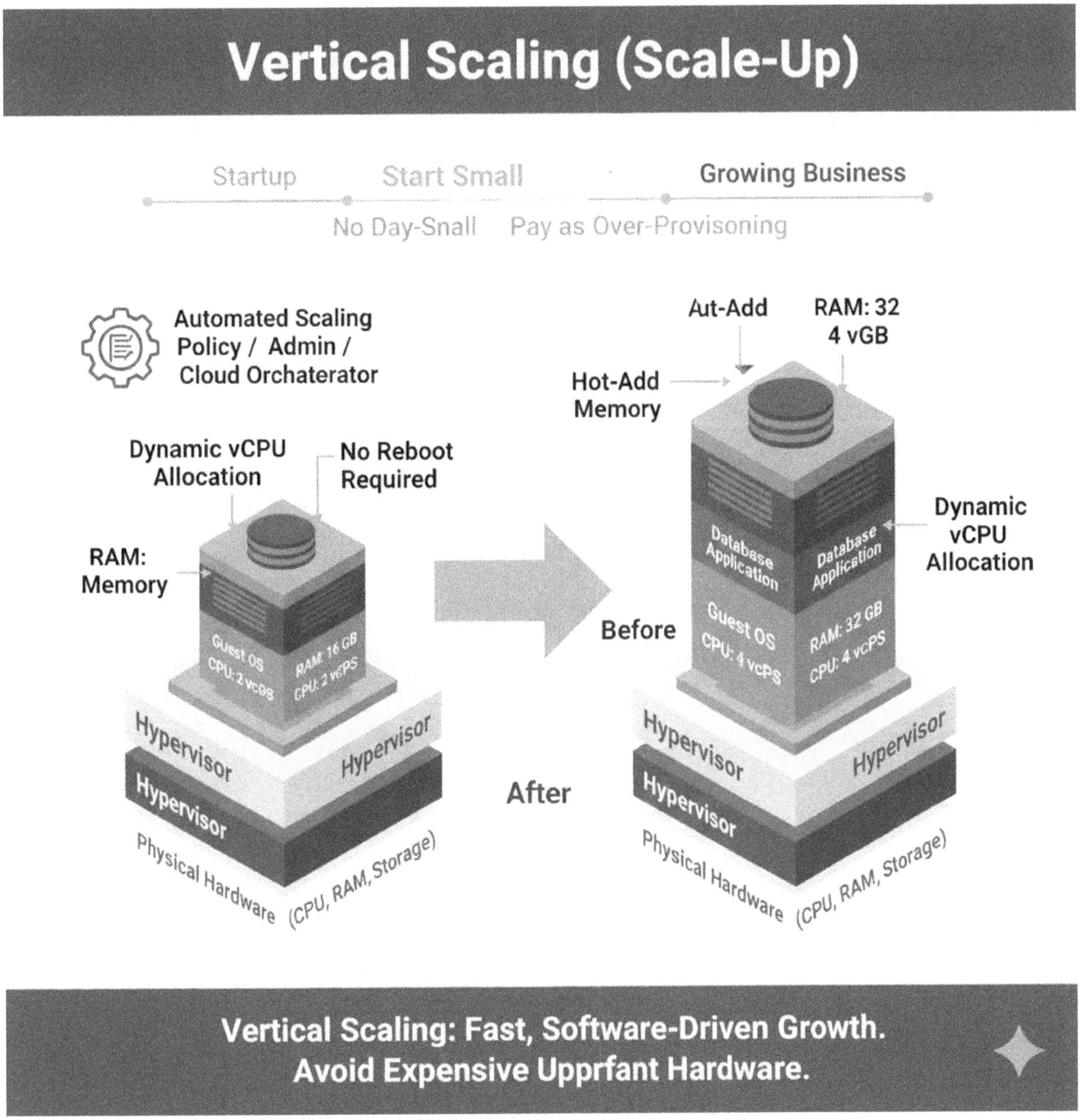

Vertical scaling involves adding more power to an existing instance. Because of virtualization, this is a "soft" operation. If a virtual machine running a database is running out of memory, an administrator (or an automated script) can simply adjust the VM's settings to grant it 32 GB of RAM instead of 16 GB. In many modern systems, this can even be done "hot," meaning the VM doesn't even need to be rebooted. This flexibility allows businesses to start small and grow their infrastructure precisely in line with their success, avoiding the cost of buying massive servers on "day one."

3.2 Horizontal Scaling (Scaling Out)

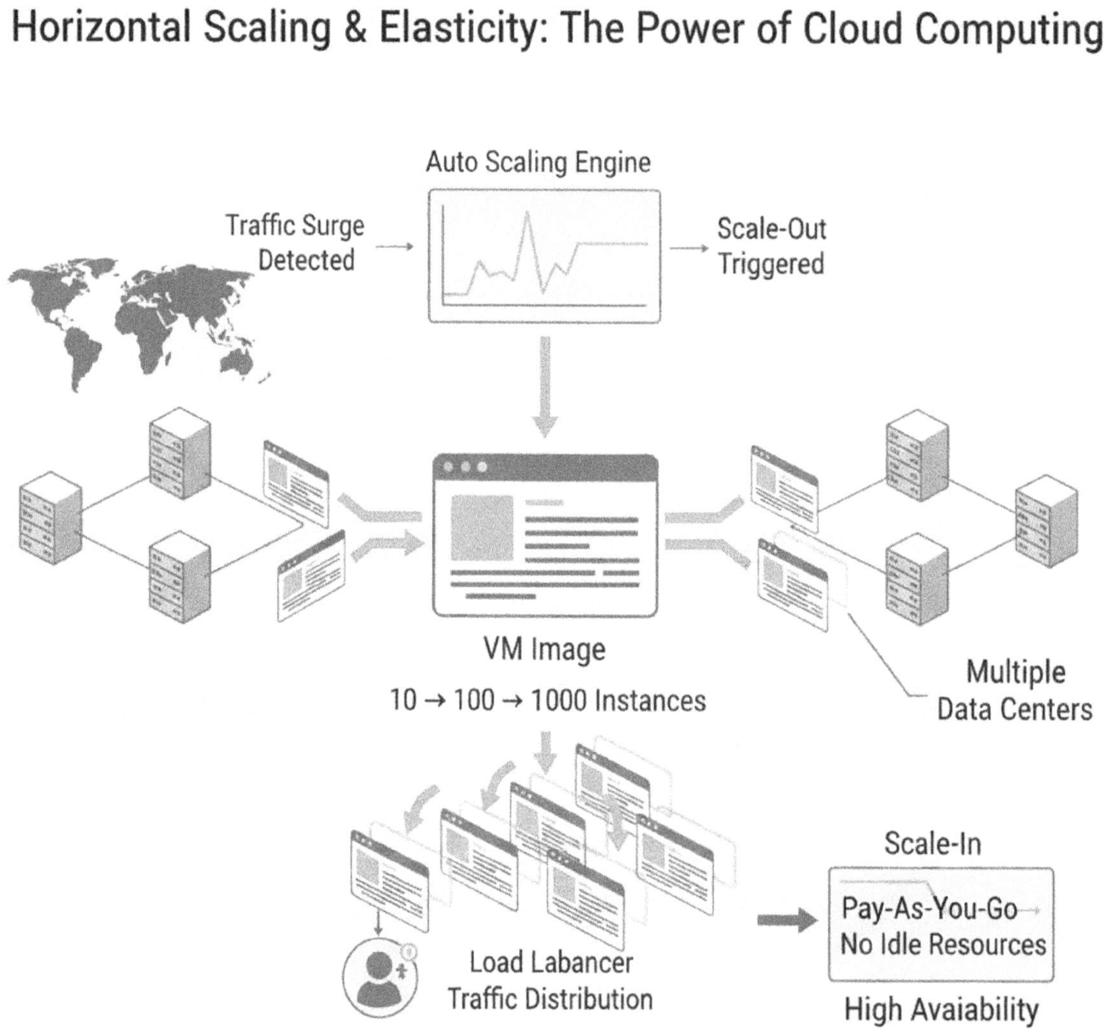

Fast, Practically Unlimited Scaling Enabled by Virtualization, Encapsulation, & Load Balnacing. Pay Only for What You Use.

While vertical scaling has a physical ceiling (you can't give a VM more RAM than the physical host possesses), **Horizontal Scaling** is theoretically infinite. This is the heart of cloud elasticity. When a web application experiences a spike in traffic, the cloud orchestration layer (like AWS Auto Scaling) uses virtualization to "clone" the existing web server VM. It can spin up 10, 100, or 1,000 identical copies of that server across a global data center network in minutes.

This is only possible because of **Encapsulation**. Since a virtual machine is just a collection of files (the "image"), it can be duplicated and moved across the network with ease. These new instances are then placed behind a **Load Balancer**, which distributes incoming traffic among all the available VMs. When the traffic spike subsides, the cloud provider simply deletes the extra virtual machines, and the customer stops paying for them. This "Elasticity" is the ultimate practical expression of virtualization.

3.3 The Role of Templates and Orchestration

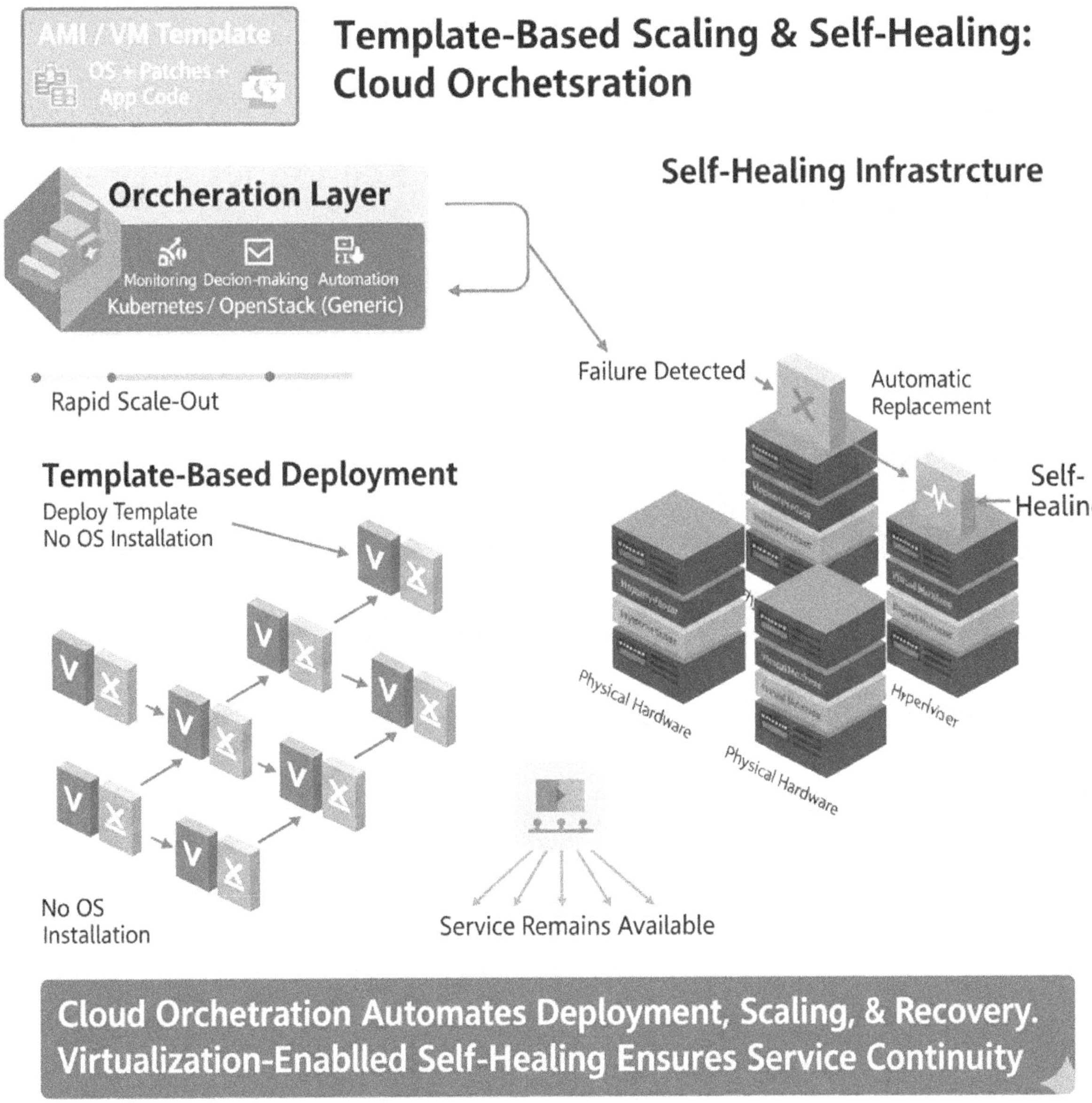

In practice, scaling is managed through **Templates** (often called Amazon Machine Images or AMIs in AWS). A template is a "frozen" golden image of a virtual machine that has the operating system, security patches, and application code pre-installed and optimized. When the cloud needs to scale, it doesn't "install" a new server; it "deploys" a template.

This process is governed by an **Orchestration Layer**. This software (such as Kubernetes for containers or OpenStack for VMs) acts as the "brain" of the cloud. It monitors the health and load of the virtualized environment. If a VM fails, the orchestrator detects the loss of the heartbeat and automatically spins up a replacement VM on a healthy host. This "Self-Healing" capability is a direct result of the abstraction provided by virtualization. It ensures that the "service" remains available even if the underlying "hardware" fails.

4. Resource Overcommitment and the Economics of Practice

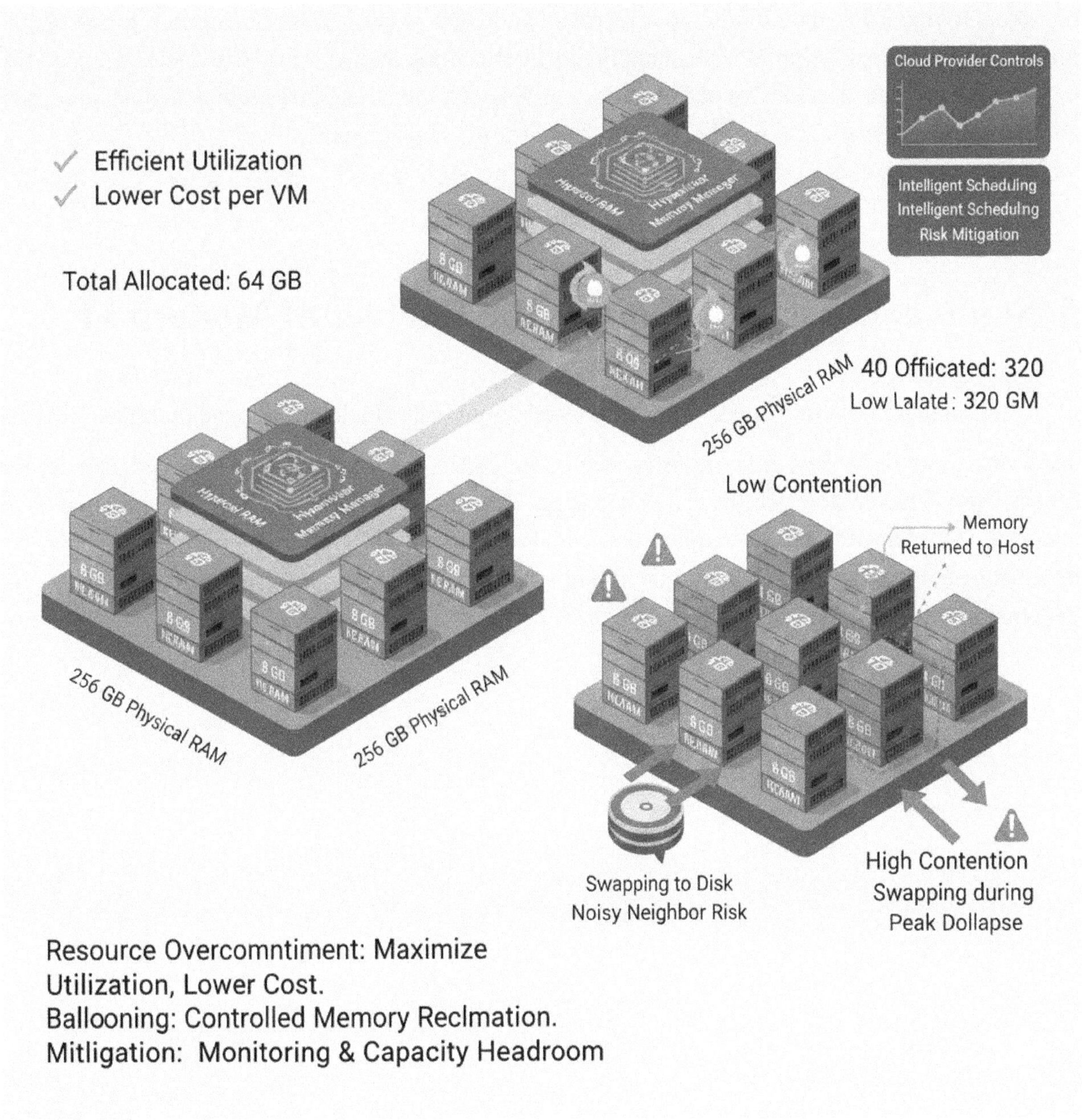

A fascinating aspect of virtualization in practice is **Resource Overcommitment**. Cloud providers frequently sell more resources than they actually possess. This is based on the statistical reality that not every customer will use 100% of their allocated CPU and RAM at the same time.

For example, a physical host with 256 GB of RAM might host 40 virtual machines that each believe they have 8 GB of RAM (totaling 320 GB). The hypervisor manages this through a technique called **Memory Ballooning**. When the physical host starts to run low on actual RAM, it communicates with a "balloon driver" inside the guest VMs. This driver "inflates," forcing the guest OS to clear out its own cache and give memory back to the hypervisor. This allows cloud providers to maximize their hardware investment and keep prices low for consumers. However, in practice, if too many "neighbors" demand their full allocation at once, it leads to "swapping" to the disk, which can cause a massive performance collapse—a scenario cloud architects must carefully avoid through sophisticated monitoring and "headroom" management.

5. Summary: Virtualization as the Enabler of Modern IT

Chapter 4 has moved from the theoretical "how" of virtualization to the practical "where" and "why." We have seen how industry giants like VMware have turned the hypervisor into a robust, enterprise-grade platform that can manage thousands of servers as a single unit. We have analyzed the trade-offs, acknowledging that while virtualization introduces a performance tax, the benefits of agility, rapid provisioning, and hardware independence far outweigh the costs for the vast majority of use cases.

Part – III
The Cloud Reference Model

Chapter – 5

Cloud Delivery Models (the SPI Model)

An exhaustive analysis of Infrastructure (IaaS), Platform (PaaS), and Software (SaaS) as a Service. It introduces the Shared Responsibility Model, detailing how management burdens shift between the provider and the customer across different layers.

1. Introduction to the SPI Model and the Shift in Responsibility

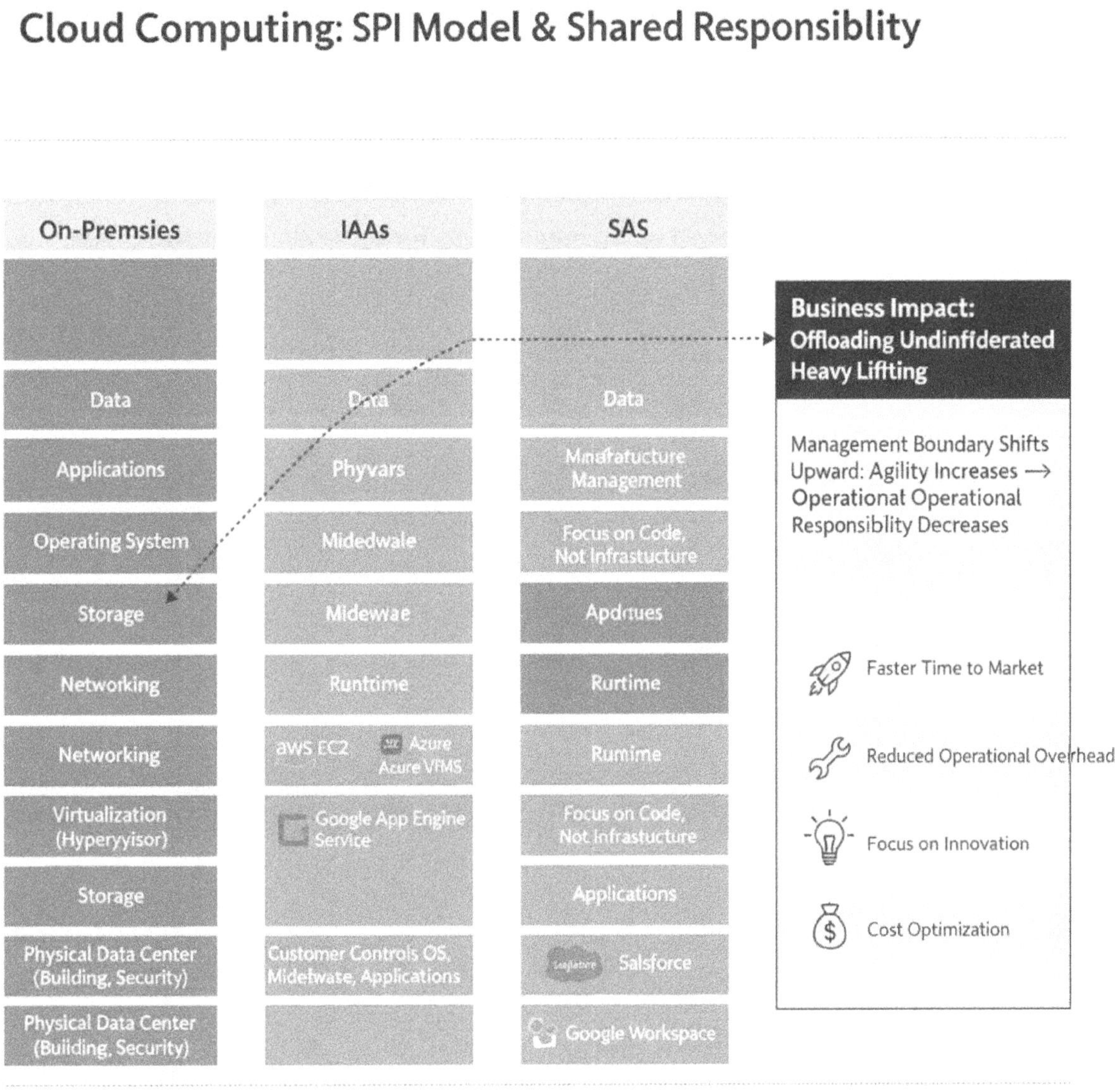

Cloud Adoption isa Progressive Transfer of Responsiblity: Higher-Lvel Services Offer More Agility with Less Operational Burden.

The landscape of modern IT is governed by a hierarchical structure known as the **SPI Model**, which stands for Software, Platform, and Infrastructure as a Service. This model represents the different layers of the computing stack that can be outsourced to a cloud provider. To understand the SPI model, one must move beyond the simple definitions and look at the "Shared Responsibility Model." In a traditional on-premises data center, the organization is responsible for everything: the physical security of the building, the cooling, the power, the hardware, the networking, the virtualization layer, the operating system, the middleware, the runtime, and finally, the application and its data.

The transition to the cloud is essentially a gradual offloading of these responsibilities. As we move from IaaS to PaaS and finally to SaaS, the "Management Boundary" shifts higher up the stack. This shift is the primary driver of organizational agility; by offloading the "undifferentiated heavy lifting" of infrastructure management to a cloud provider, businesses can reallocate their human and capital resources toward innovation and customer value. This chapter provides an exhaustive deep dive into each of these three models, examining their technical foundations, their impact on the development lifecycle, and the strategic implications for the digital economy.

2. Infrastructure as a Service (IaaS): The Foundational Layer

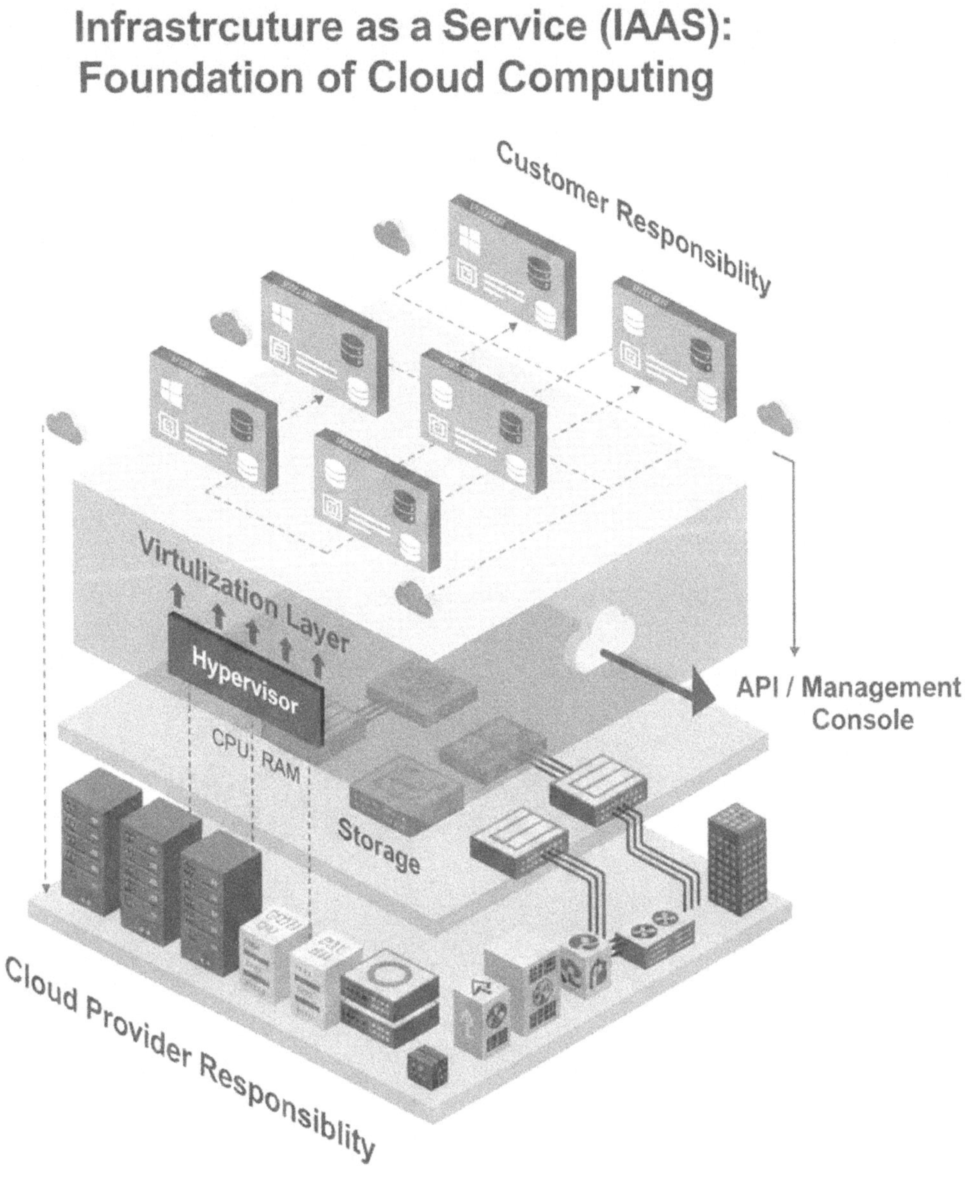

Infrastructure as a Service (IaaS) is the most basic and flexible category of cloud computing services. It provides the fundamental building blocks of computing: virtualized server instances, storage, and networking. In the IaaS model, the cloud provider manages the physical infrastructure—the data centers, the servers, the storage arrays, and the networking hardware—as well as the virtualization layer (the hypervisor). The customer, however, remains responsible for everything from the operating system upward.

2.1 Technical Architecture of IaaS

IAAS Workflow: From API Call to Running Virtual Machine

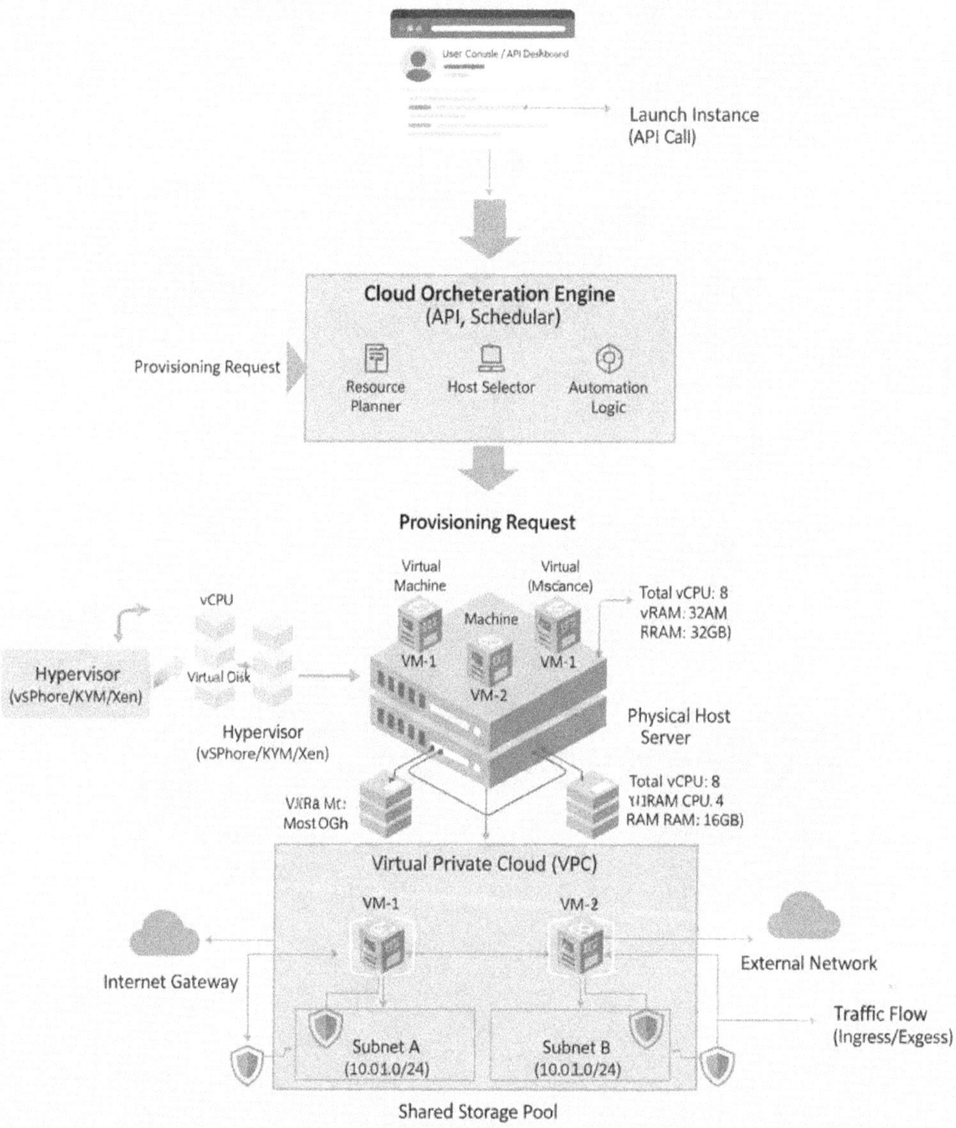

In an IaaS environment, the user interacts with the infrastructure through an API or a web-based dashboard. When a user requests a "virtual machine," the cloud provider's orchestration engine selects a physical host with available capacity, uses the hypervisor to carve out a set of virtual CPUs (vCPUs) and RAM, and attaches a virtual disk image. This process is nearly instantaneous, allowing for a level of agility that was impossible in the era of physical hardware.

The networking component of IaaS is equally sophisticated. Customers can create **Virtual Private Clouds (VPCs)**, which are logically isolated sections of the provider's network. Within a VPC, a customer has total control over their IP address range, creation of subnets, and configuration of route tables and network gateways. This allows for the creation of complex, multi-tier architectures that mirror traditional on-premises networks but with the added benefit of software-defined flexibility. For example, a security group (a virtual firewall) can be applied to a group of servers with a single command, ensuring consistent security posture across a global fleet.

2.2 Use Cases and Strategic Value of IaaS

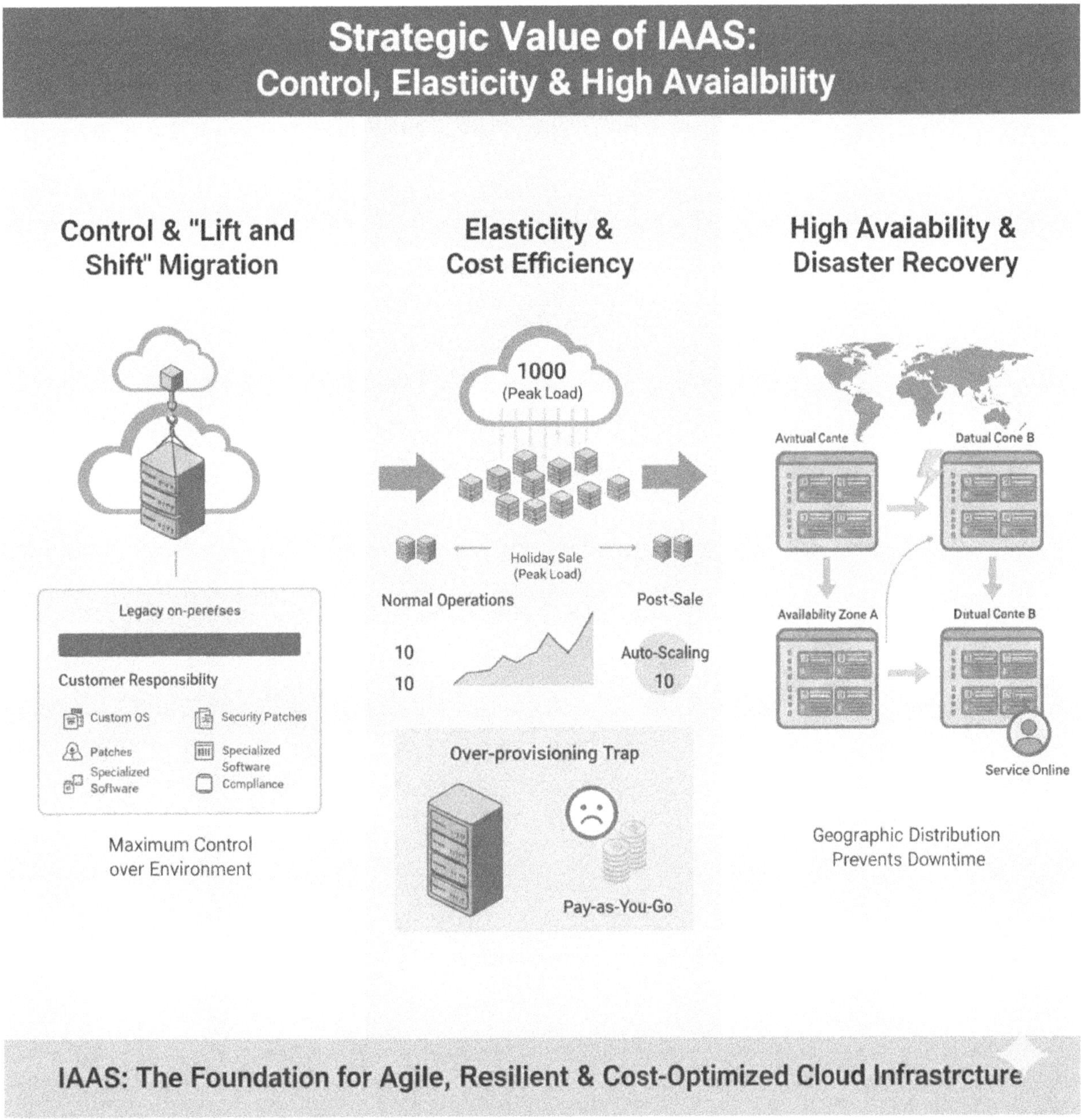

IaaS is the preferred choice for organizations that require maximum control over their environment. It is ideal for "Lift and Shift" migrations, where a company moves its existing legacy applications from local servers to the cloud without rewriting the code. Since the customer manages the operating system, they can install any specialized software, apply custom security patches, or configure the kernel to meet specific regulatory requirements.

The strategic value of IaaS lies in its **Elasticity**. For a retail company, the ability to scale their infrastructure from 10 servers to 1,000 servers during a holiday sale and then back down to 10 servers afterward is a game-changer. This prevents the "Over-provisioning" trap, where companies spend millions on hardware that sits idle for 90% of the year. Furthermore, IaaS enables "High Availability" through geographic distribution. A company can deploy identical infrastructure across different "Availability Zones" (separate data centers) to ensure that even if one facility fails due to a power outage or natural disaster, the application remains online.

2.3 Challenges and Management Burdens of IaaS

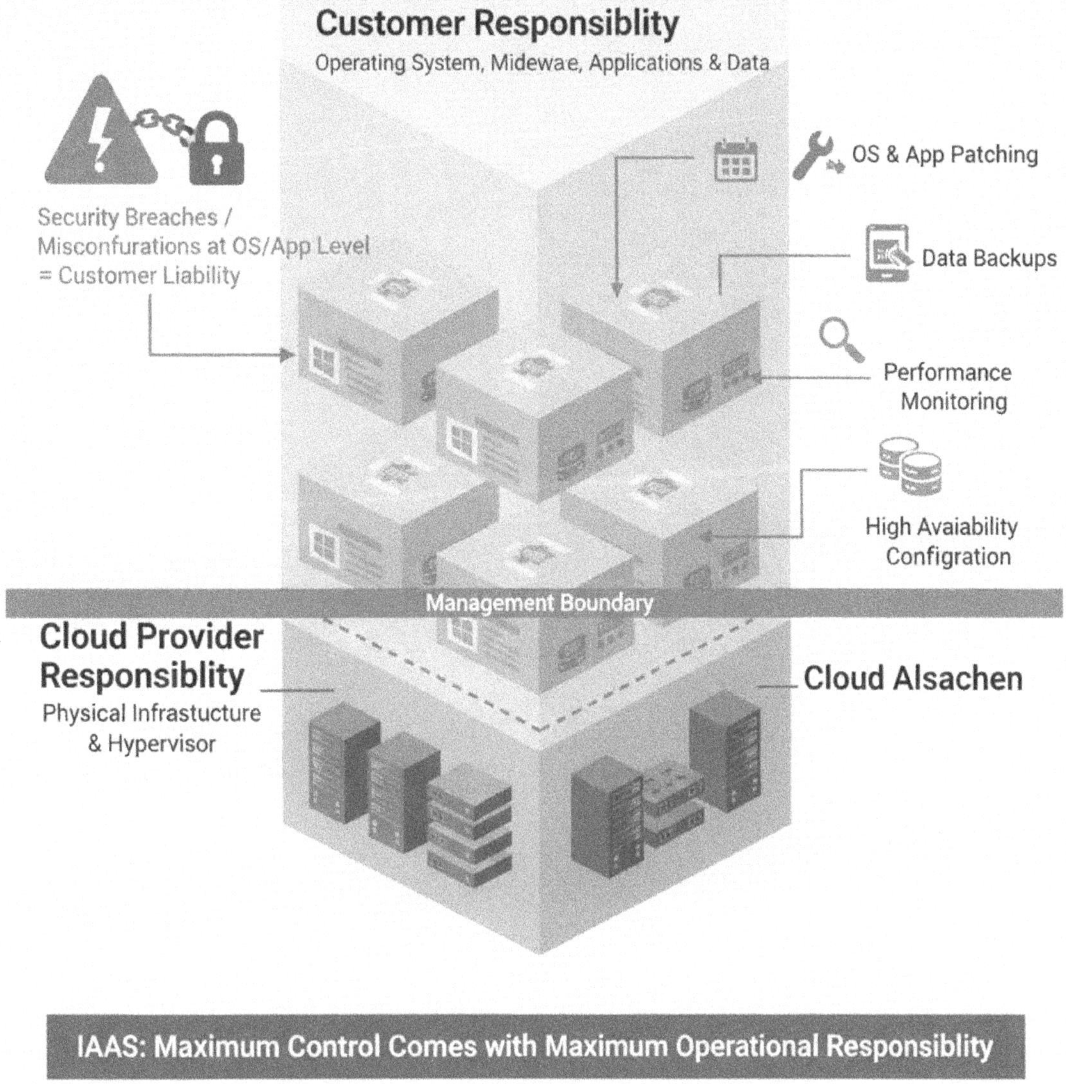

Despite its flexibility, IaaS comes with a significant "Management Burden." Because the customer owns the operating system, they are responsible for all maintenance. This includes patching vulnerabilities, managing backups, monitoring performance, and configuring high availability. If a server is hacked because the customer forgot to update the OS, the responsibility lies solely with the customer, not the cloud provider. This "Administrative Overhead" can be taxing for small teams, leading many to look toward the next layer of the SPI model: PaaS.

3. Platform as a Service (PaaS): The Developer's Playground

Platform as of Service (Paas): Focus on Code, Not Infrostcture

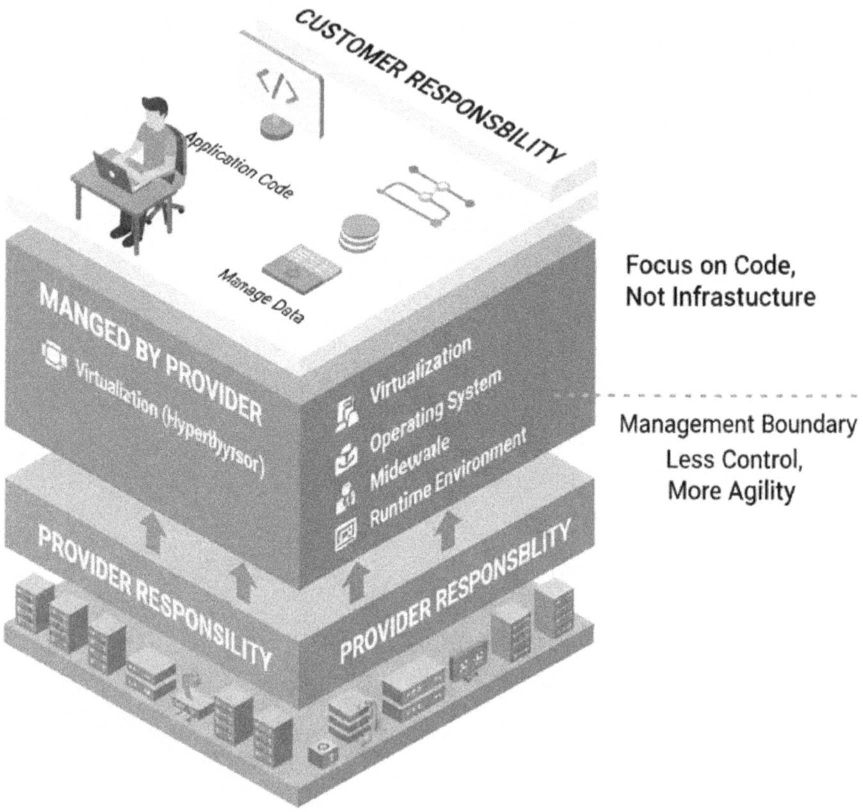

Pass: Abstracting the Stack, Empowering Developers

Platform as a Service (PaaS) elevates the abstraction layer. In this model, the cloud provider manages not only the hardware and virtualization but also the operating system, middleware, and runtime environment. The developer is responsible only for the application code and the data. PaaS is designed to streamline the entire software development lifecycle, from coding and testing to deployment and scaling.

3.1 The Architecture of Abstraction in PaaS

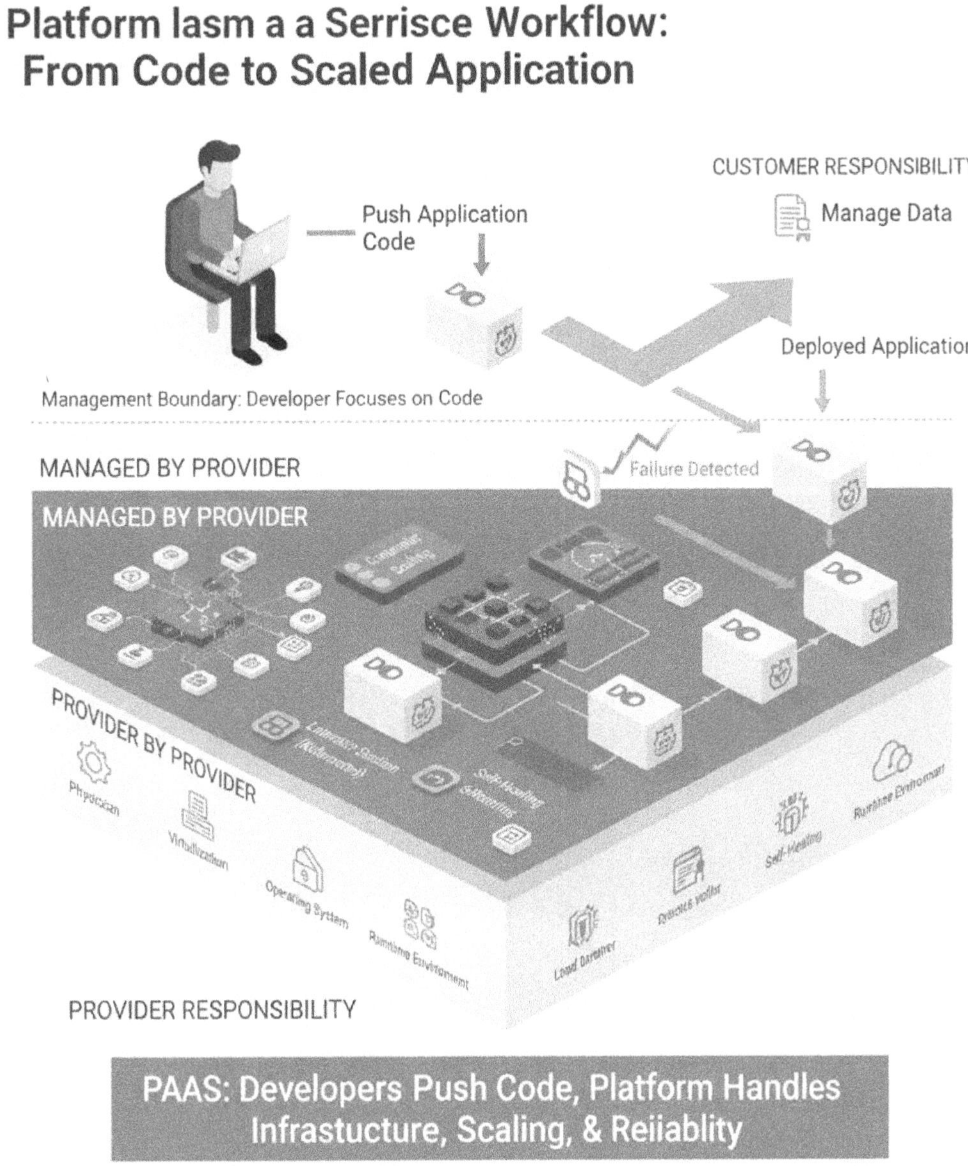

In a PaaS environment, the concept of a "server" largely disappears for the developer. Instead of worrying about how many gigabytes of RAM a server has or which version of Linux is running, the developer focuses on the "Runtime." Whether they are writing in Python, Java, Node.js, or .NET, the PaaS provider offers a ready-made environment where the code can simply be "pushed" and executed.

Modern PaaS solutions often utilize **Containerization** (like Docker and Kubernetes) behind the scenes. When a developer deploys an application, the PaaS platform packages the code into a lightweight container and handles the orchestration. This includes automatic load balancing, health monitoring, and scaling. If the traffic increases, the PaaS platform automatically spins up more instances of the application. If an instance fails, the platform kills it and starts a new one instantly. This "Self-Healing" nature of PaaS allows developers to focus entirely on feature development rather than infrastructure plumbing.

3.2 Accelerating the DevOps Pipeline

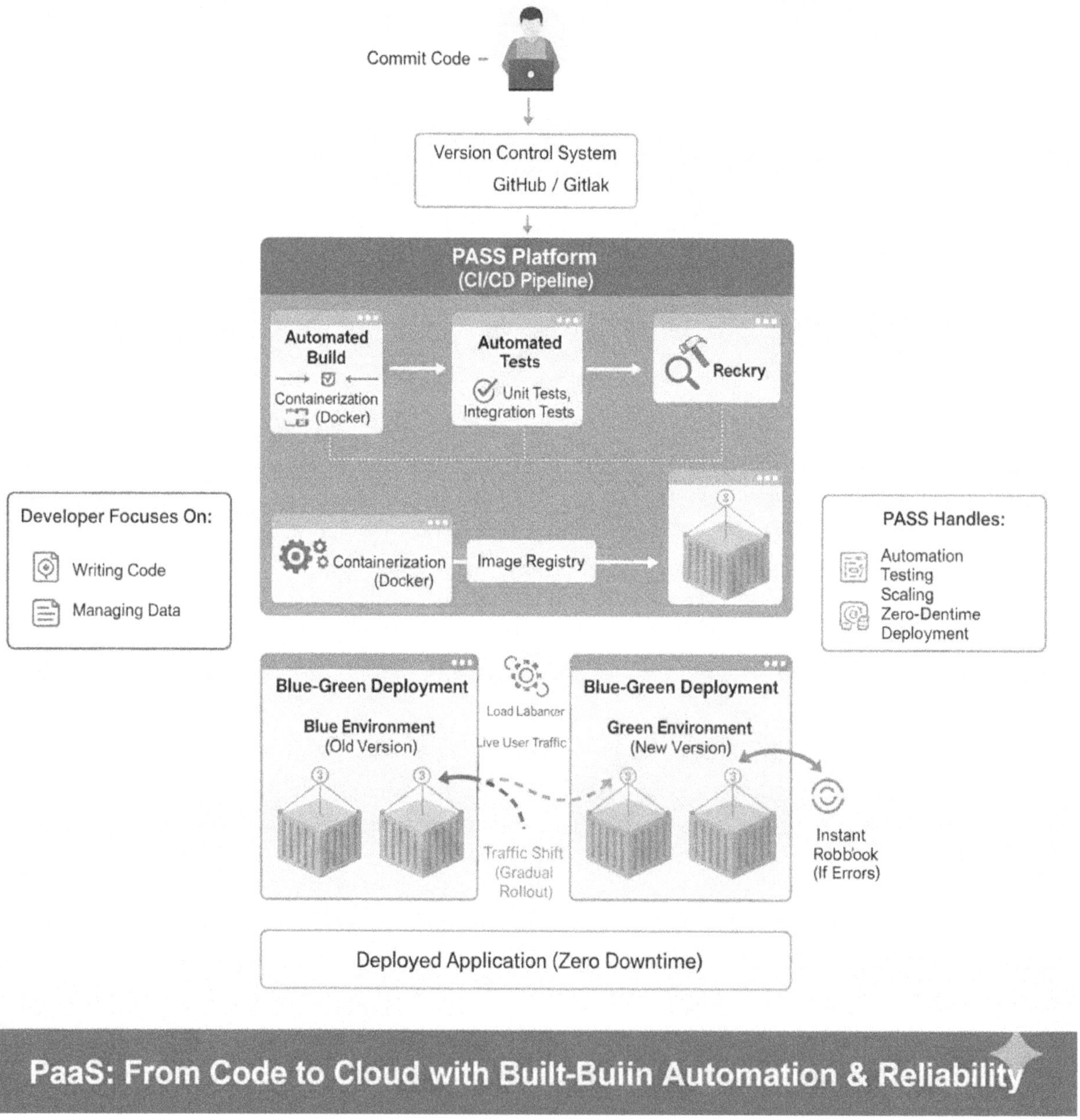

PaaS is the engine of the modern **CI/CD (Continuous Integration / Continuous Deployment)** pipeline. Because the environment is standardized, developers can be certain that the code that works on their local machine will work exactly the same way in production. PaaS platforms often integrate directly with version control systems like GitHub or GitLab. When a developer commits code, the PaaS platform can automatically trigger a build, run a battery of tests, and deploy the new version to a staging environment for review.

This level of automation reduces the "Time to Market" for new products. In a traditional environment, deploying a new version of an app might take hours of manual work by a "SysAdmin." In a PaaS environment, it happens in seconds. Furthermore, PaaS offers "Blue-Green Deployments," where a new version of the app is deployed alongside the old one. Traffic is gradually shifted to the new version, and if any errors are detected, the platform can instantly roll back all traffic to the "Green" (old) version, ensuring zero downtime for users.

3.3 The Trade-off: Convenience vs. Lock-in

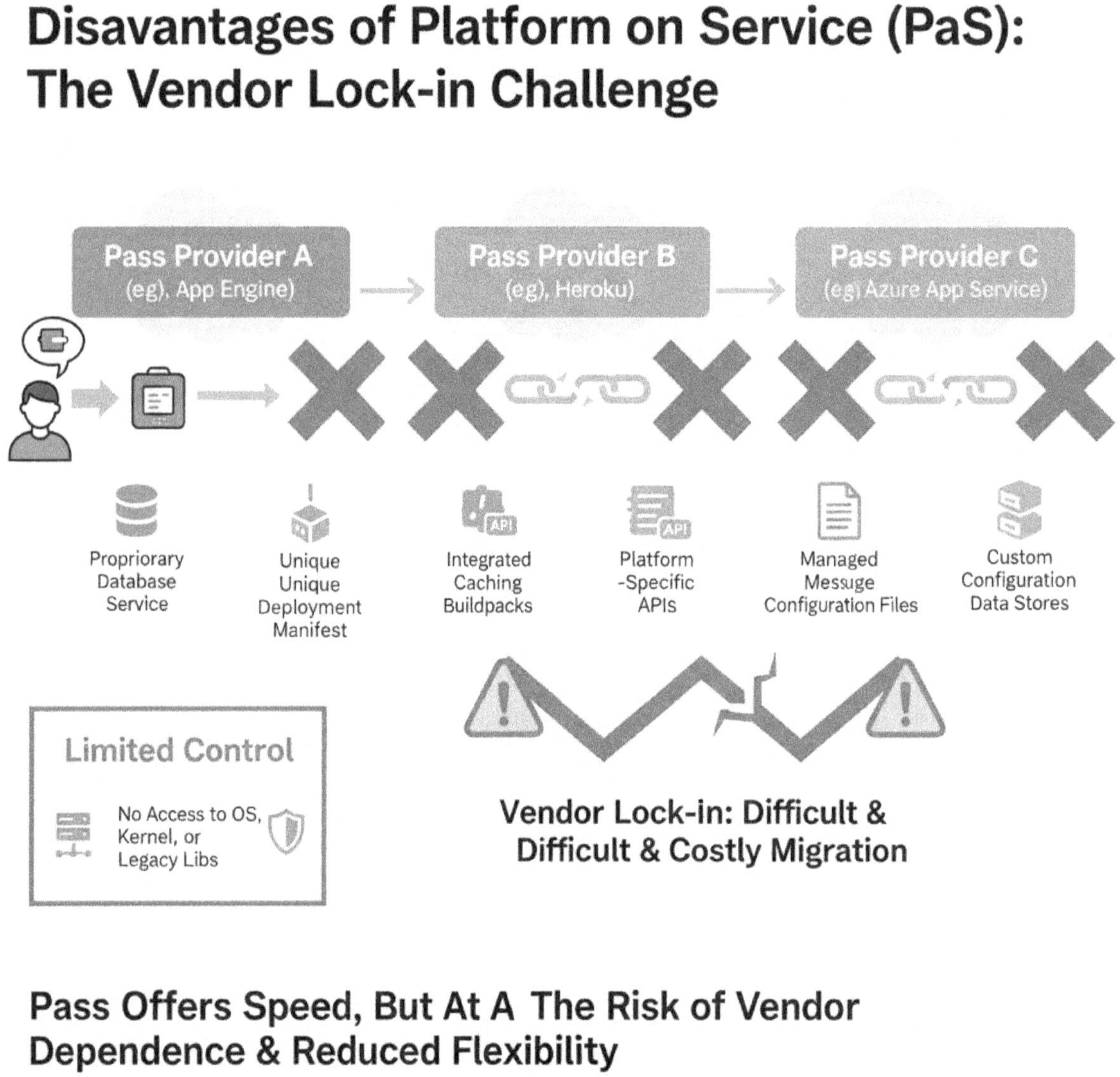

The primary disadvantage of PaaS is **Vendor Lock-in**. Because PaaS platforms often use proprietary APIs, deployment configurations, and integrated services (like specialized databases or caching layers), it can be difficult to move an application from one PaaS provider to another. For example, an app built specifically for Google App Engine might require significant rewriting to run on Heroku or Azure App Service. Additionally, the lack of control over the underlying operating system means that if an application requires a specific, non-standard kernel module or a legacy library that the provider doesn't support, the developer is out of luck. PaaS trades "Control" for "Speed."

4. Software as a Service (SaaS): The End-User Experience

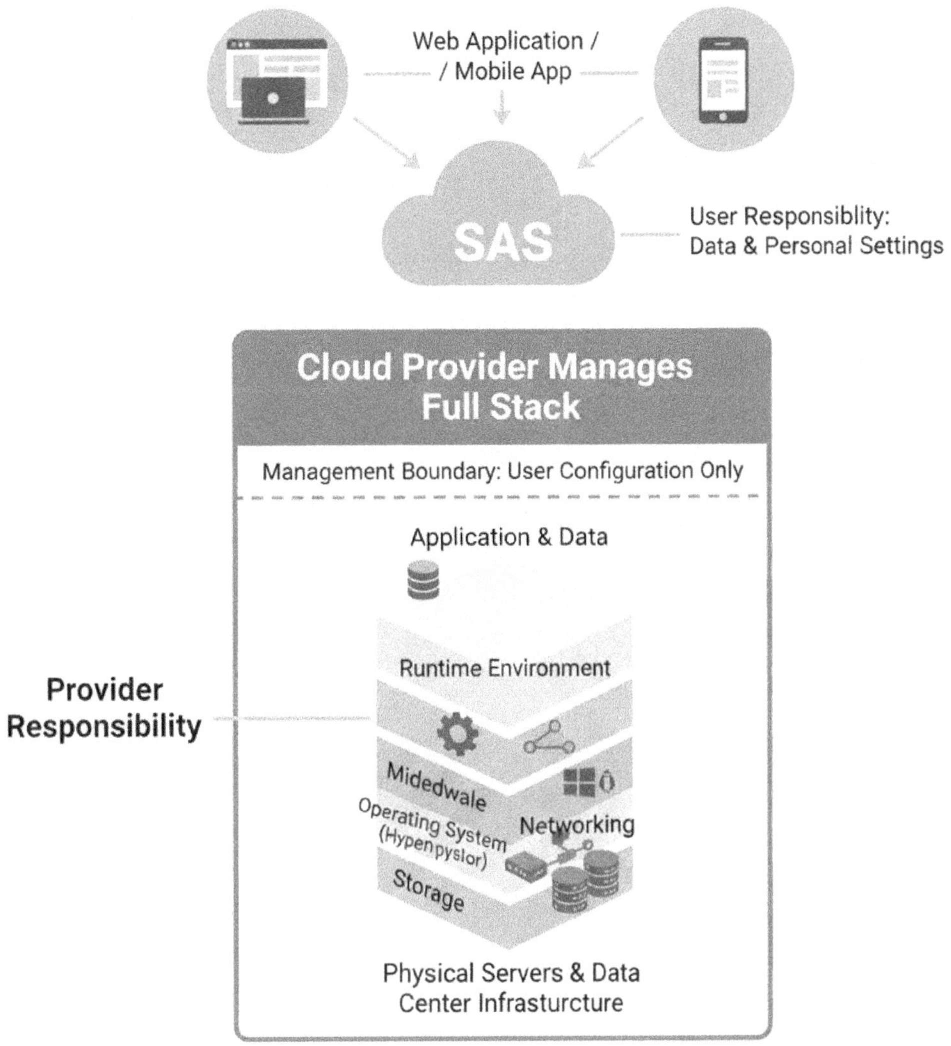

SAAS: Application Delivery, Zero Infrastructure Management

Software as a Service (SaaS) is the most complete cloud model, providing a fully functional application delivered via the web or a mobile app. In this model, the provider manages the entire stack—from the physical hardware and networking up to the application code and the user interface. The user is responsible only for their own data and their internal configuration settings.

4.1 The SaaS Economy and Multi-Tenancy

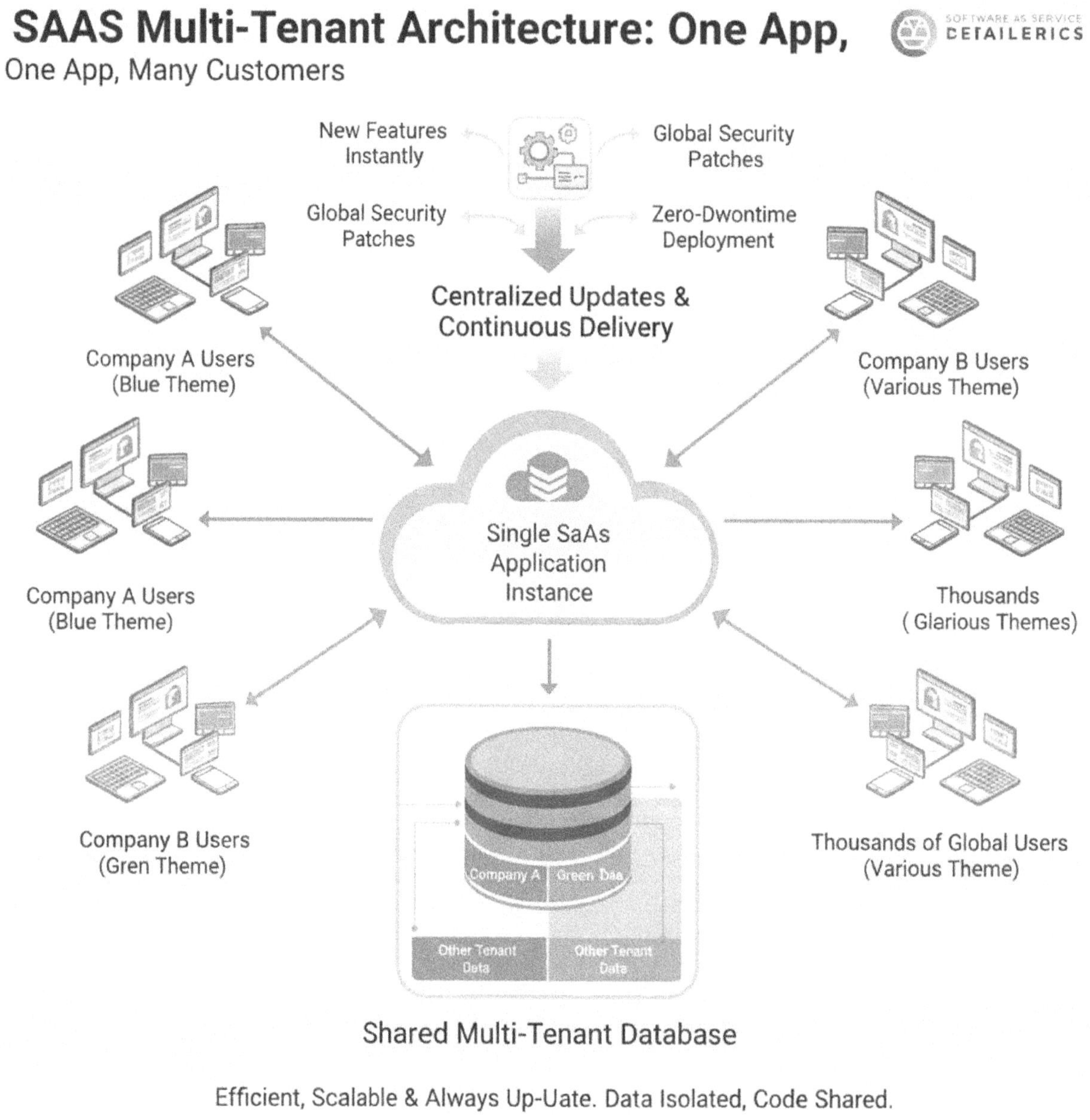

SaaS is the ultimate expression of the "Utility Computing" vision. It turns software from a product you buy and install into a service you subscribe to. The technical backbone of SaaS is **Multi-Tenancy**, where a single instance of the software serves thousands of different customers. Each customer's data is logically isolated within the database, but they all share the same code base and hardware resources.

This multi-tenant architecture is what allows SaaS providers like Salesforce, Zoom, or Slack to offer high-end enterprise software at a fraction of the traditional cost. Updates are managed centrally; when the provider releases a new feature or a security patch, it is instantly available to every user globally. There is no such thing as "Version 2.0" or "Version 3.0" in SaaS; the software is in a state of "Permanent Beta," constantly evolving and improving without requiring any action from the user.

4.2 Accessibility and Collaborative Innovation

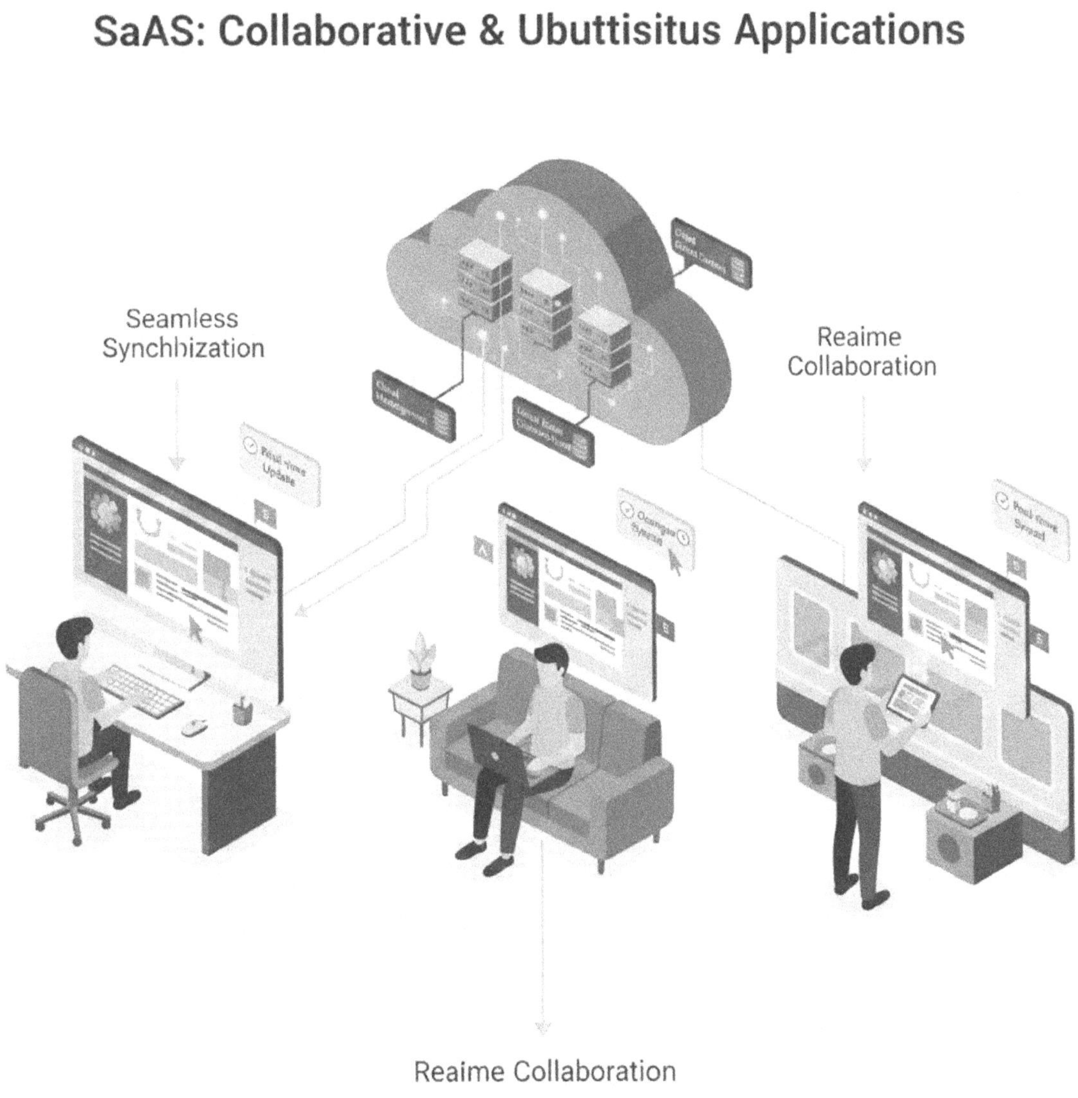

SaaS has revolutionized the way we work by enabling **Ubiquitous Access**. Because the application lives in the cloud, a user can start a document on a desktop in the office, edit it on a smartphone during a commute, and present it from a laptop at home. This seamless synchronization is facilitated by the SaaS provider's global data centers.

Furthermore, SaaS has enabled a new era of "Collaborative Innovation." Applications like Google Docs or Figma allow multiple users from different parts of the world to work on the same file simultaneously. The cloud handles the complex "State Management"—ensuring that everyone sees the changes in real-time and managing the "Collision Detection" if two people try to edit the same sentence. This level of collaboration would be technically impossible with traditional, locally installed software.

4.3 Security and Data Sovereignty in SaaS

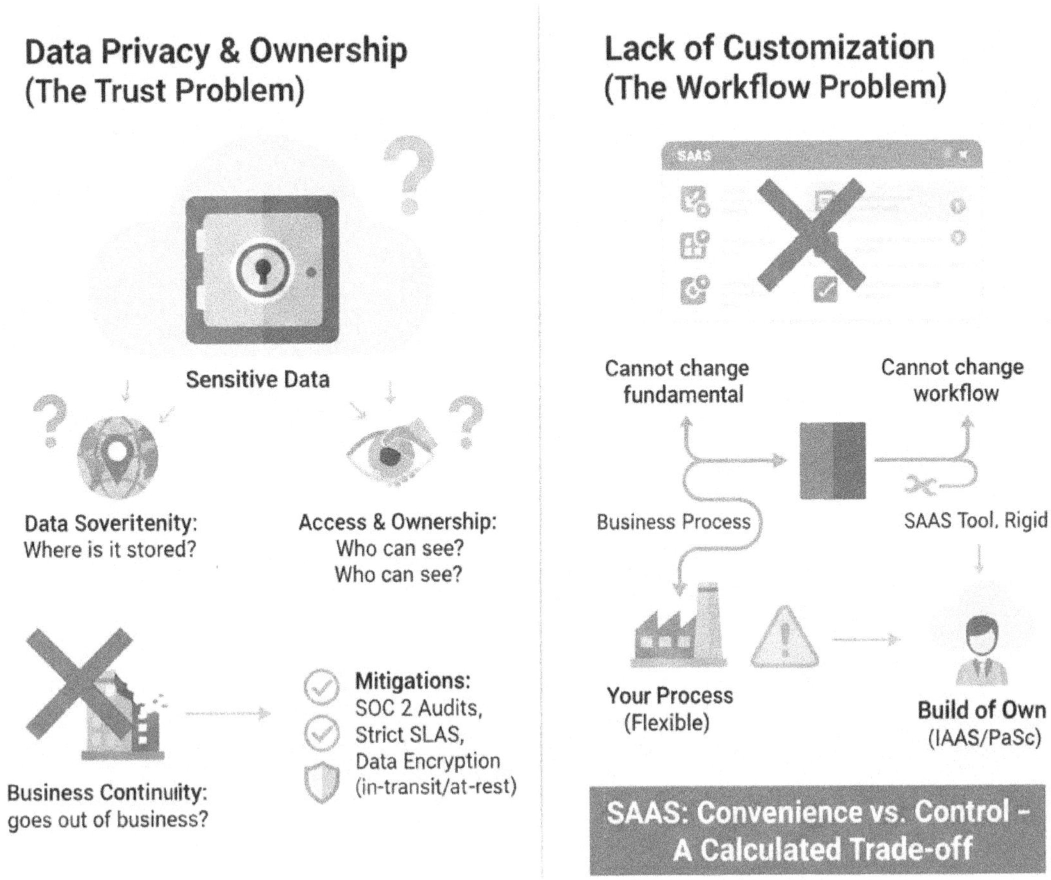

The biggest concern with SaaS is **Data Privacy and Ownership**. When an organization uses a SaaS provider, they are essentially entrusting their most sensitive data to a third party. This raises questions about **Data Sovereignty**: Where is the data physically stored? Who has access to it? What happens to the data if the SaaS provider goes out of business?

To address these concerns, modern SaaS providers undergo rigorous third-party audits (like SOC 2) and provide detailed "Service Level Agreements" (SLAs) that guarantee 99.9% uptime and specify data encryption standards. However, the "Lack of Customization" remains a hurdle. While SaaS apps offer configuration options, you cannot change the fundamental way the software works. If your business process doesn't fit the SaaS tool's workflow, you must either change your process or build your own solution using IaaS or PaaS.

5. Comparative Analysis: Which Model to Choose?

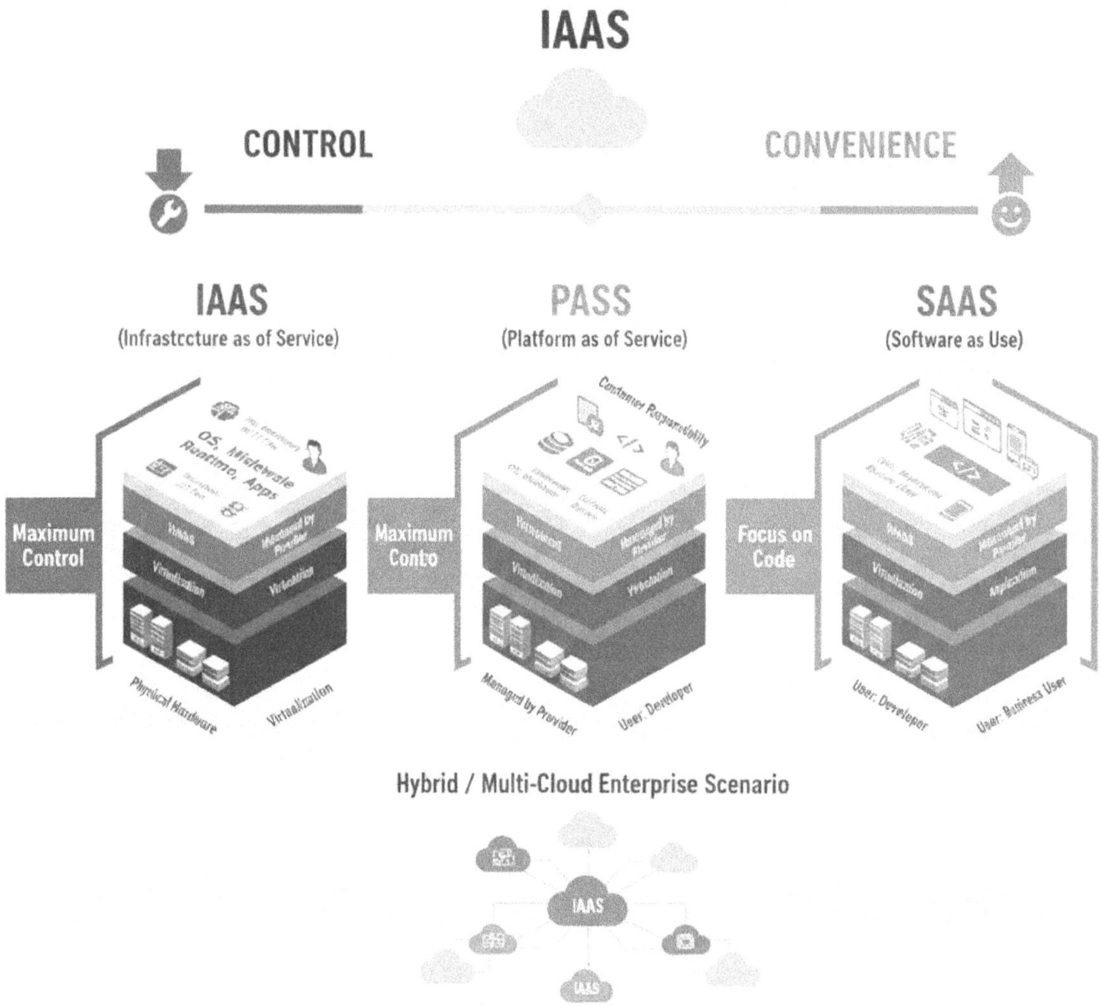

Choosing between IaaS, PaaS, and SaaS is not a matter of which is "better," but which is "most appropriate" for the specific business objective. This is often described as a balance between **Control and Convenience**.

- **IaaS is for the Architect.** It provides the raw materials. Use IaaS when you need to build a custom, highly specific infrastructure or when migrating complex legacy systems that require specific OS configurations. It offers the most control but requires the most expertise and manual labor.
- **PaaS is for the Developer.** It provides the tools. Use PaaS when the goal is to develop and deploy new applications as quickly as possible. It removes the distraction of server management, allowing the team to focus 100% on the user experience and business logic.
- **SaaS is for the Business User.** It provides the solution. Use SaaS for standard business functions that do not provide a competitive advantage if built from scratch—such as email, CRM, or HR management. It is the most cost-effective and easiest to deploy but offers the least flexibility.

In a modern enterprise, a "Multi-Cloud" or "Hybrid Model" is common. A company might host its proprietary core engine on IaaS for maximum control, use PaaS for its front-end mobile app development to ensure rapid updates, and use SaaS for its day-to-day operations like Slack and Microsoft 365.

6. The Future of Delivery: FaaS and Serverless

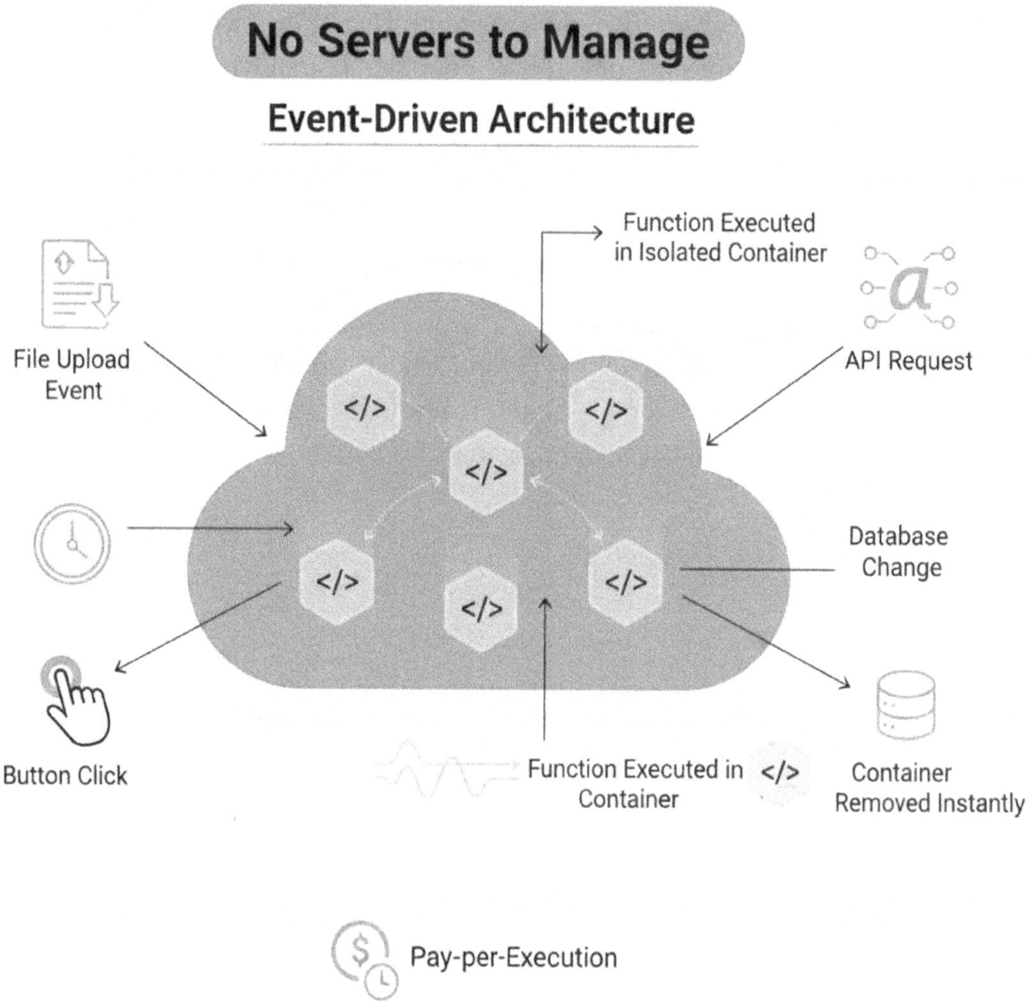

As the SPI model evolves, a new layer has emerged: **Function as a Service (FaaS)**, often called "Serverless Computing." If PaaS abstracts the operating system, FaaS abstracts the "Application" itself. In FaaS, the developer writes a single function—a small piece of code that does one specific thing (e.g., "Resize an Image" or "Calculate Sales Tax"). This code sits idle until it is triggered by an event, such as a user uploading a file or clicking a button.

The cloud provider handles everything: spinning up a container, executing the function, and then instantly destroying the container. The user pays only for the milliseconds the code was running. This represents the ultimate optimization of the cloud model. It eliminates "Idle Capacity" entirely.

With FaaS, the concept of a "server" is so far removed from the developer's consciousness that the infrastructure becomes truly invisible. FaaS is the next logical step in the historical journey we tracked in Chapter 2—moving from the monolithic mainframe to the fluid, event-driven, and infinitely granular digital world of tomorrow.

7. Economic Impact: From Ownership to Access

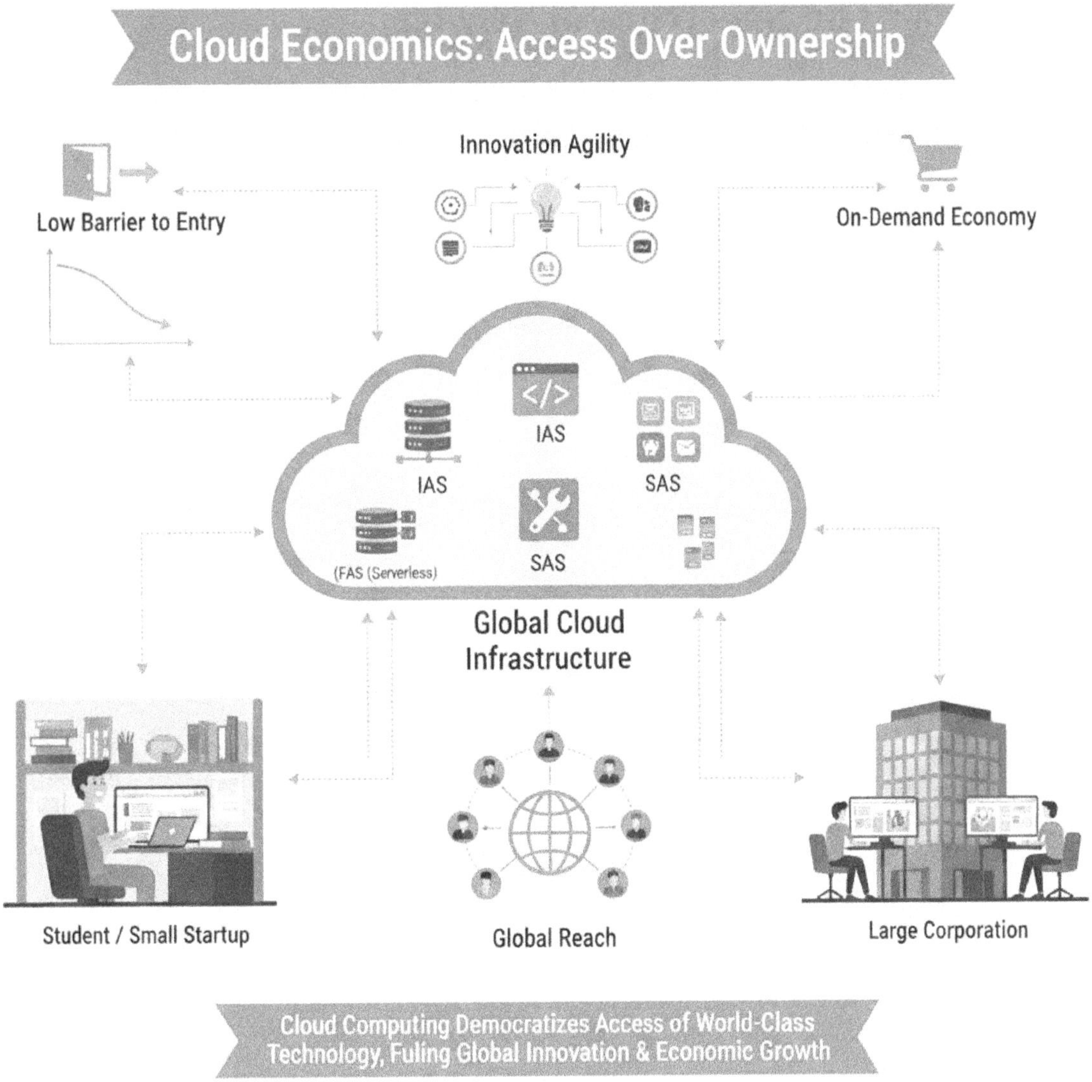

The SPI model has fundamentally changed the global economy. By turning technology into a "Service," the cloud has lowered the "Barrier to Entry" for innovation. In the past, starting a tech company required hundreds of thousands of dollars in capital to buy servers. Today, a student in a dorm room can access the same world-class infrastructure as a multinational corporation for the price of a cup of coffee.

This shift from "Ownership" to "Access" has created an "On-Demand Economy." It encourages experimentation; because the cost of failure is low, companies can try out ten different ideas on the cloud, keep the one that works, and "Turn Off" the nine that don't. This agility is what allows the digital economy to move at its current breakneck speed.

8. Summary: The Spectrum of Service

Chapter 5 has mapped the diverse landscape of cloud delivery models. We have seen how IaaS provides the resilient foundation of virtualized hardware, how PaaS empowers the developer with standardized runtimes and automated pipelines, and how SaaS delivers the finished product to the end-user with unprecedented accessibility.

Chapter – 6

Cloud Deployment Models

examines the "where" and "how" of cloud hosting, covering Public, Private, Hybrid, and Community clouds. It also pulls back the curtain on physical data center engineering, including cooling, power redundancy, and the CAPEX-to-OPEX economic transition.

1. Introduction: The Strategic Selection of Cloud Environments

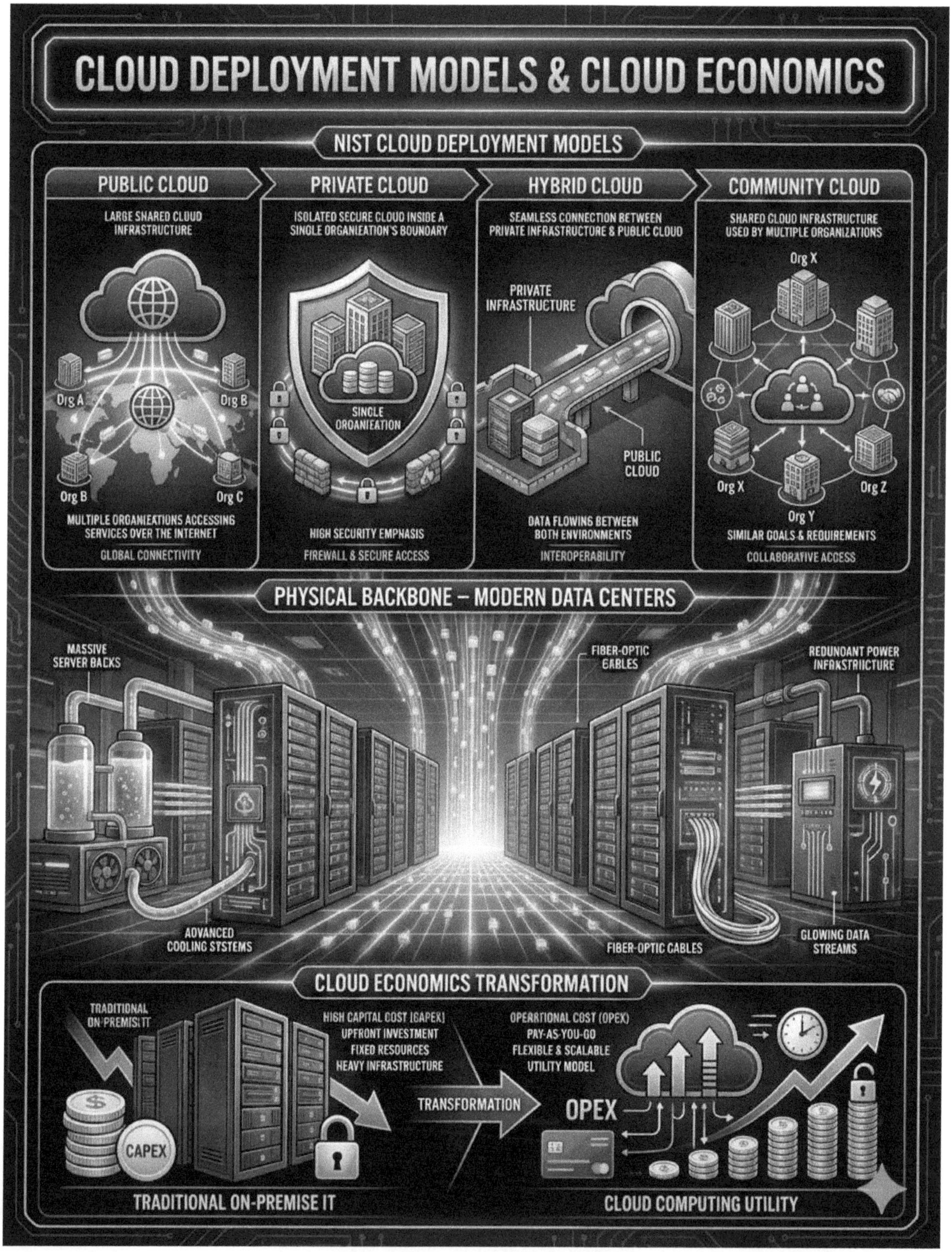

While the SPI model (Chapter 5) defines *what* is being delivered, Cloud Deployment Models define *how* those services are hosted and who has access to the underlying infrastructure. The choice of a deployment model is one of the most consequential decisions an organization can make, as it dictates the levels of security, control, scalability, and cost efficiency available to the enterprise.

This chapter examines the four primary deployment models recognized by the NIST (National Institute of Standards and Technology): Public, Private, Hybrid, and Community clouds. Furthermore, we will pull back the curtain on the "Physical Backbone" of these virtual environments—the Data Center—and analyze the fundamental shift in Cloud Economics that has transformed IT from a capital-heavy burden into a flexible, operational utility.

2. Public Cloud: The Model of Global Scale

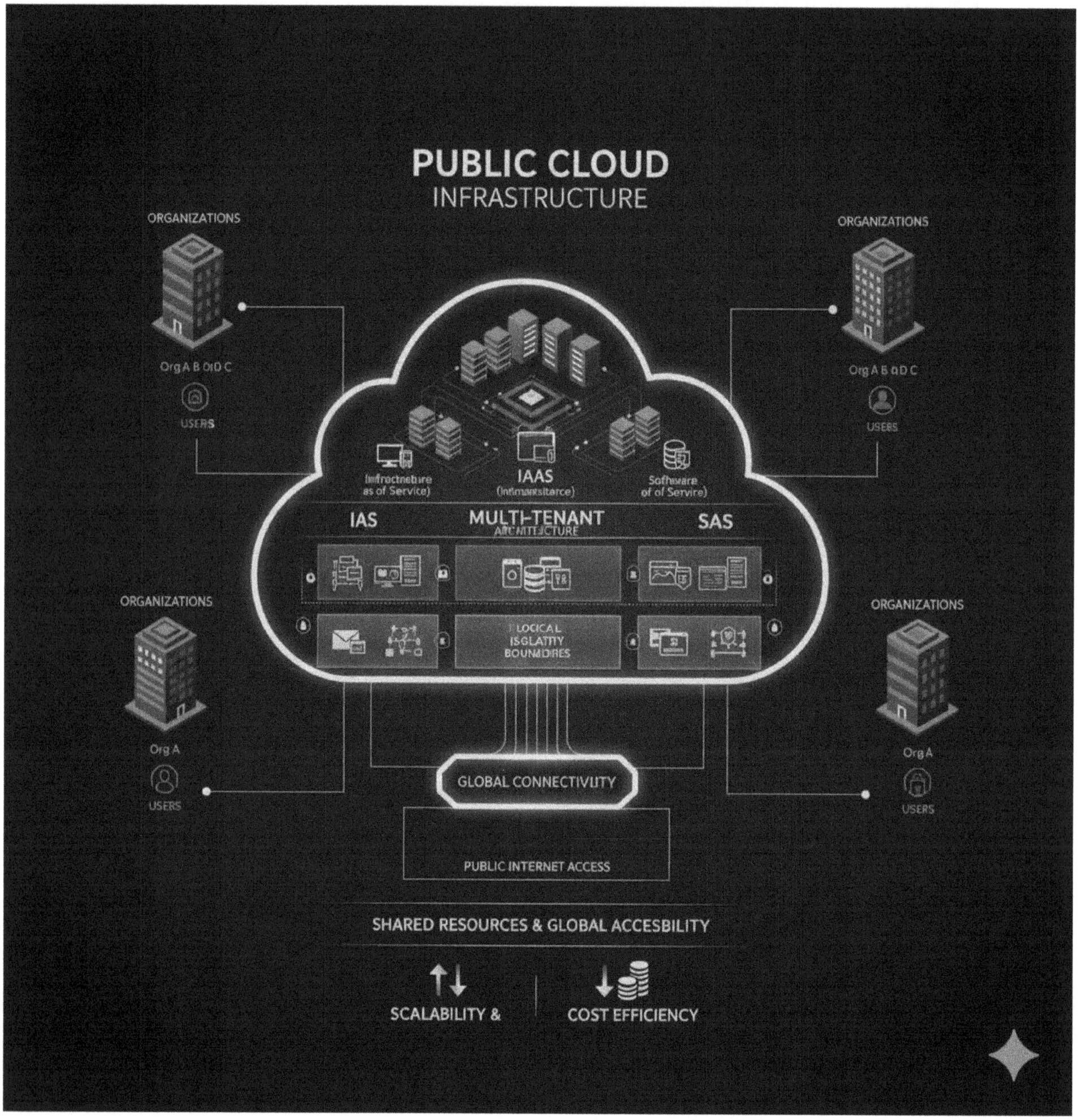

The **Public Cloud** is the most recognizable and widely used deployment model. In this setup, cloud services (IaaS, PaaS, or SaaS) are owned and operated by a third-party provider and delivered over the public internet. The infrastructure—servers, storage, and networking—is shared among multiple organizations (tenants), though each tenant's data and workloads remain logically isolated.

2.1 Characteristics and Technical Advantages

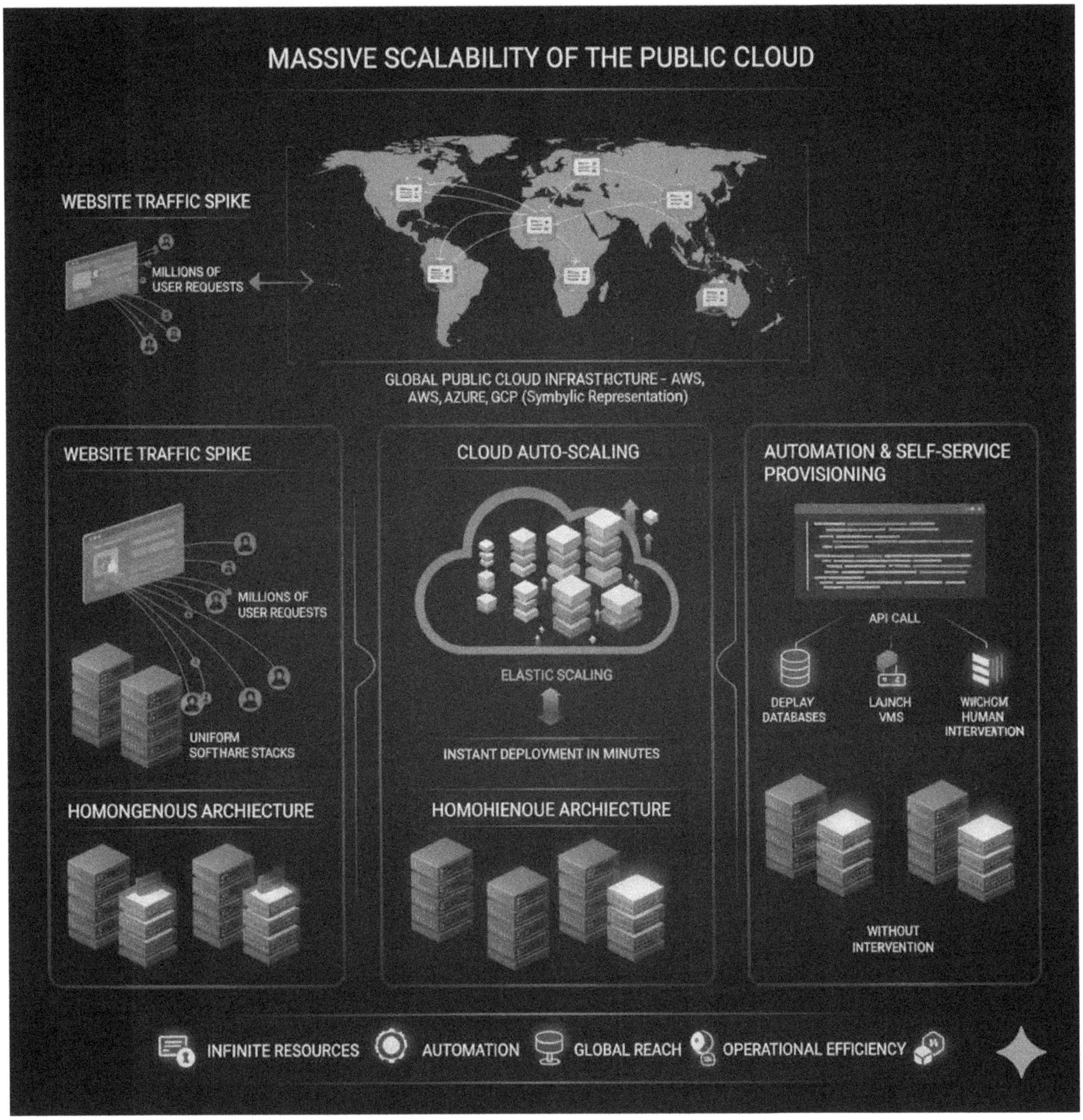

The defining characteristic of the public cloud is **Massive Scalability**. Providers like Amazon Web Services (AWS), Microsoft Azure, and Google Cloud Platform (GCP) operate millions of servers across dozens of geographic regions. For a customer, this means that resources are essentially infinite. If a viral marketing campaign suddenly drives millions of users to a website, the public cloud can automatically provision thousands of additional virtual instances in minutes to handle the load.

Technically, public clouds utilize a **Homogeneous Architecture**. By using standardized hardware and software stacks across their entire global footprint, providers can automate management at a scale that is impossible for a single company to replicate. This automation includes self-service provisioning, where a developer can launch a database or a machine learning cluster with a single API call, without any human intervention from the provider.

2.2 The Economic Appeal of Public Cloud

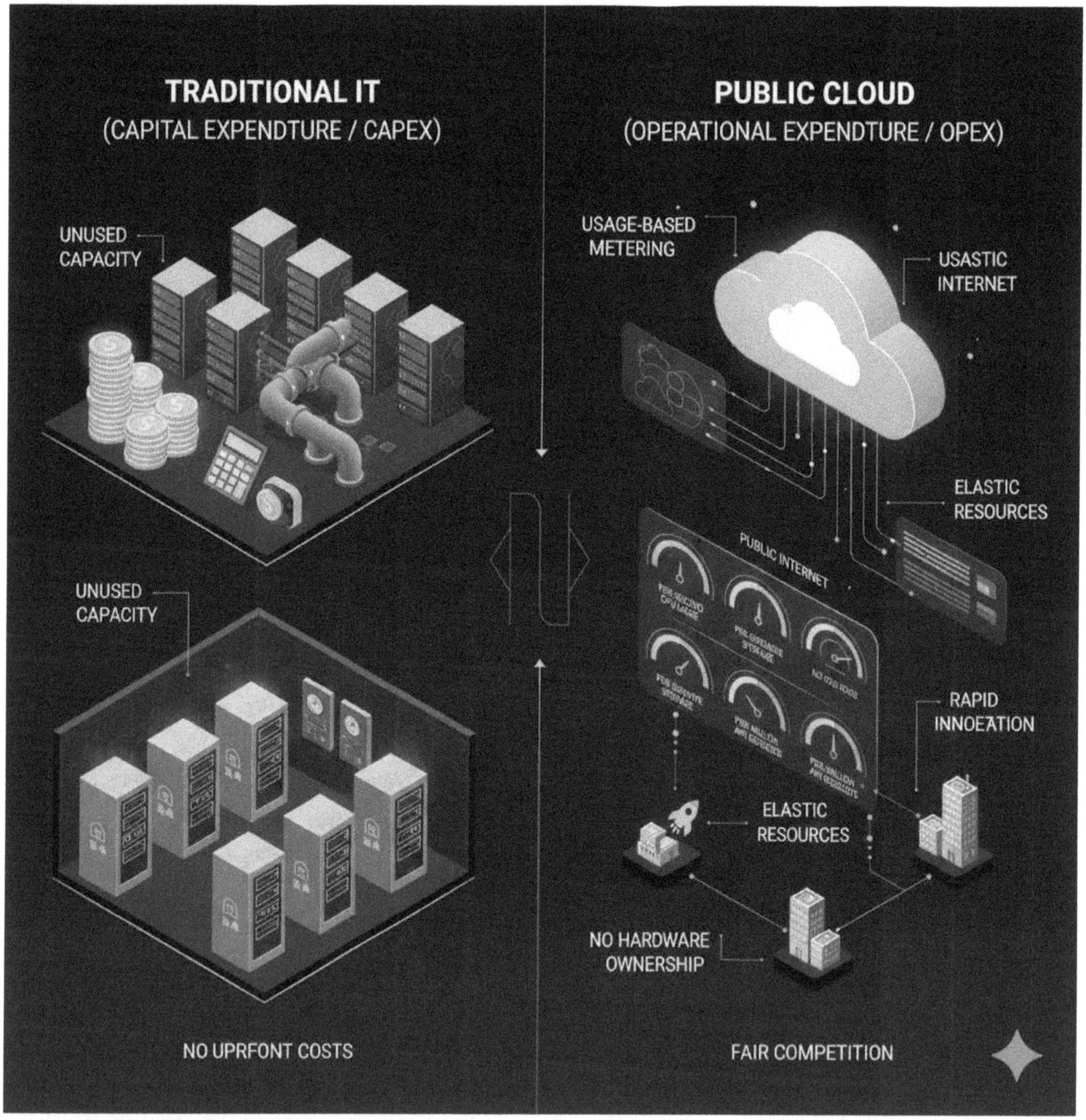

The public cloud is the primary driver of the **"Pay-as-you-go"** philosophy. Because the provider owns the hardware, the customer avoids all upfront costs. There are no servers to buy, no data centers to build, and no electricity bills to pay. Instead, the customer is billed based on actual consumption—per second of CPU time, per gigabyte of storage, or per million API requests. This eliminates the risk of "Shelfware" (purchased software or hardware that is never used) and allows startups to compete with established giants on an even playing field.

2.3 Challenges: Security, Compliance, and the "Black Box"

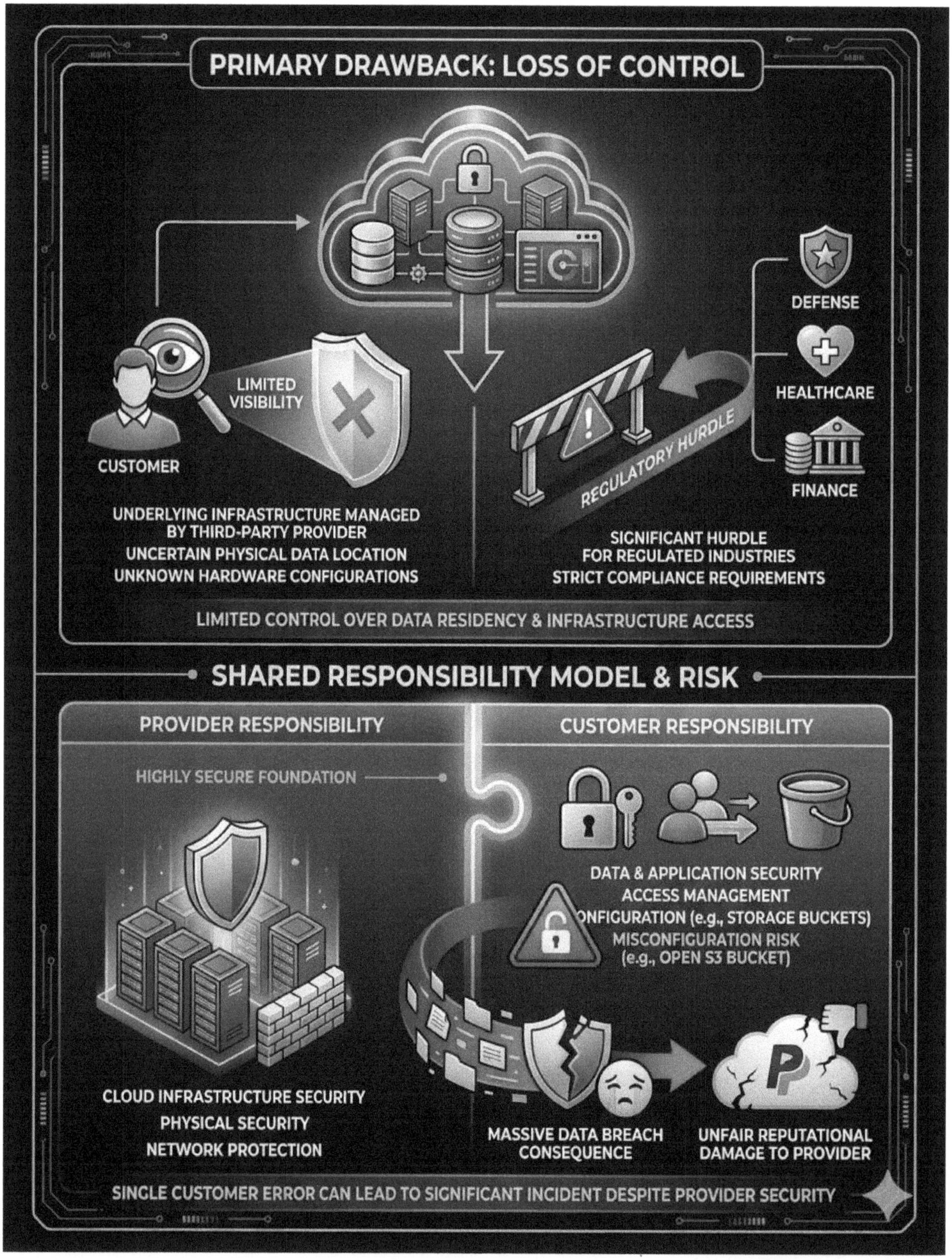

The primary drawback of the public cloud is the **Loss of Control**. Because the provider manages the underlying infrastructure, the customer has limited visibility into the exact physical location of their data or the specific hardware configurations. This can be a significant hurdle for industries with strict regulatory requirements, such as defense, healthcare, or finance. Furthermore, while the cloud is highly secure, the "Shared Responsibility" model means that a single misconfiguration by the customer (such as an open S3 bucket) can lead to a massive data breach, often unfairly tarnishing the provider's reputation.

3. Private Cloud: The Model of Total Control

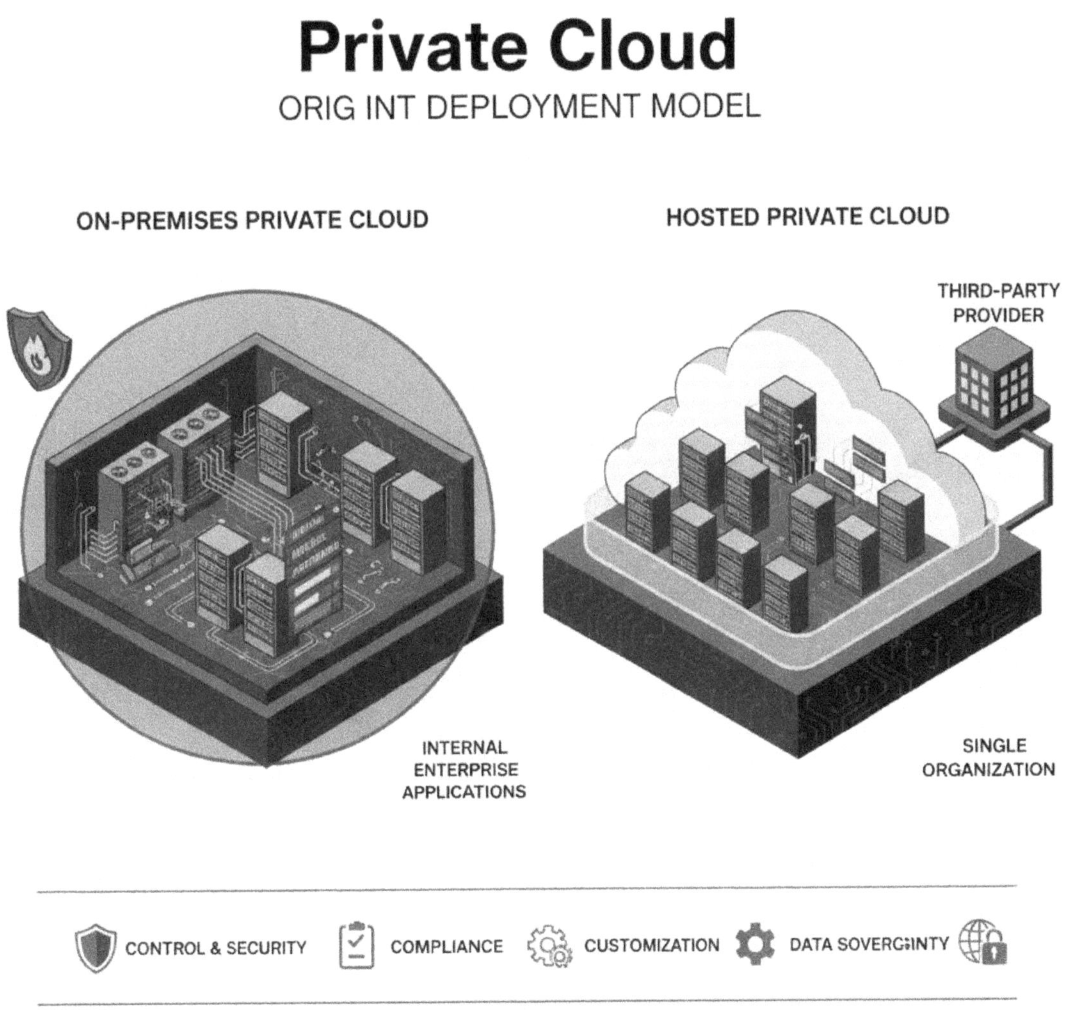

A **Private Cloud** is a cloud environment dedicated exclusively to a single organization. It can be hosted on-premises (in the company's own data center) or managed by a third party (hosted private cloud). The key distinction is that the infrastructure is not shared with any other tenants.

3.1 Why Choose Private Cloud?

The primary drivers for private cloud are **Security and Compliance**. For organizations dealing with highly sensitive intellectual property or government secrets, the "Multi-Tenancy" of the public cloud is often seen as an unacceptable risk. A private cloud allows for "Physical Isolation," ensuring that no other company's code ever runs on the same silicon.

Furthermore, a private cloud provides **Customization**. In a public cloud, you are limited to the instance types and configurations the provider offers. In a private cloud, an organization can build a bespoke environment optimized for specific, high-performance workloads—such as a specialized GPU cluster for medical imaging or a high-frequency trading platform with ultra-low latency networking that public providers cannot guarantee.

3.2 Technical Implementation: The Software-Defined Data Center (SDDC)

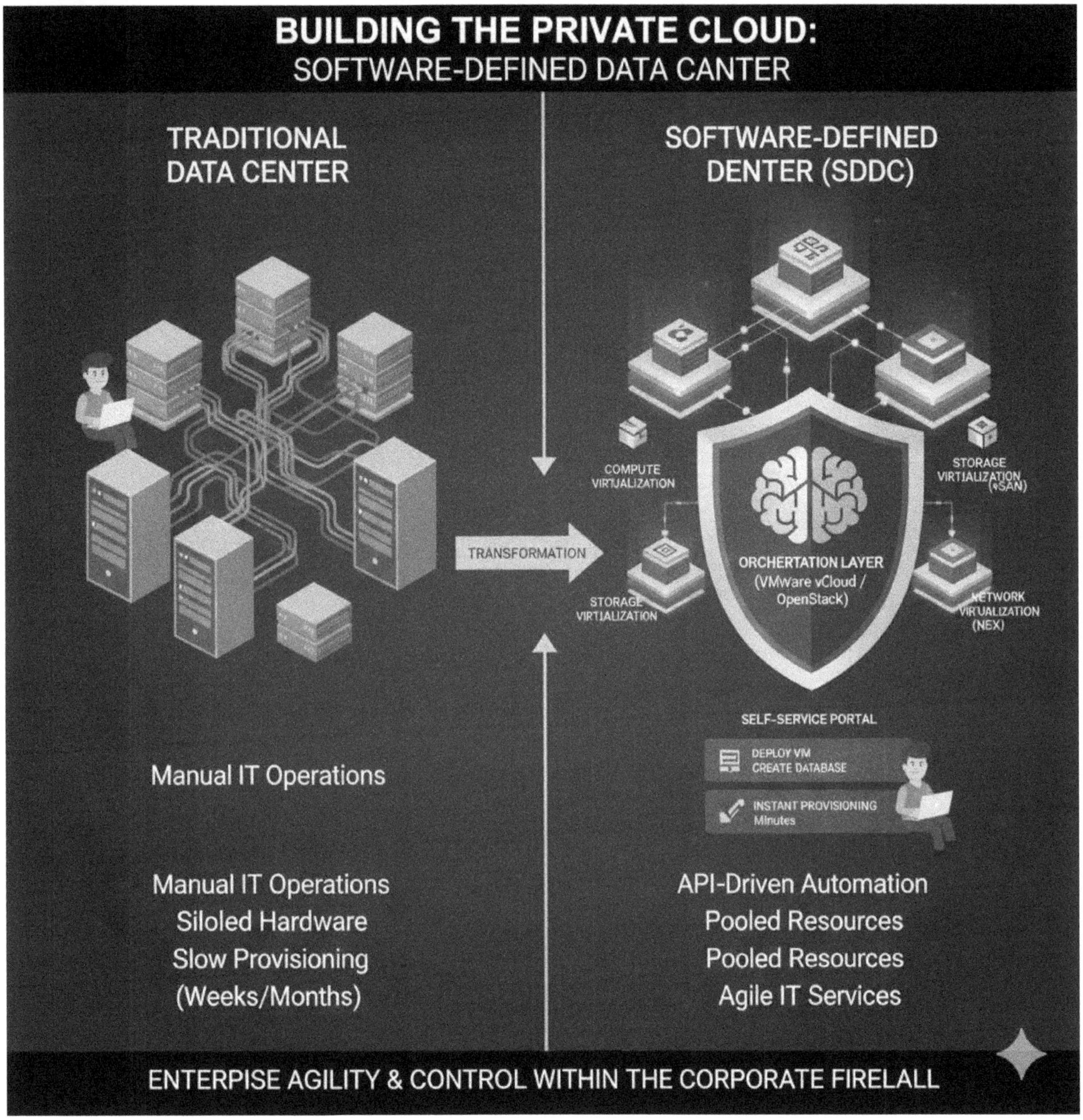

Building a private cloud is more than just buying servers; it requires transforming a traditional data center into a **Software-Defined Data Center (SDDC)**. This involves implementing a comprehensive orchestration layer (such as VMware vCloud or OpenStack) that virtualizes not just compute, but also storage (vSAN) and networking (NSX). The goal is to provide internal developers with the same "Self-Service" experience they would find in the public cloud, but within the safety of the corporate firewall.

3.3 The Downside: High CAPEX and Complexity

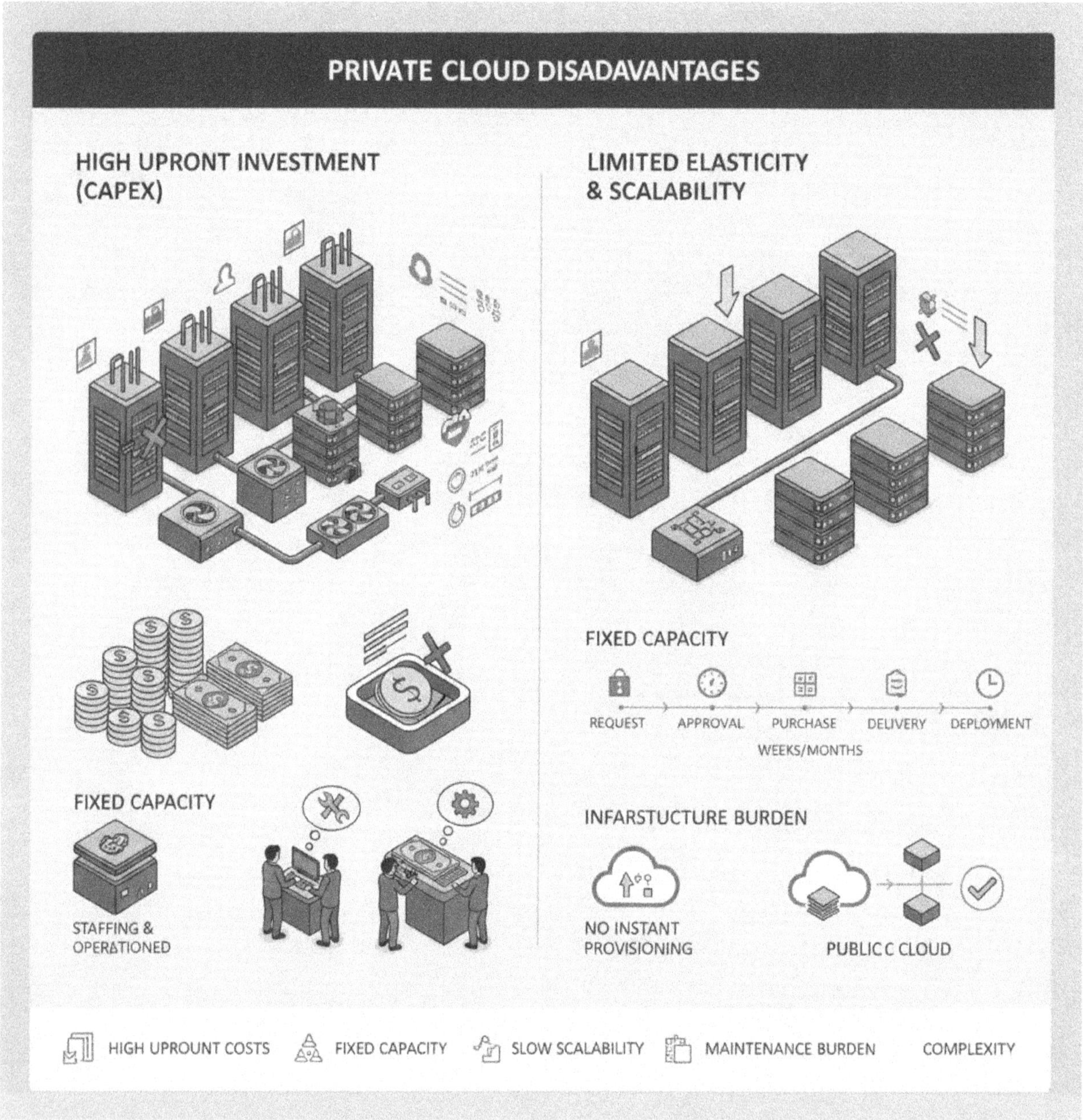

The disadvantage of the private cloud is the return to **Capital Expenditure (CAPEX)**. The organization must once again buy the hardware, pay for the cooling, and employ a large team of specialized engineers to maintain the infrastructure. A private cloud is also less elastic than a public cloud; if the company runs out of physical capacity, it cannot instantly "scale up"—it must go through the traditional procurement cycle to buy more servers.

4. Hybrid Cloud: The Best of Both Worlds

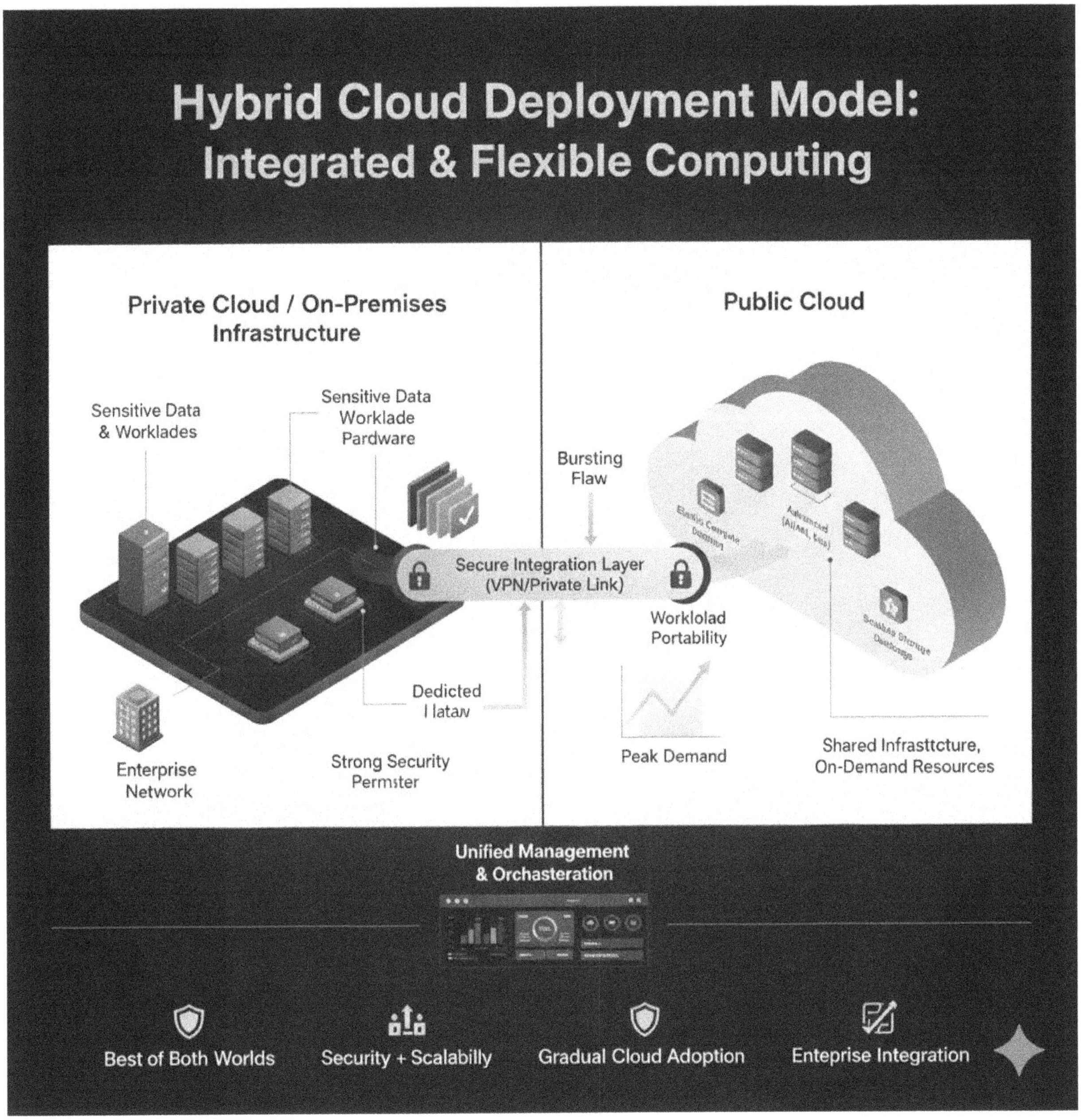

The **Hybrid Cloud** is the most complex and increasingly the most popular deployment model. It is a computing environment that combines a private cloud (or on-premises infrastructure) with a public cloud, allowing data and applications to be shared between them.

4.1 "Cloud Bursting" and Strategic Flexibility

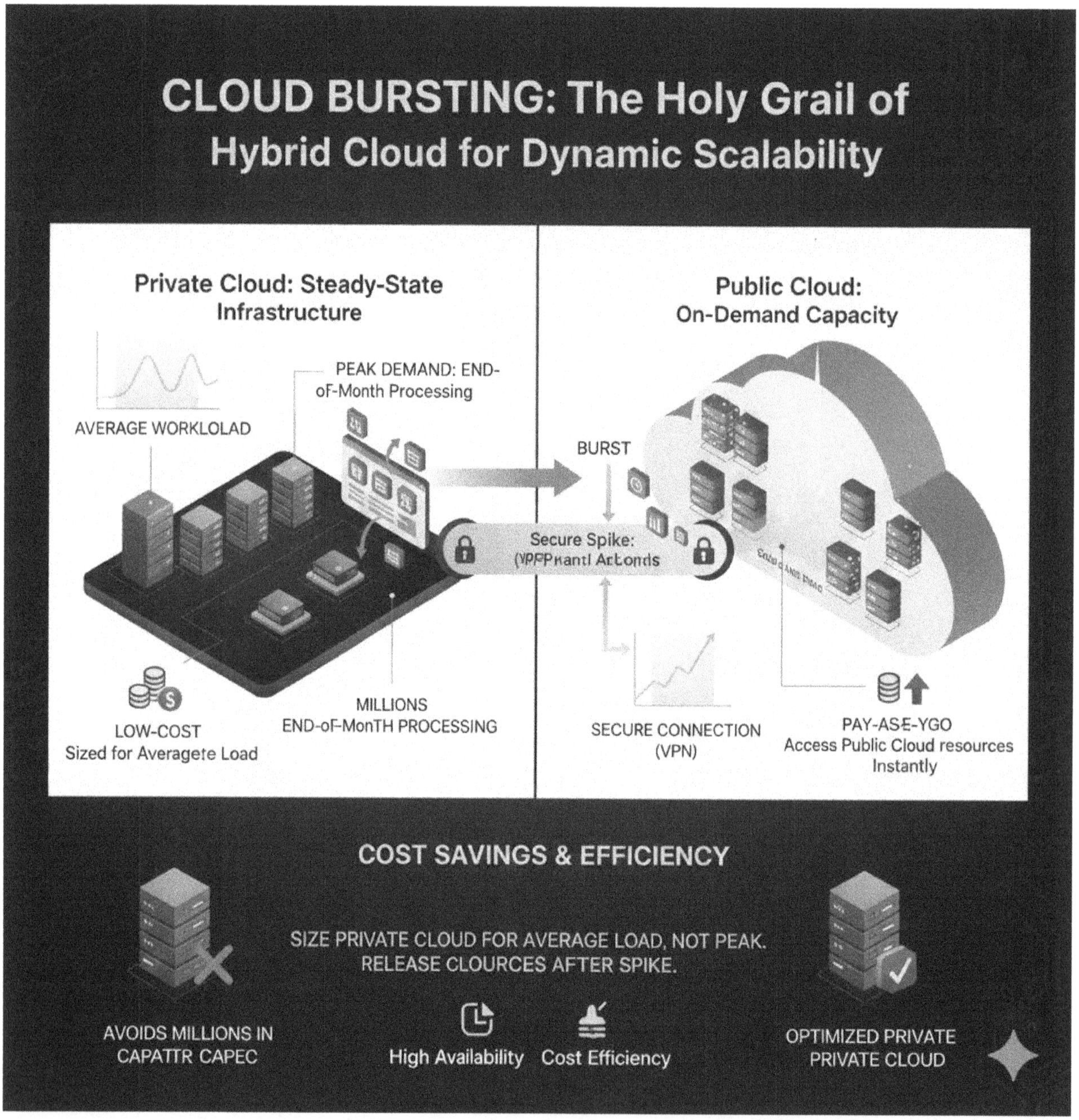

The "Holy Grail" of hybrid cloud is **Cloud Bursting**. In this scenario, an organization runs its steady-state workloads in its own low-cost private cloud. When a spike in demand occurs (such as end-of-month financial processing), the application "bursts" into the public cloud to access additional capacity. Once the spike is over, the public cloud resources are released. This allows the company to size its private data center for the "average" load rather than the "peak" load, saving millions in hardware costs.

4.2 Data Sovereignty and Tiering

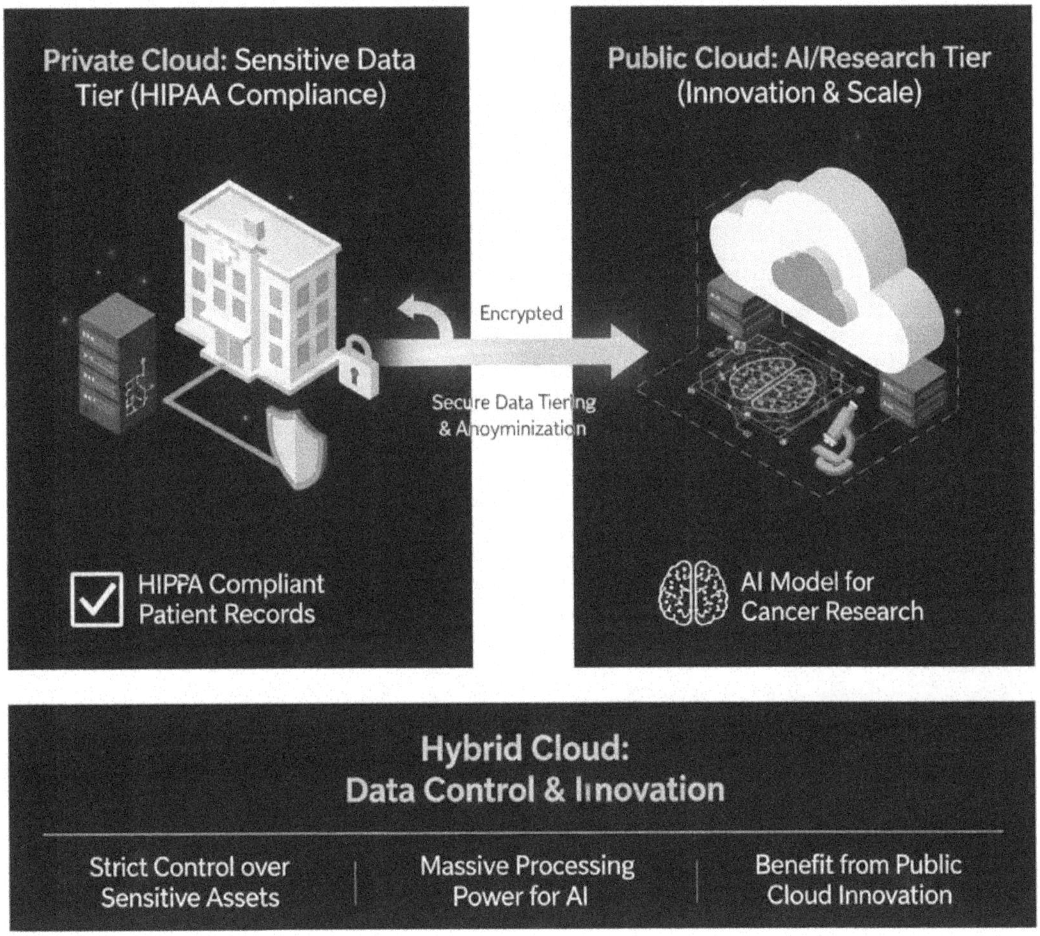

Hybrid cloud also enables **Data Tiering**. A hospital might keep sensitive patient records in its private cloud to comply with HIPAA regulations, while using the public cloud's massive processing power to run anonymous, aggregated data through an AI model for cancer research. This allows the organization to benefit from the public cloud's innovation while maintaining strict control over its most sensitive assets.

4.3 Technical Challenges: Latency and Connectivity

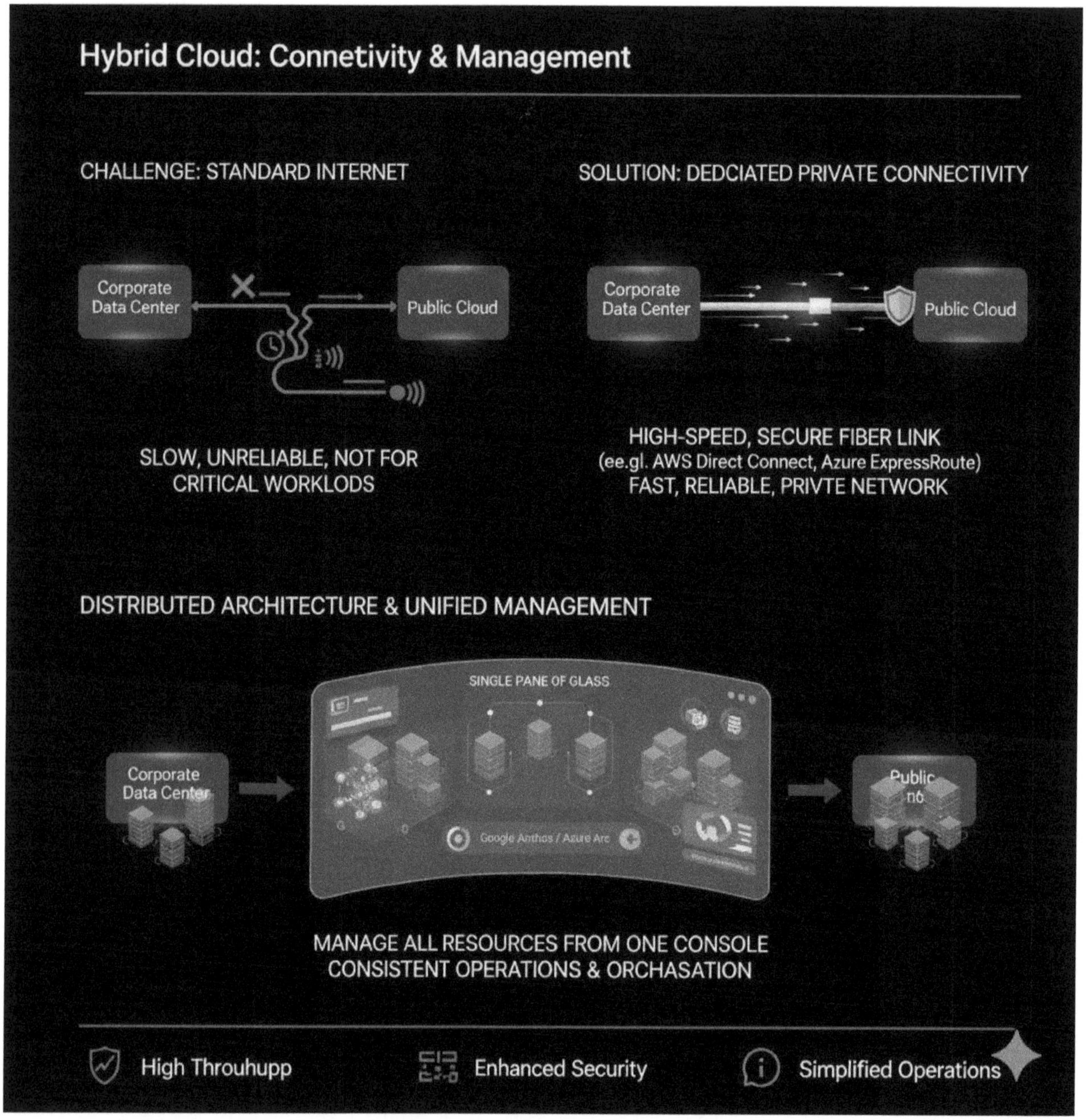

The success of a hybrid cloud depends on the connectivity between the two environments. Standard internet connections are often too slow or unreliable for hybrid workloads. Instead, organizations use dedicated connections like **AWS Direct Connect** or **Azure ExpressRoute,** which provide a private, high-speed fiber link between the corporate data center and the cloud provider. Managing this "Distributed Architecture" requires sophisticated tools (like Google Anthos or Azure Arc) that can provide a "Single Pane of Glass" view of resources regardless of where they are physically located.

5. Community Cloud: The Model of Shared Interest

The **Community Cloud** is a specialized model where the infrastructure is shared by several organizations with similar concerns, such as a common mission, security requirements, policy, or compliance considerations.

5.1 Use Cases in Government and Research

A classic example is a **Government Cloud**. Multiple federal agencies might share a cloud environment that meets specific high-security clearances (such as FedRAMP High). No commercial entities are allowed in this "Community," ensuring that the environment is optimized for the specific regulatory and security needs of the state.

Similarly, in **Higher Education and Research**, several universities might pool their resources to build a community cloud for massive scientific simulations (like the Large Hadron Collider data analysis). By sharing the cost and the management burden, these institutions can access supercomputing capabilities that none of them could afford individually.

6. The Physical Backbone: The Modern Data Center

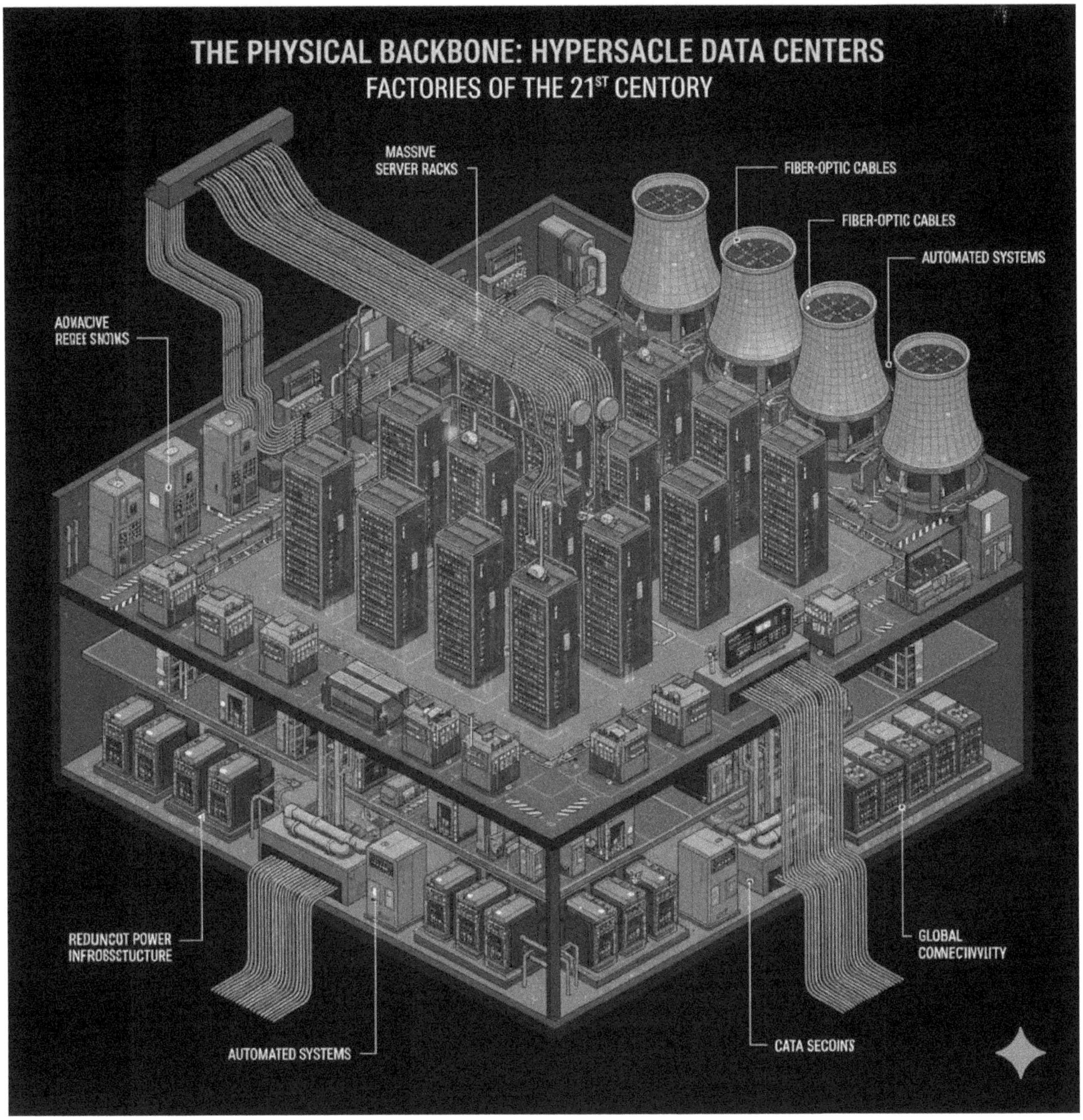

While the cloud is often described as "virtual," it is anchored in the most sophisticated physical structures ever built by humans: the **Hyper-scale Data Center**. These facilities are the factories of the 21st century.

6.1 Power and Cooling: The Silent Giants

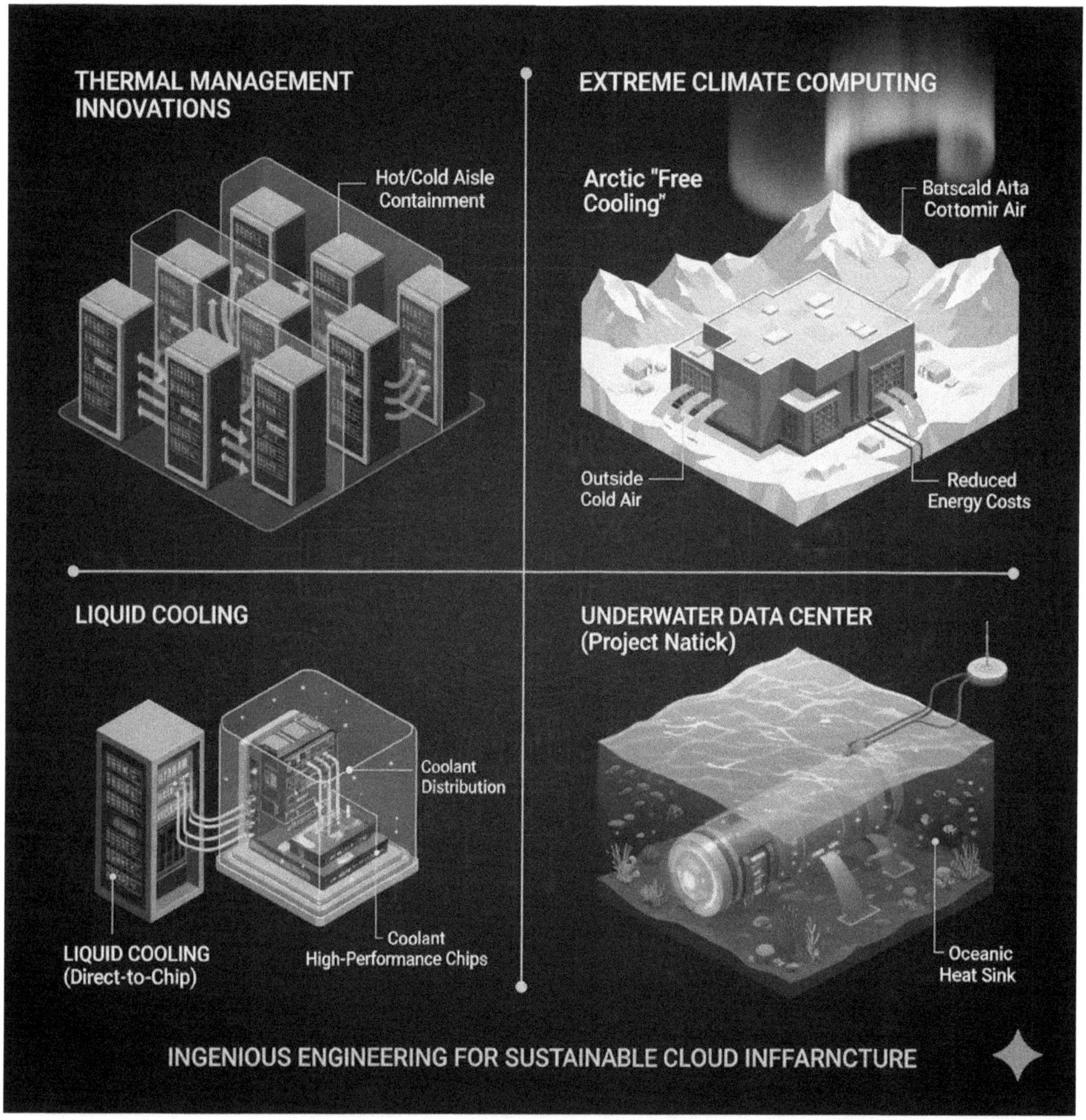

A single hyper-scale data center can consume as much electricity as a small city (up to 100 megawatts). Managing this heat is a monumental engineering task. Modern data centers have moved away from traditional air conditioning toward **Liquid Cooling** and **Hot/Cold Isle Containment**. Some providers, like Microsoft, have even experimented with underwater data centers (Project Natick) to use the ocean as a natural heat sink, while others build in the Arctic to take advantage of the "Free Cooling" provided by the climate.

6.2 Redundancy and Reliability

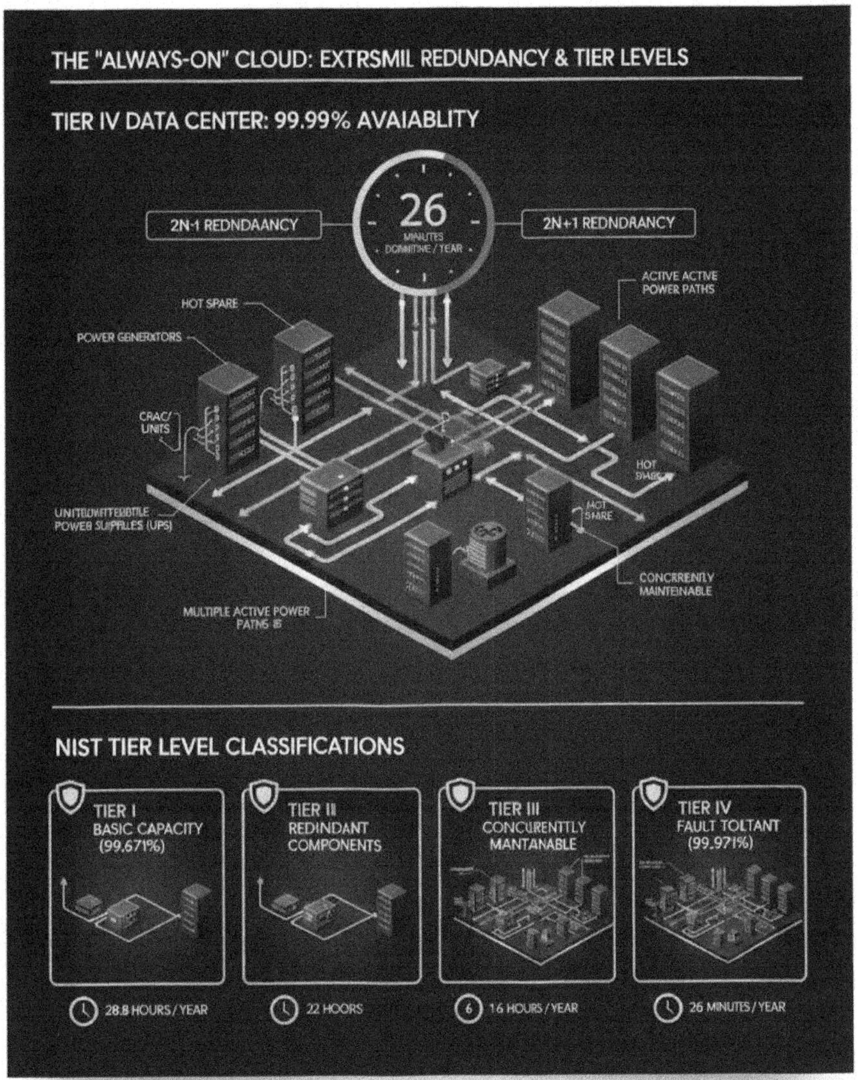

The "Always-On" nature of the cloud is achieved through extreme physical redundancy. This is categorized by **Tier Levels** (Tier I to Tier IV). A Tier IV data center is designed for 99.995% availability, meaning it can have no more than 26 minutes of downtime *per year*. This is achieved through "2N+1" redundancy: for every critical component (like a generator or a chiller), there are two backups plus one extra spare.

6.3 Geographic Regions and Availability Zones

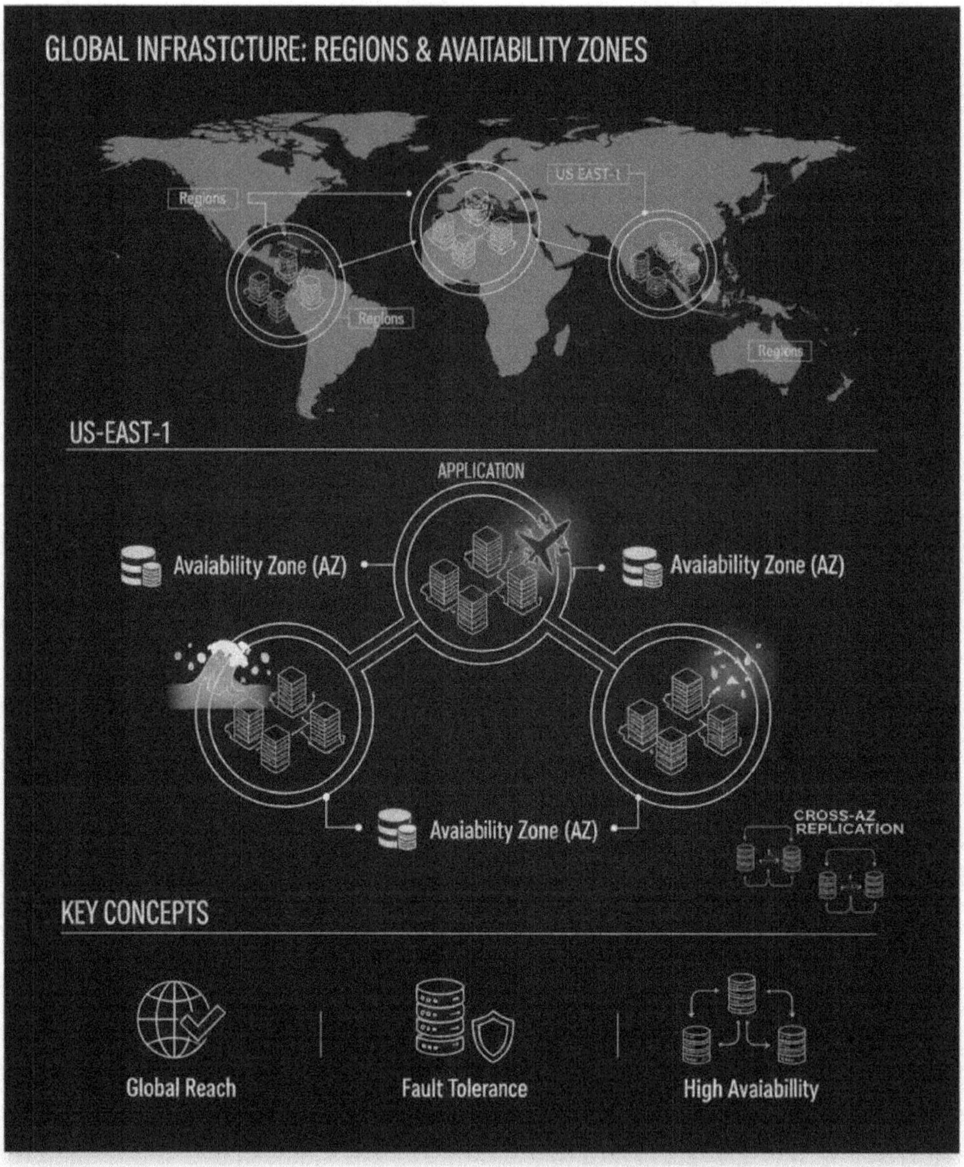

Cloud providers organize their data centers into **Regions** (e.g., US-East-1). Each region consists of multiple **Availability Zones (AZs)**. An AZ is one or more discrete data centers with redundant power, networking, and connectivity. By deploying an application across multiple AZs, a developer ensures that even if a catastrophic event (like a flood or a plane crash) destroys an entire data center, the application continues to run in the other AZs within that region.

7. Cloud Economics: The CAPEX to OPEX Revolution

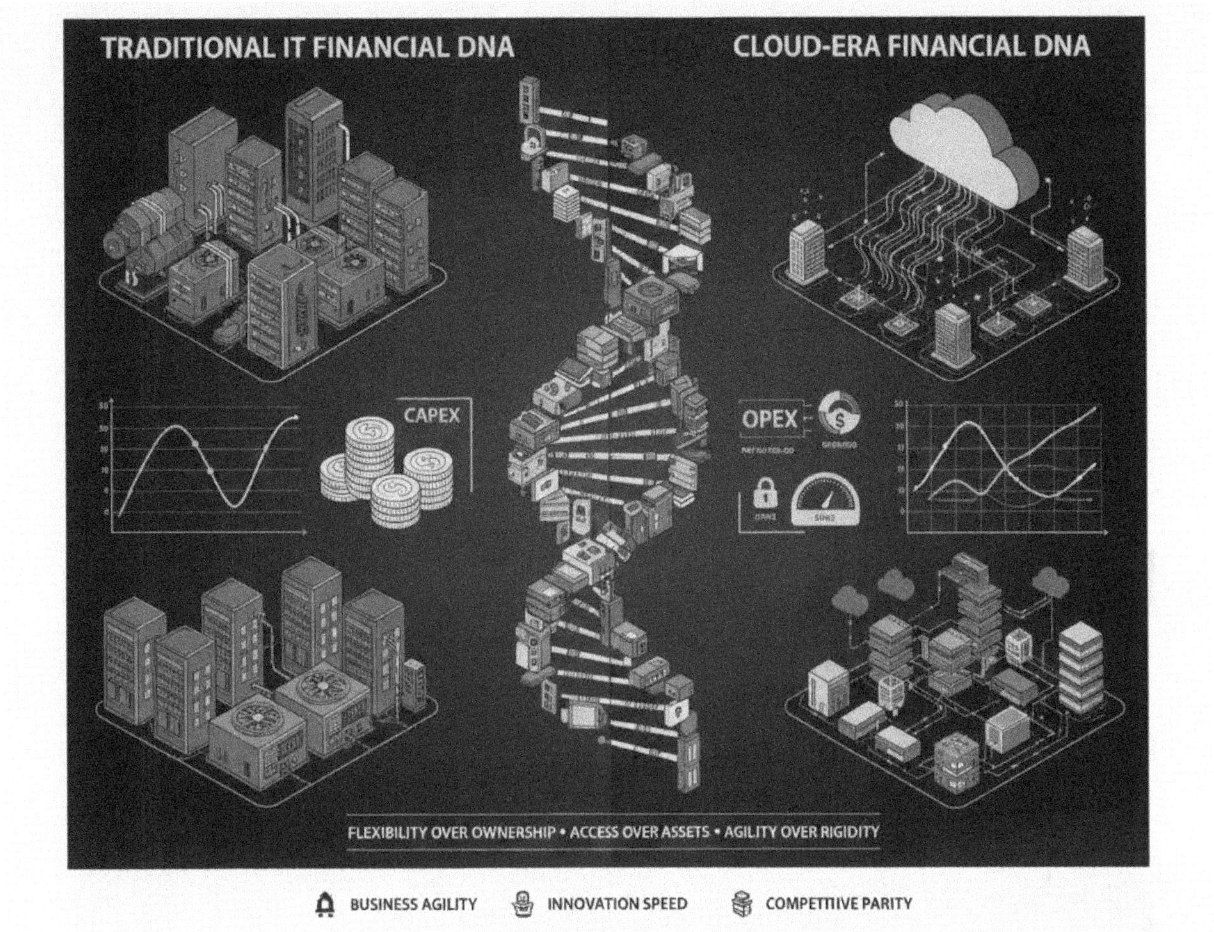

The shift to cloud deployment models has fundamentally changed the financial DNA of modern business.

7.1 CAPEX (Capital Expenditure)

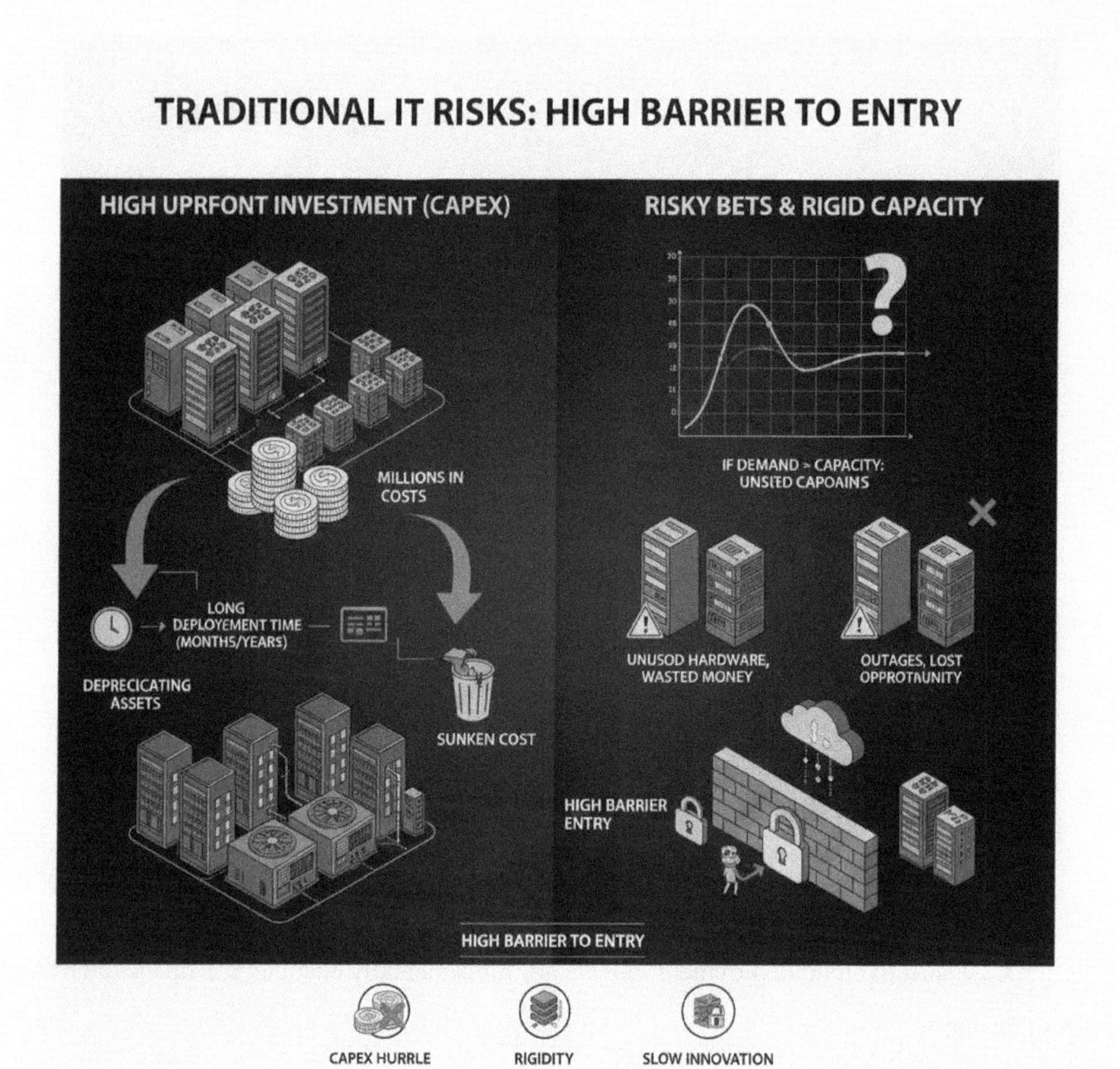

In the traditional IT model, a company had to spend millions of dollars upfront (**CAPEX**) to build a data center. This money was "sunk" into depreciating assets. If the project failed, the company was still stuck with the hardware. This created a "High Barrier to Entry" for new ideas and forced companies to make risky bets on how much capacity they would need five years in the future.

7.2 OPEX (Operational Expenditure)

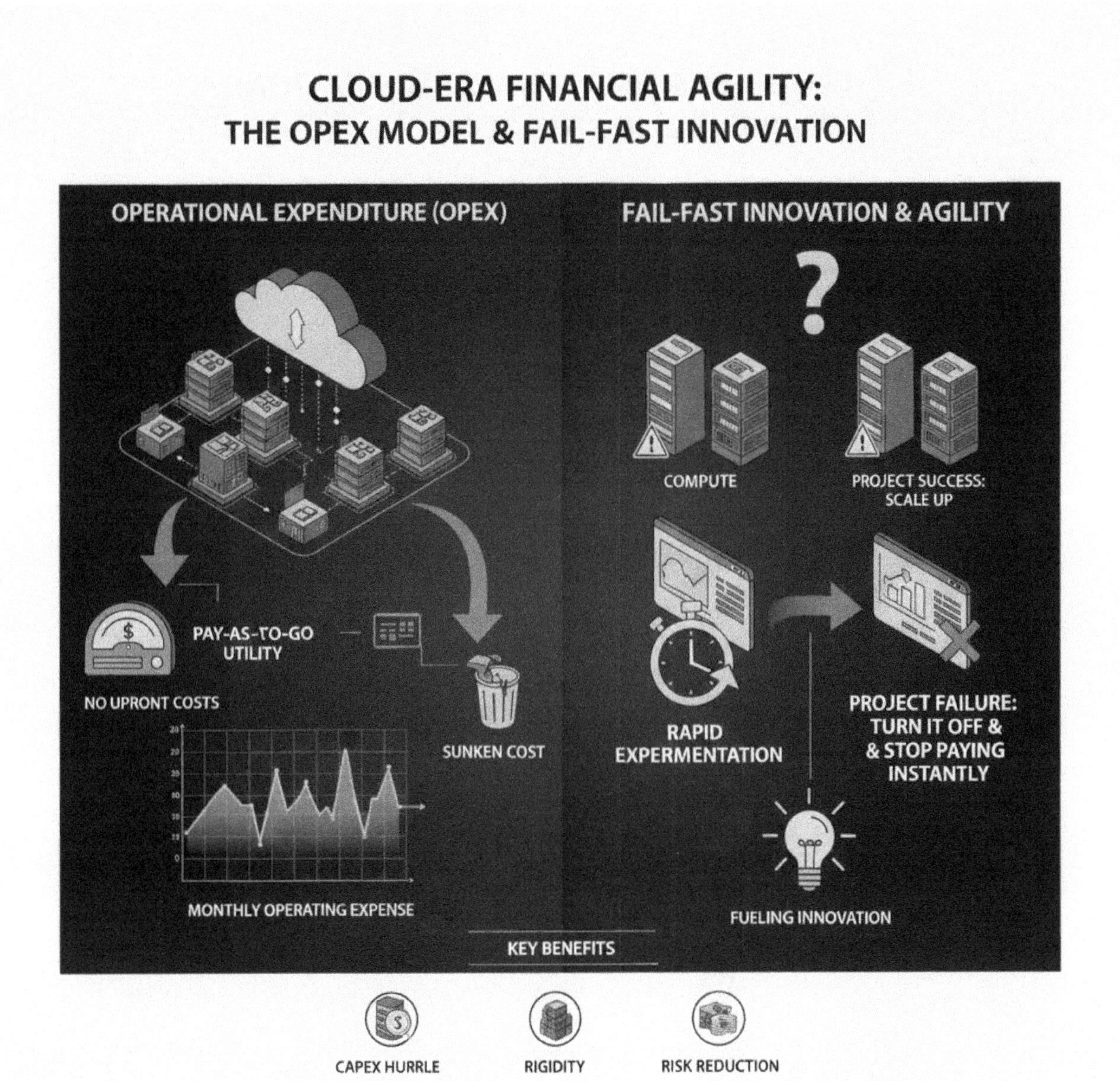

Cloud computing transforms IT into an **OPEX** model. There is no upfront cost; instead, the cost is an ongoing operational expense, much like a utility bill. This shift provides **Financial Agility**. If a project isn't working, the company can "Turn it off" and immediately stop paying. This "Fail Fast" mentality is what has fueled the rapid innovation of the last decade.

7.3 The Philosophy of "Pay-as-you-go"

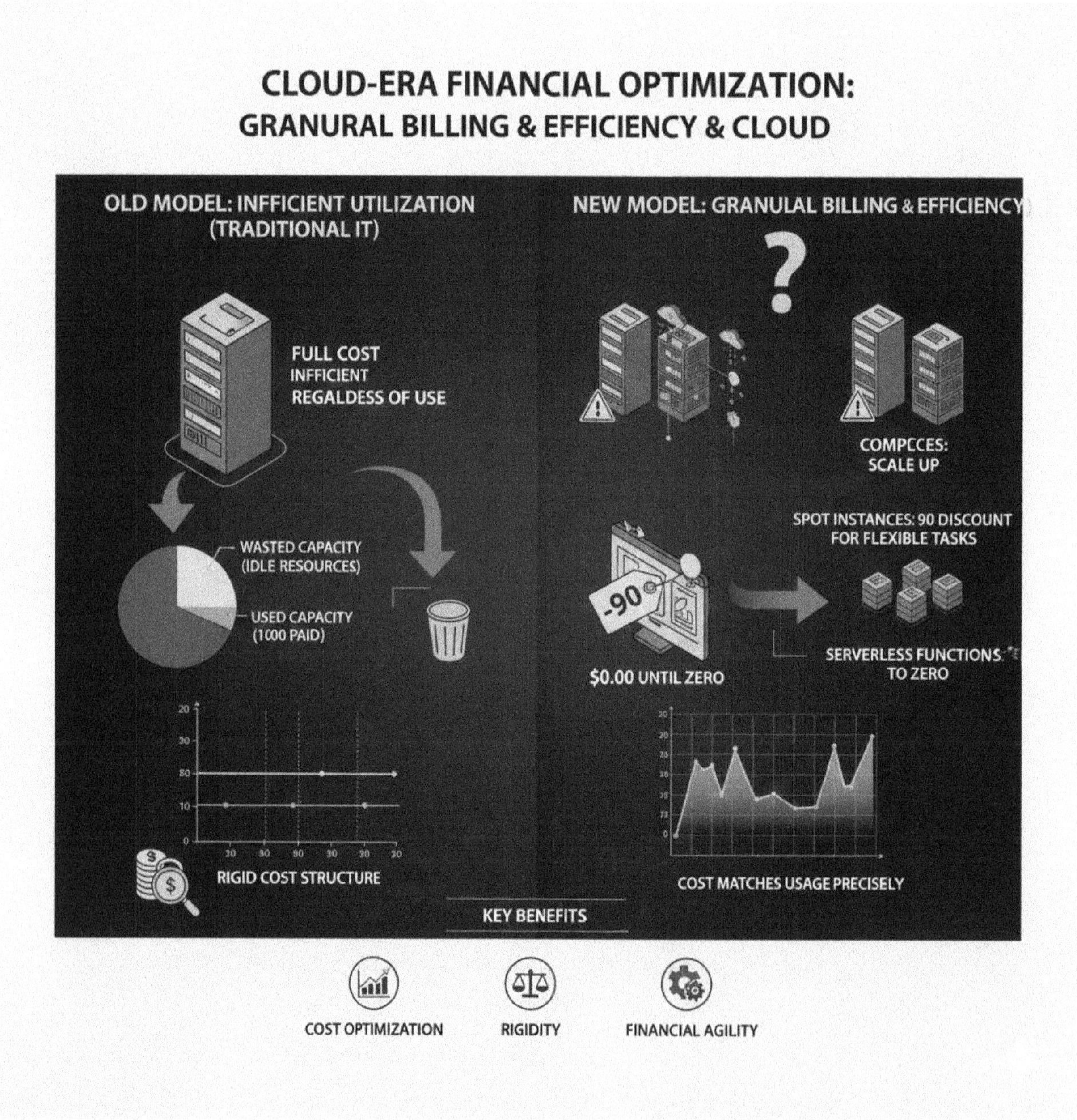

The **Pay-as-you-go** model also introduces the concept of **Granular Billing**. In a traditional model, if you bought a server, you paid for it whether it was 1% busy or 100% busy. In the cloud, you can use "Spot Instances"—excess capacity that the provider sells at a 90% discount—for non-critical tasks. You can also "Scale to Zero," where a serverless function costs absolutely nothing until the exact millisecond it is called by a user. This efficiency allows companies to optimize their margins to a degree that was previously impossible.

8. Summary: Choosing the Right Fit

The selection of a cloud deployment model is not a technical formality; it is a strategic decision that balances the competing needs of security, cost, and speed.

- **Public Cloud** is the engine of innovation and global scale.
- **Private Cloud** is the fortress of security and customization.
- **Hybrid Cloud** is the bridge of flexibility, allowing organizations to navigate the transition from legacy to modern.
- **Community Cloud** is the collaborative space for shared missions.

Underpinning all of these models is the massive physical reality of the data center and the transformative logic of cloud economics. As we move into **Chapter 7: Cloud Security and Governance**, we will build upon these deployment models to understand how to protect data in a world where the physical boundaries of the "Computer" have effectively disappeared. The cloud is not just "someone else's computer"—it is a global, elastic, and economically optimized ecosystem that has redefined what is possible in the digital age.

Part – IV

The Ecosystem and Future Challenges

Chapter – 7

Commercial and Open Source Platforms

A comparative study of AWS, Azure, and GCP. It also explores the pioneer PaaS (Google AppEngine) and the open-source big data ecosystem (Hadoop, HDFS, and MapReduce) that allows for massive-scale data processing.

1. Introduction: The Industrialization of the Cloud

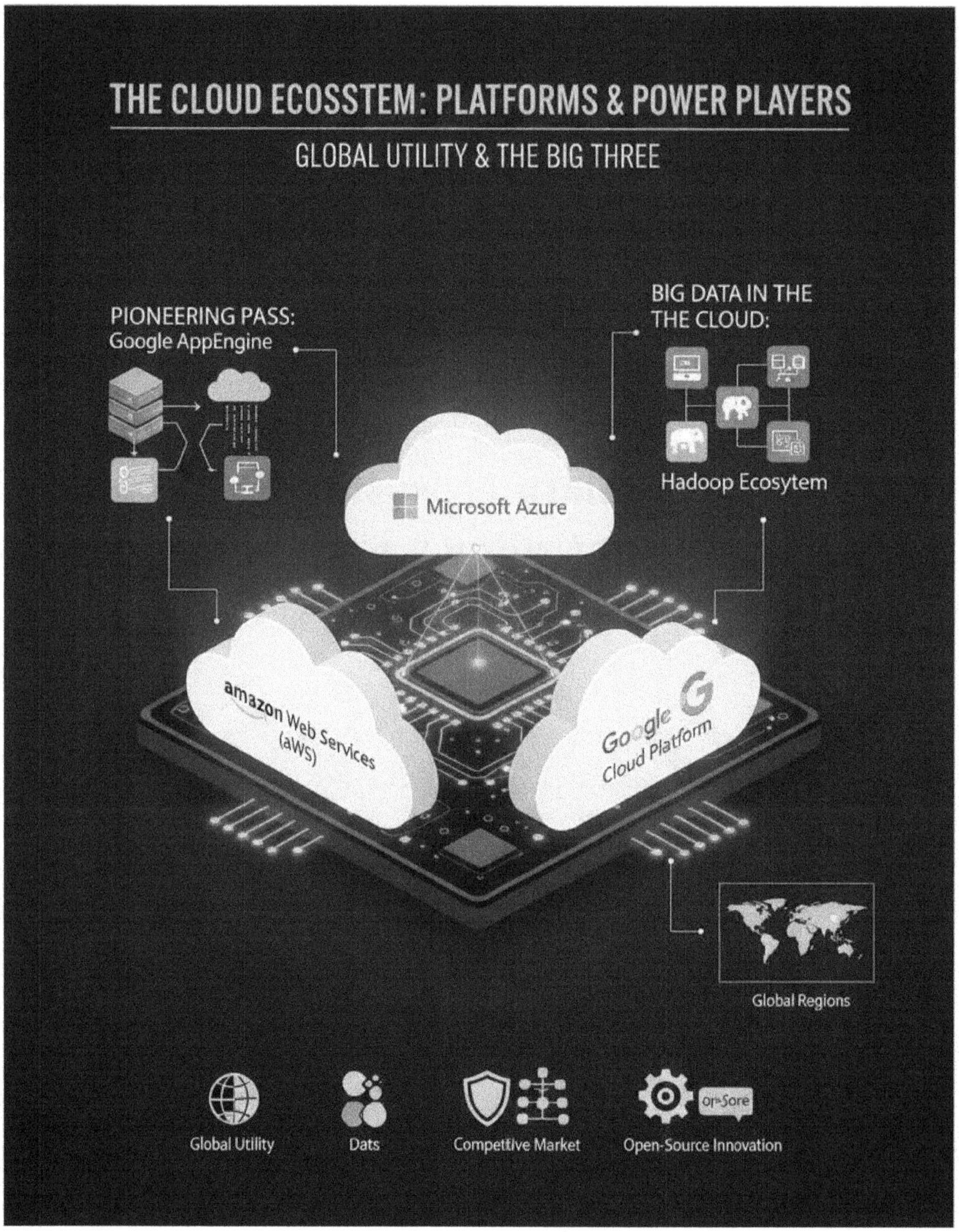

The theoretical evolution of virtualization (Chapter 3) and the definitions of delivery models (Chapter 5) have culminated in a massive, competitive market of commercial and open-source platforms. Today, the cloud is no longer an experimental technology but a global utility controlled by a few dominant players—the "Big Three"—and supported by a vibrant ecosystem of open-source projects.

This chapter provides a comprehensive analysis of **Amazon Web Services (AWS)**, **Microsoft Azure**, and **Google Cloud Platform (GCP)**. We will explore their unique architectural philosophies, their specialized services, and how they have shaped the modern enterprise. Furthermore, we will examine **Google AppEngine** as a pioneer of the PaaS model and delve into the world of **Big Data in the Cloud**, specifically focusing on the open-source **Hadoop** ecosystem and the mechanics of distributed storage and processing.

2. The Big Three: Amazon Web Services (AWS), Microsoft Azure, and GCP

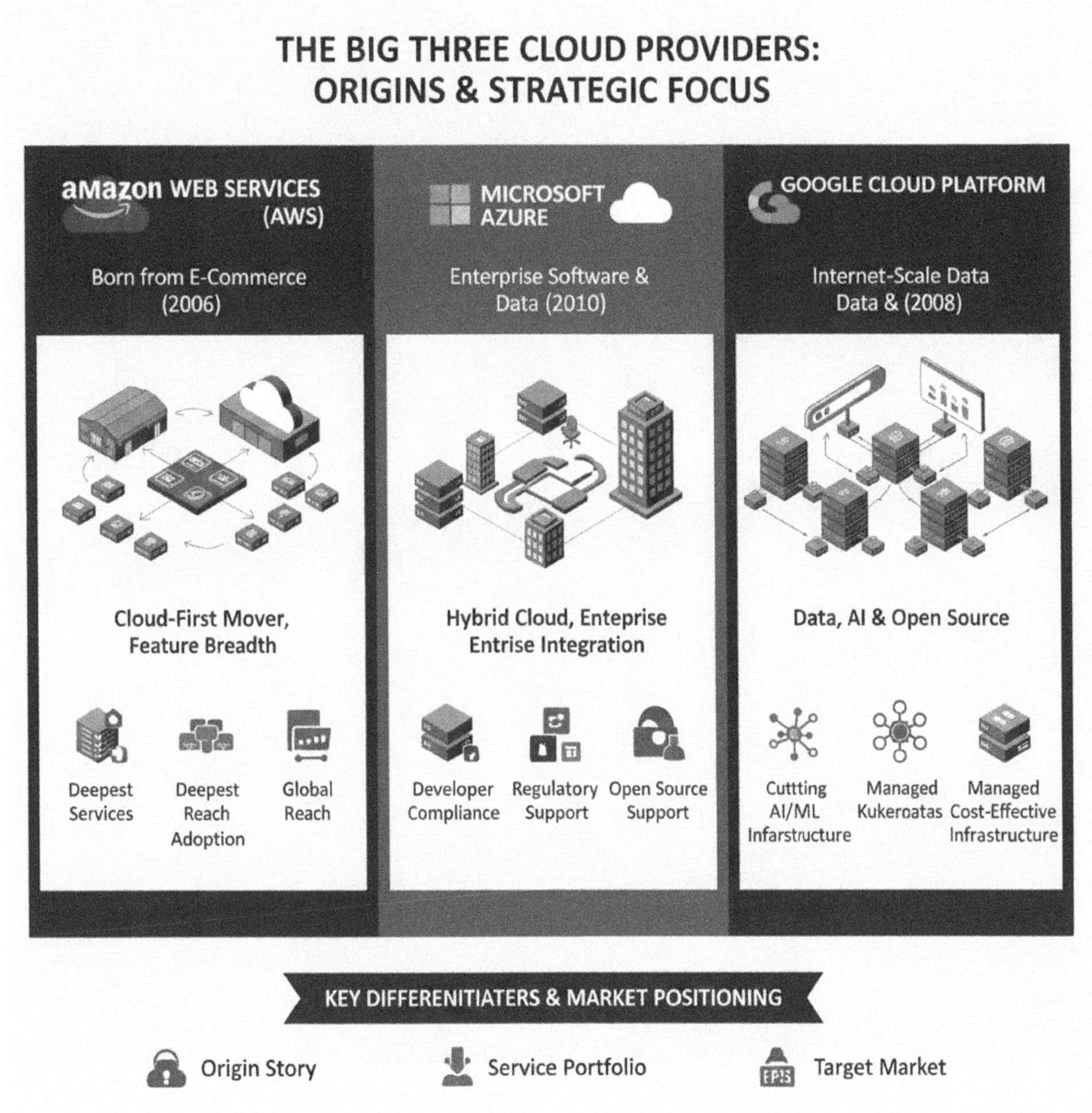

The commercial cloud market is dominated by three hyper-scale providers, often referred to as "The Big Three." While they all offer similar core services (Compute, Storage, Networking), they arrived at the cloud from very different origins, which has influenced their current capabilities and market positioning.

2.1 Amazon Web Services (AWS): The First Mover

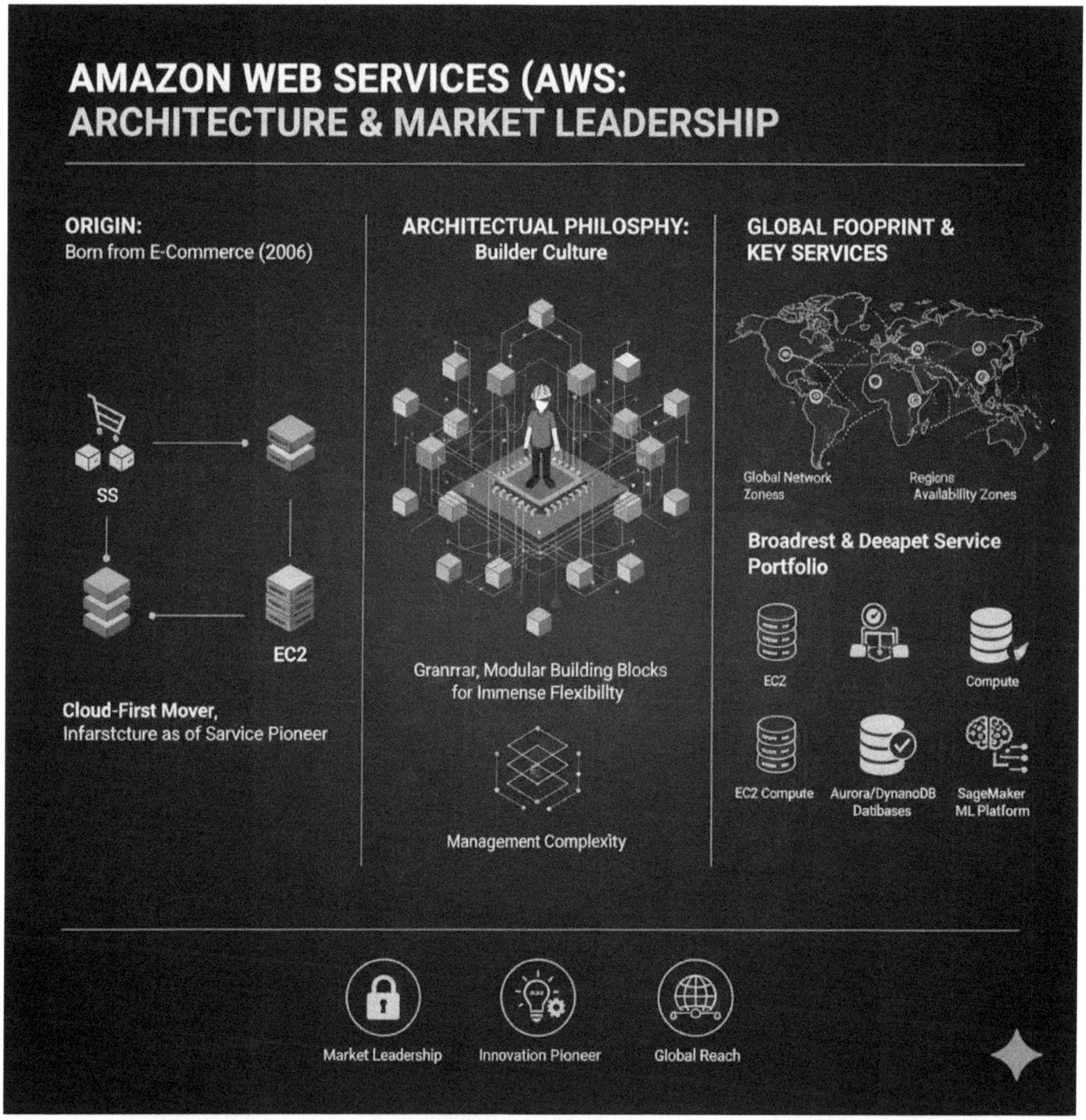

AWS is the undisputed market leader, having launched its first services (S3 and EC2) in 2006. Born out of Amazon's internal need to manage its massive e-commerce infrastructure, AWS pioneered the concept of "Infrastructure as a Service."

- **Architectural Philosophy**: AWS is known for its "Builder Culture." Its services are designed as granular, modular building blocks. This offers developers immense flexibility but can lead to significant complexity in management.
- **Key Services**: AWS offers the broadest and deepest set of services, ranging from standard compute (**EC2**) to specialized databases (**Aurora**, **DynamoDB**) and advanced machine learning platforms (**SageMaker**).
- **Global Footprint**: AWS operates the most extensive global network of Regions and Availability Zones, providing the highest level of redundancy and low-latency access for global applications.

2.2 Microsoft Azure: The Enterprise Standard

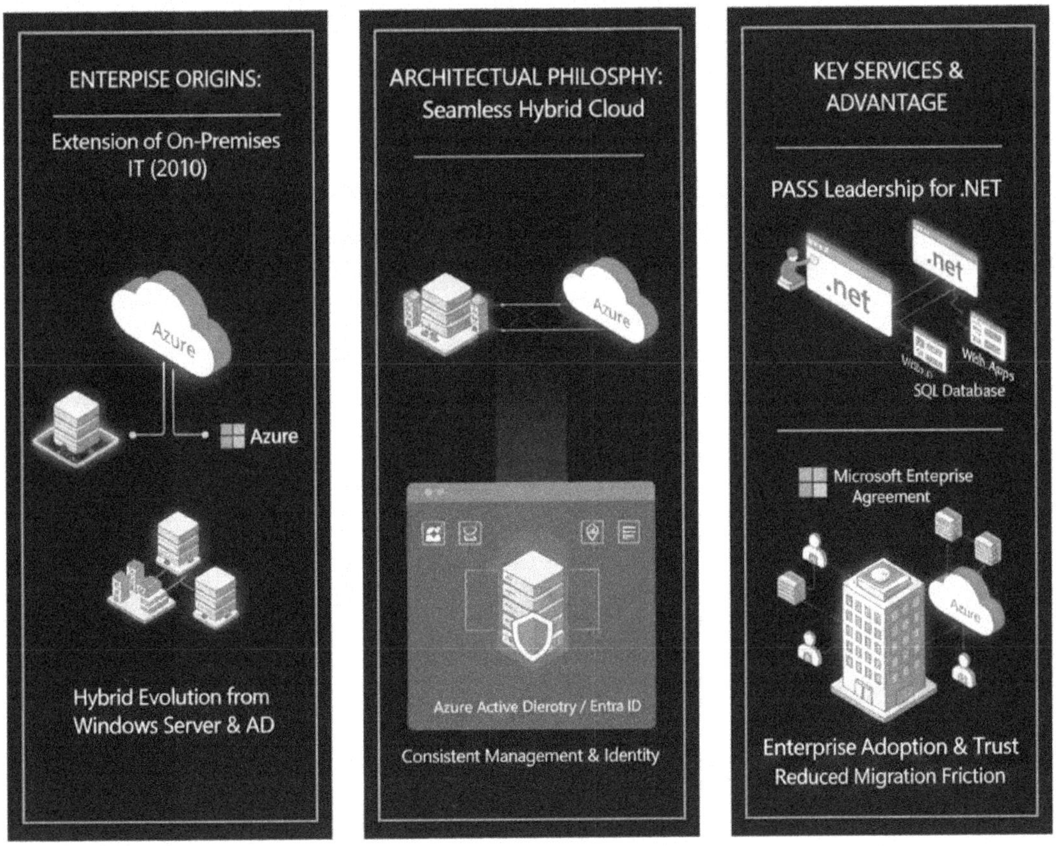

Azure was Microsoft's response to AWS, launched in 2010. Leveraging its dominant position in the corporate world, Microsoft positioned Azure as the natural extension of the Windows Server and Active Directory ecosystems.

- **Architectural Philosophy**: Azure focuses on the "Hybrid Cloud" and seamless integration. It is designed to look and feel like an extension of an organization's existing on-premises Windows environment.
- **Key Services**: Azure is the leader in PaaS services, particularly for .NET developers. Its **Azure Active Directory** (now Microsoft Entra ID) is the gold standard for identity management in the cloud.
- **Strategic Advantage**: Microsoft's ability to bundle Azure with existing enterprise agreements (Office 365, Windows) makes it the most attractive option for large, established corporations looking to transition to the cloud without abandoning their existing software investments.

2.3 Google Cloud Platform (GCP): The Innovation Specialist

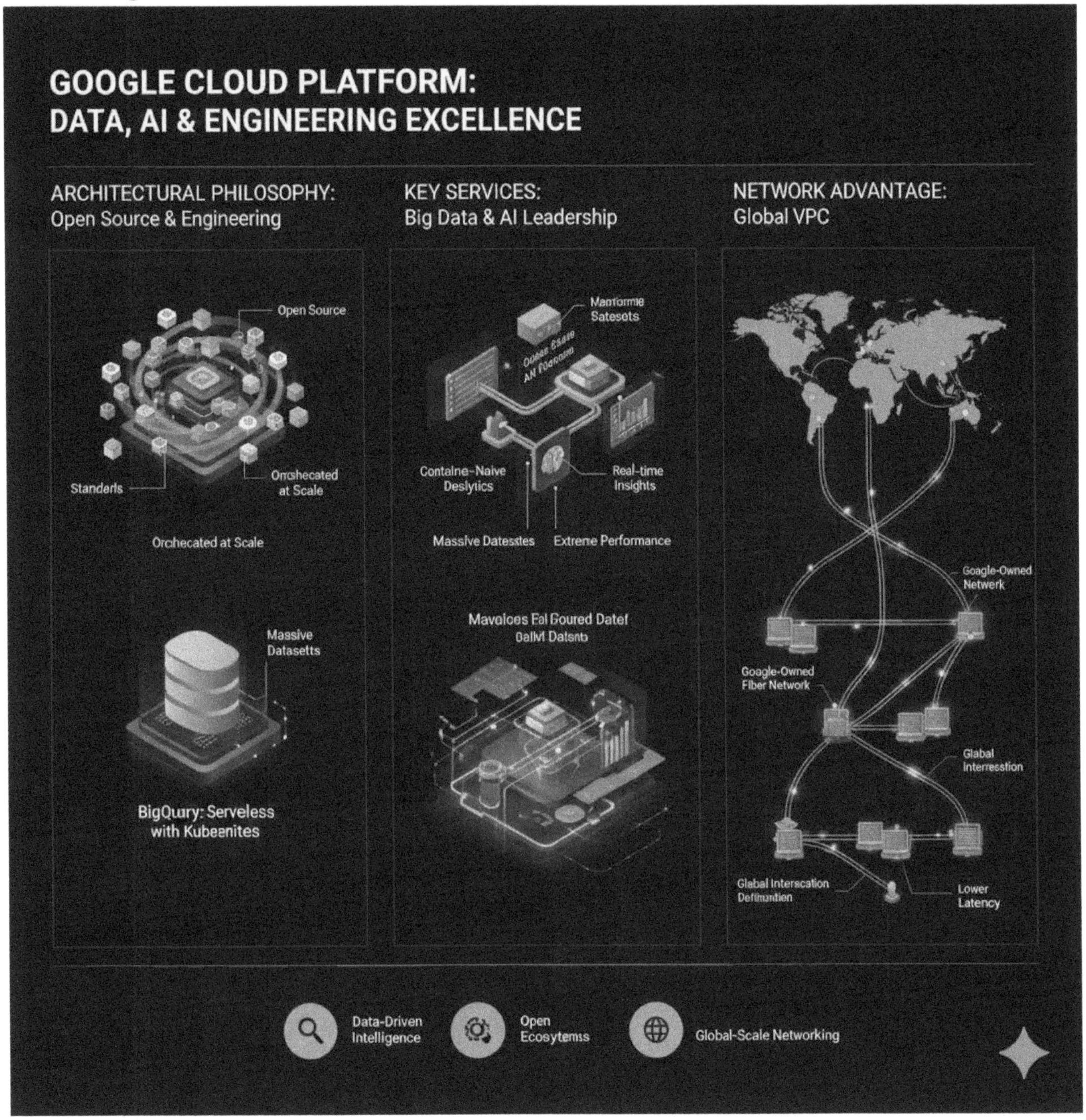

GCP is the "Data Scientist's Cloud." Launched later than its rivals, Google leveraged its expertise in managing the world's most massive data sets and search algorithms to create a cloud platform optimized for analytics and high-speed networking.

- **Architectural Philosophy**: Google focuses on open-source standards and high-end engineering. GCP is the birthplace of **Kubernetes**, and it remains the premier platform for containerized workloads.
- **Key Services**: GCP excels in Big Data and AI. **BigQuery**, Google's serverless data warehouse, is widely considered the most performant analytics engine in the cloud market.

- **Network Advantage**: Unlike its competitors, Google owns and operates much of the undersea fiber-optic cables that connect its data centers, providing a "Global VPC" that offers lower latency and higher security than the public internet.

3. Google AppEngine and the PaaS Revolution

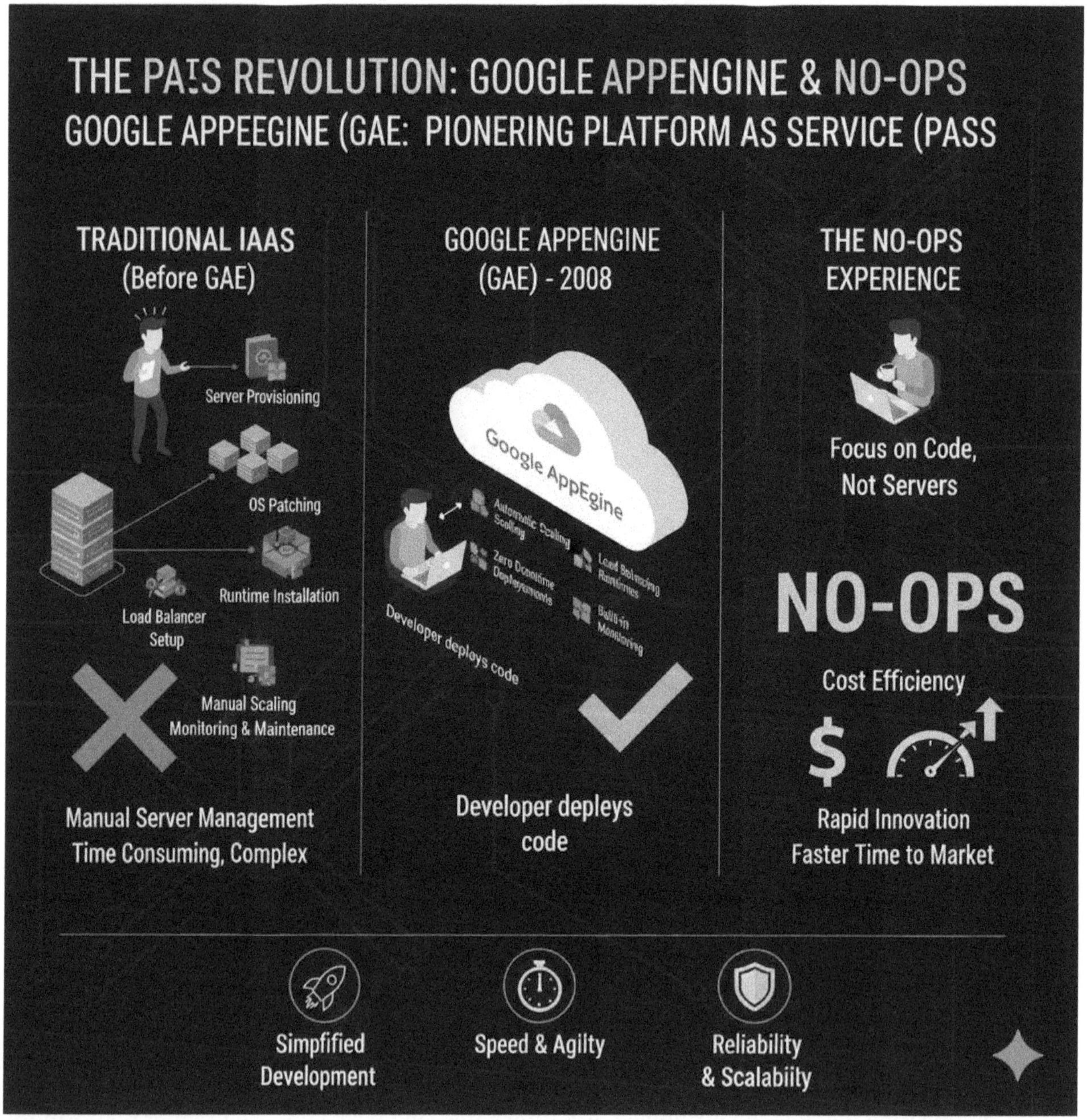

While AWS focused on IaaS, Google's first major foray into the cloud was **Google AppEngine (GAE)** in 2008. GAE was a revolutionary Platform as a Service (PaaS) that offered a "No-Ops" experience for developers.

3.1 The "No-Ops" Philosophy

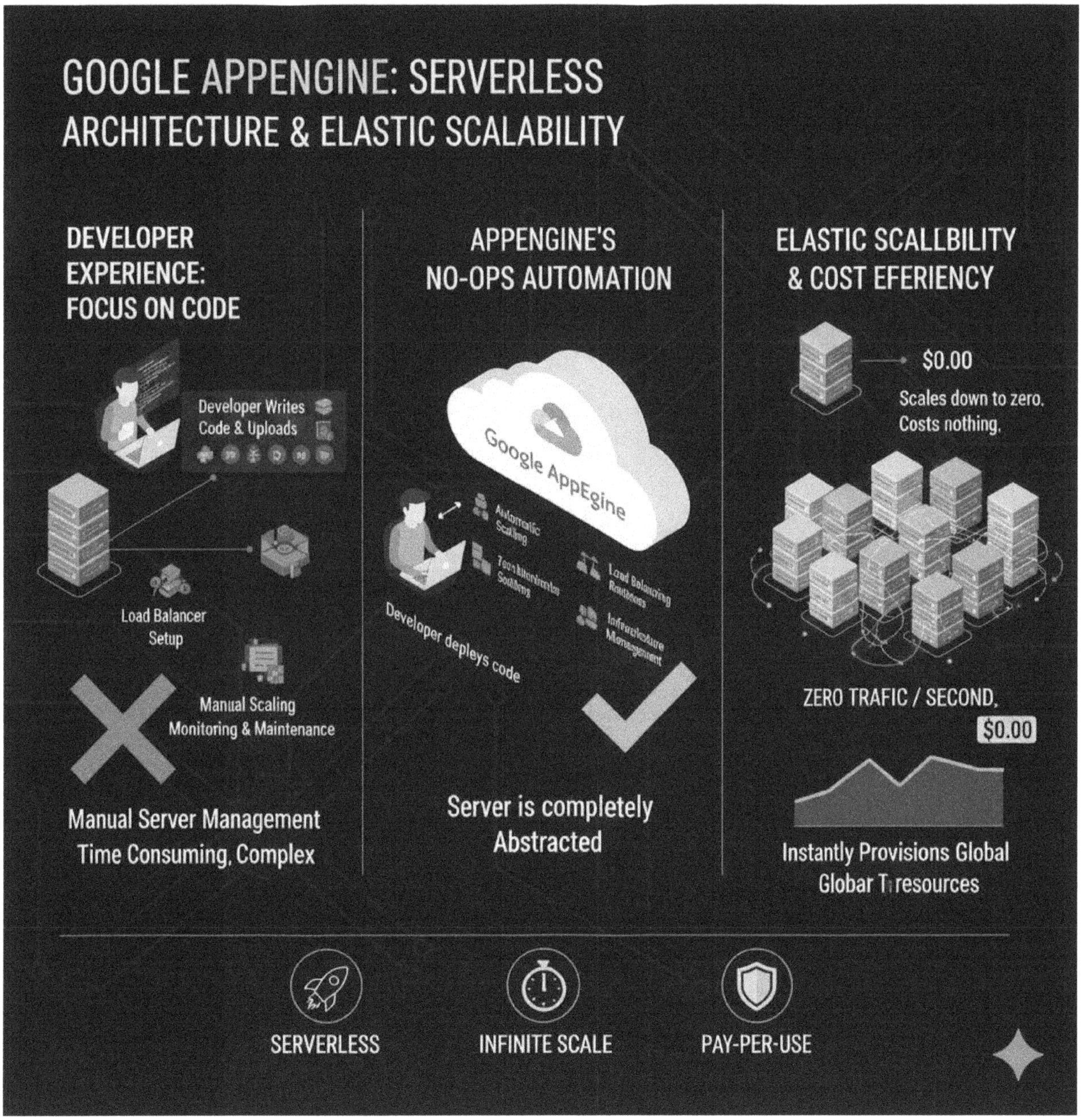

In AppEngine, the concept of a server is completely abstracted. A developer simply writes their code (originally only in Python, later expanding to Java, Go, PHP, and more) and uploads it to Google. AppEngine handles all the scaling, load balancing, and health monitoring automatically. If an app receives zero traffic, it scales down to zero and costs nothing. If it receives a million hits, Google instantly provisions the necessary resources across its global infrastructure.

3.2 Standard vs. Flexible Environments

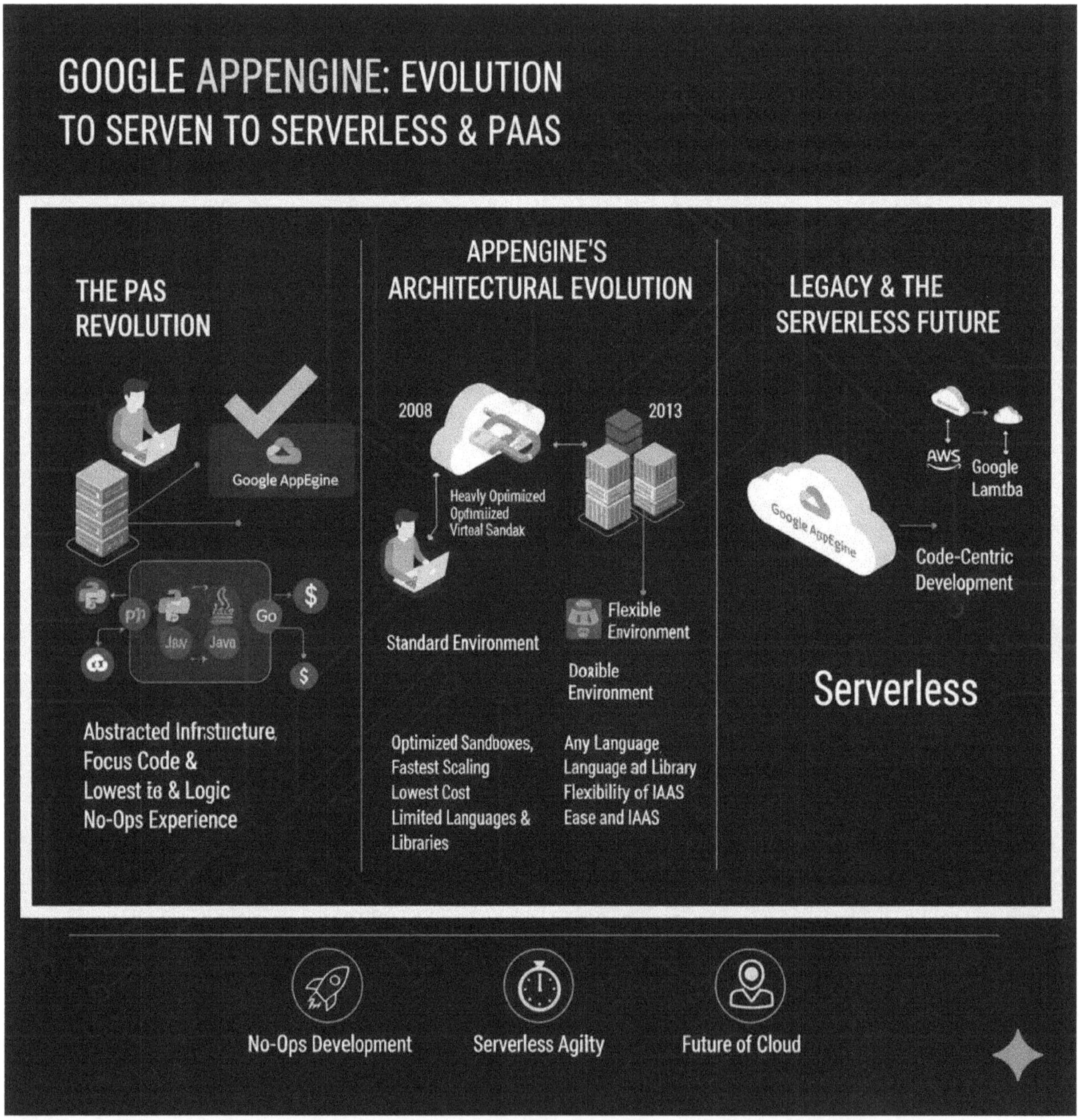

AppEngine evolved into two distinct models:

1. **Standard Environment**: Uses specialized, highly optimized sandboxes. It offers the fastest scaling and the lowest cost but limits the developer to specific versions of supported languages and restricted libraries.
2. **Flexible Environment**: Uses Docker containers. This allows developers to use any language or library they choose, providing the flexibility of IaaS with the management ease of PaaS.

AppEngine proved that the future of cloud development was not in managing virtual machines, but in managing **Code and Logic**. It paved the way for the "Serverless" movement that would eventually culminate in technologies like AWS Lambda and Google Cloud Functions.

4. Big Data in the Cloud: The Power of Distributed Systems

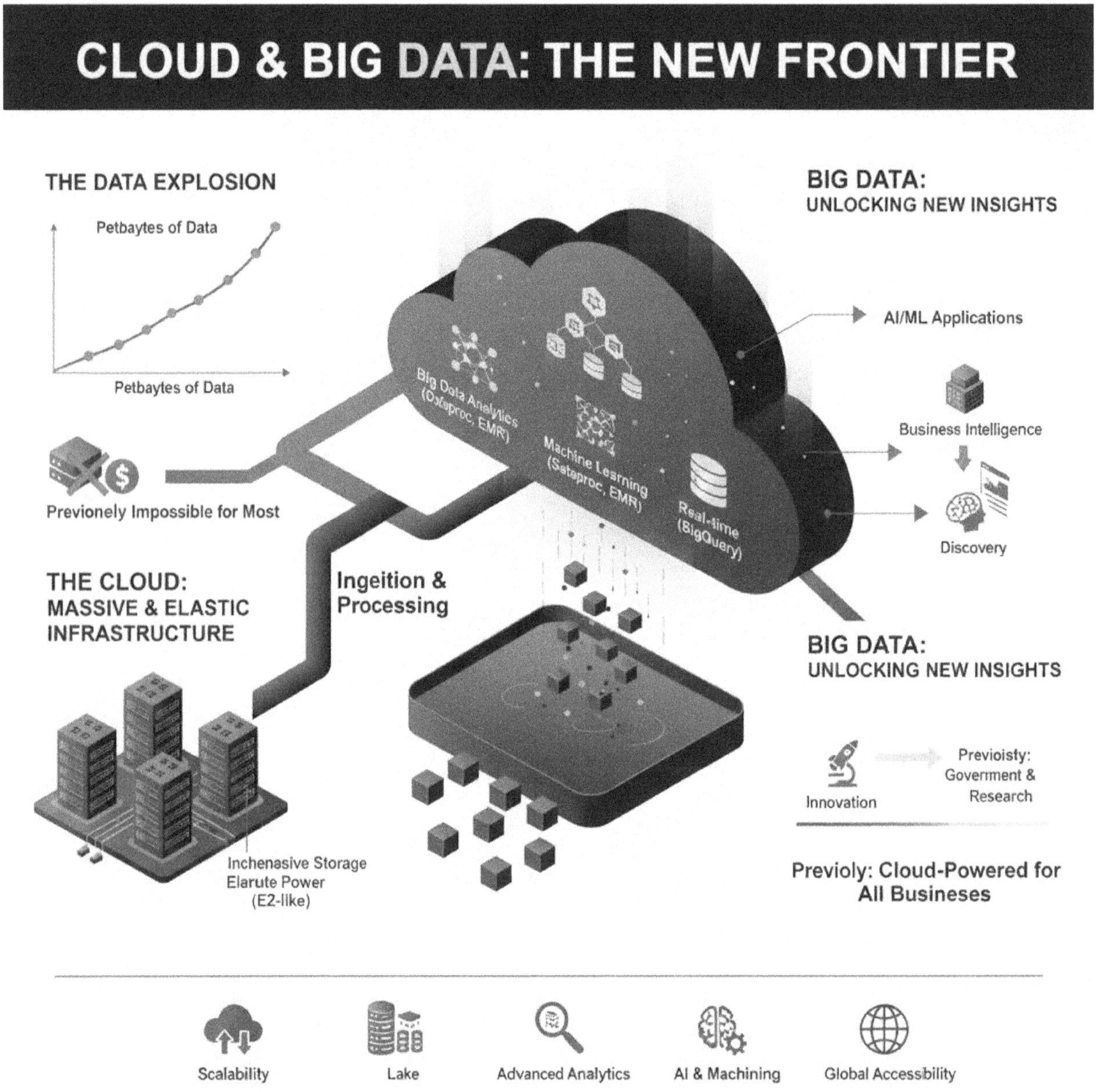

The "Cloud" and "Big Data" are inextricably linked. The cloud provides the massive, inexpensive storage and compute power required to process petabytes of data—tasks that were previously only possible for government agencies or massive research institutions.

4.1 Introduction to the Hadoop Ecosystem

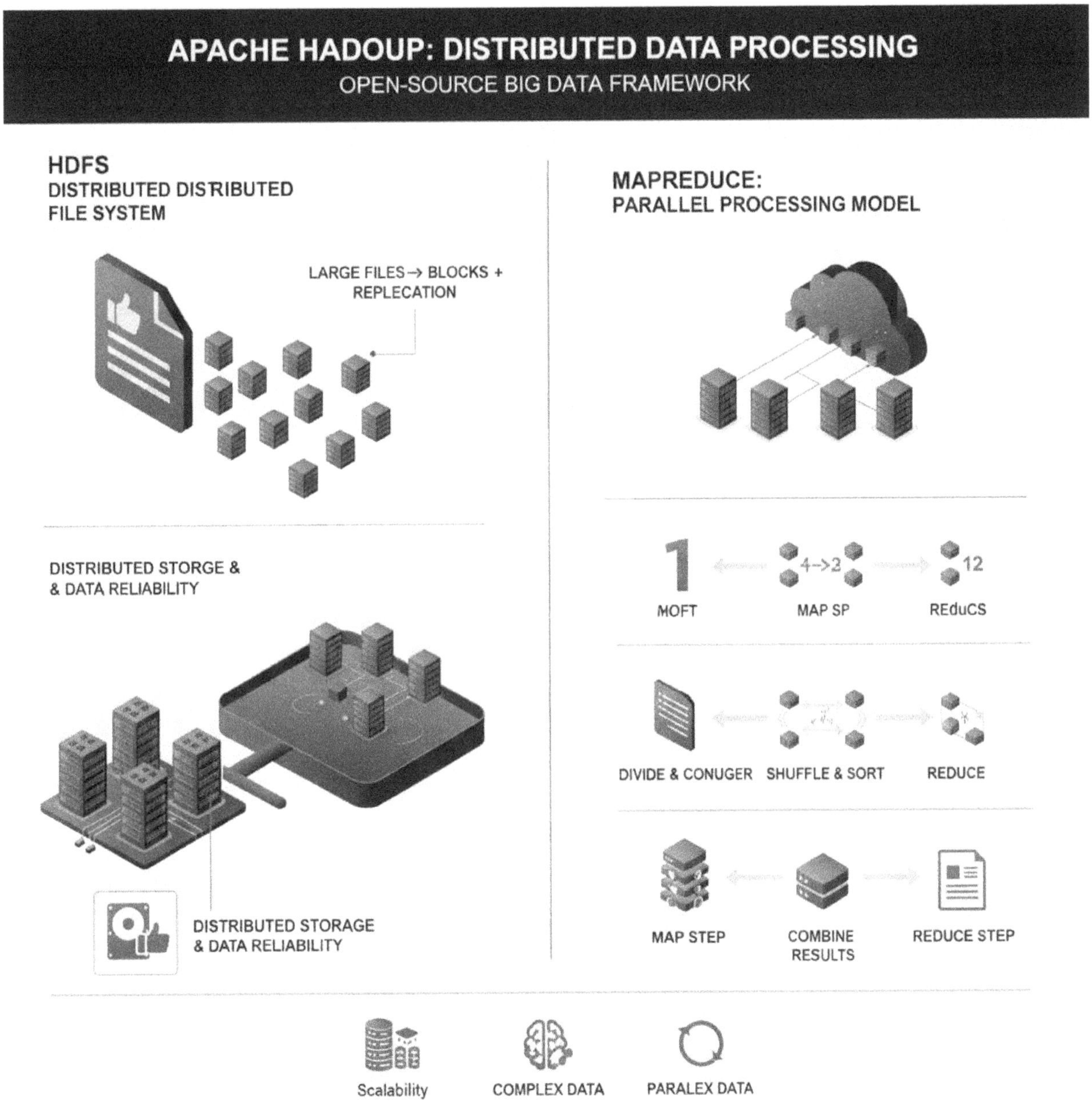

Apache Hadoop is the open-source framework that redefined how the world handles data. Inspired by Google's proprietary MapReduce and Google File System papers, Hadoop allows for the distributed processing of large data sets across clusters of computers using simple programming models.

The Hadoop ecosystem consists of two core components:

- **HDFS (Hadoop Distributed File System)**: A distributed file system that provides high-throughput access to application data. It breaks large files into "blocks" and replicates them across multiple nodes in a cluster to ensure data reliability even if individual hard drives or servers fail.
- **MapReduce**: A software framework for easily writing applications which process vast amounts of data in parallel on large clusters. The "Map" step divides the task into smaller sub-problems, and the "Reduce" step combines the results from those sub-problems into a final output.

4.2 Distributed Storage: From HDFS to Object Storage

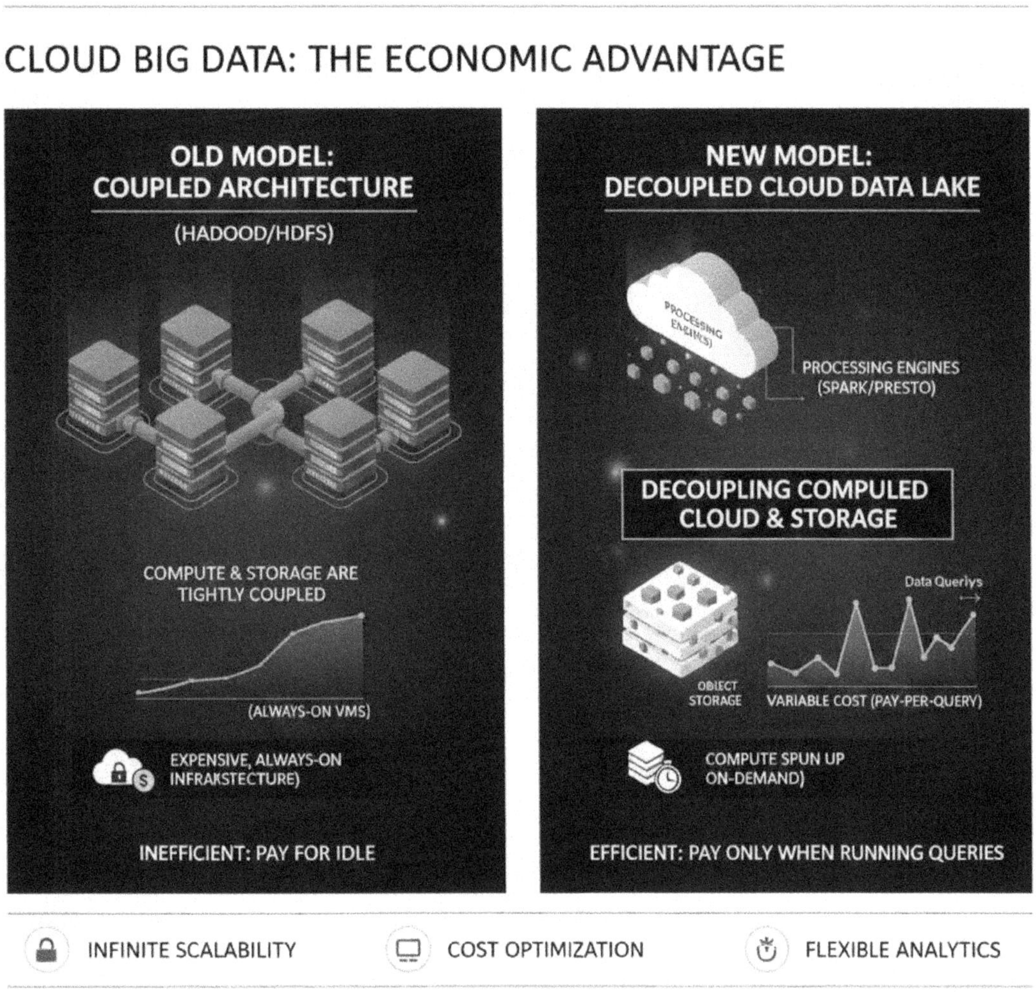

In the cloud, the "Distributed Storage" model has evolved beyond HDFS. While HDFS is excellent for high-performance clusters, it requires expensive, always-on virtual machines. Cloud providers introduced **Object Storage** (like Amazon S3 or Google Cloud Storage) as a more flexible alternative.

Object storage separates metadata from the data itself, allowing for nearly infinite scalability. In the modern cloud "Data Lake" architecture, raw data is stored in inexpensive object storage, and distributed processing engines (like **Apache Spark** or **Presto**) are spun up on-demand to analyze that data. This "Decoupling of Compute and Storage" is the primary economic advantage of big data in the cloud; you only pay for the "Processing" power when you are actually running a query.

4.3 NoSQL and the End of "One Size Fits All"

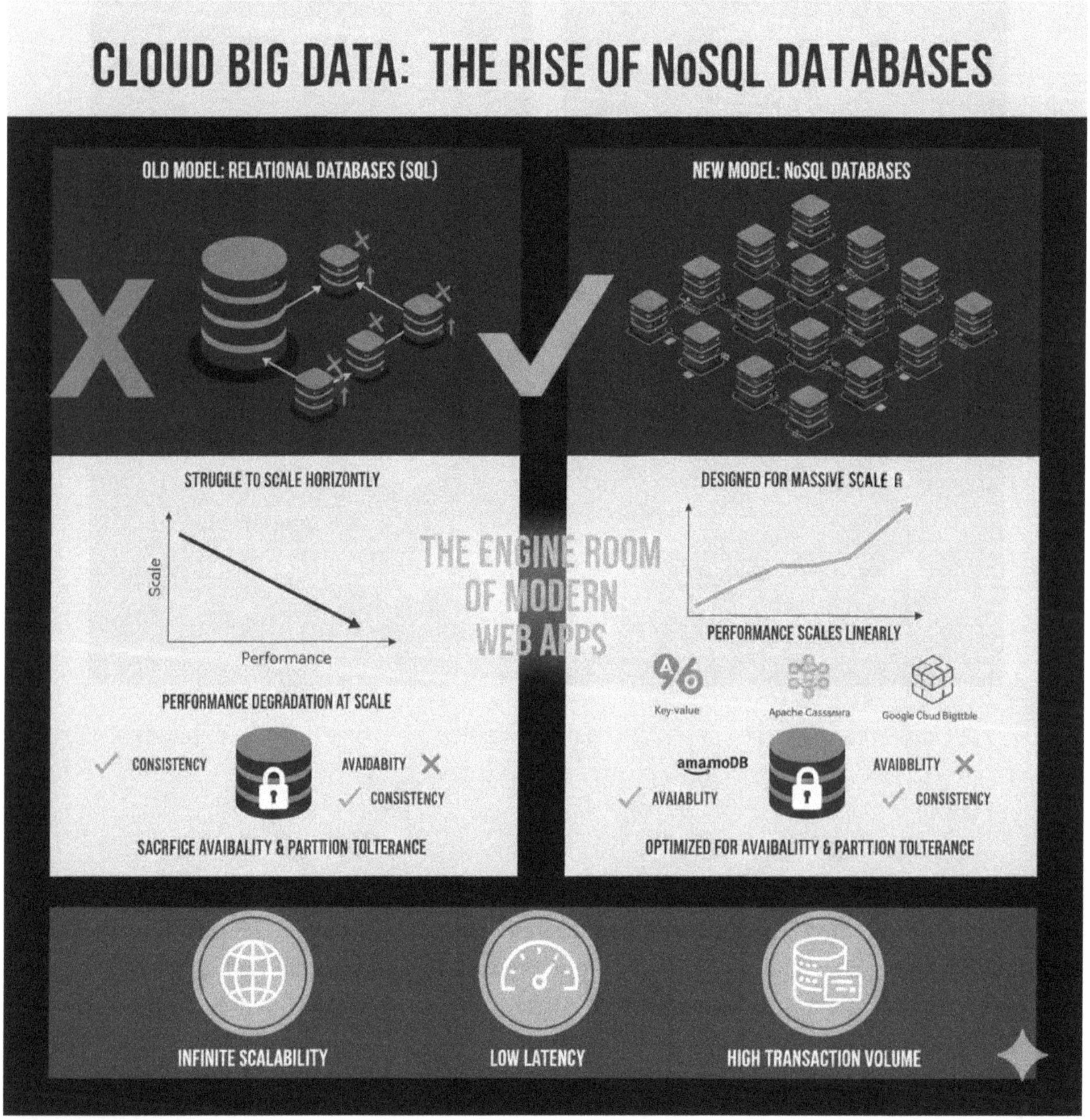

Big Data in the cloud also led to the rise of **NoSQL Databases**. Traditional relational databases (SQL) struggle to scale horizontally across hundreds of nodes. NoSQL databases, such as **Amazon DynamoDB**, **Apache Cassandra**, and **Google Cloud Bigtable**, sacrifice some consistency (following the CAP Theorem) to achieve massive scale and low latency. These databases are the "Engine Room" of modern web applications, handling the billions of transactions generated by users of Netflix, Facebook, and Amazon.

5. Open Source Platforms: OpenStack and the Private Cloud

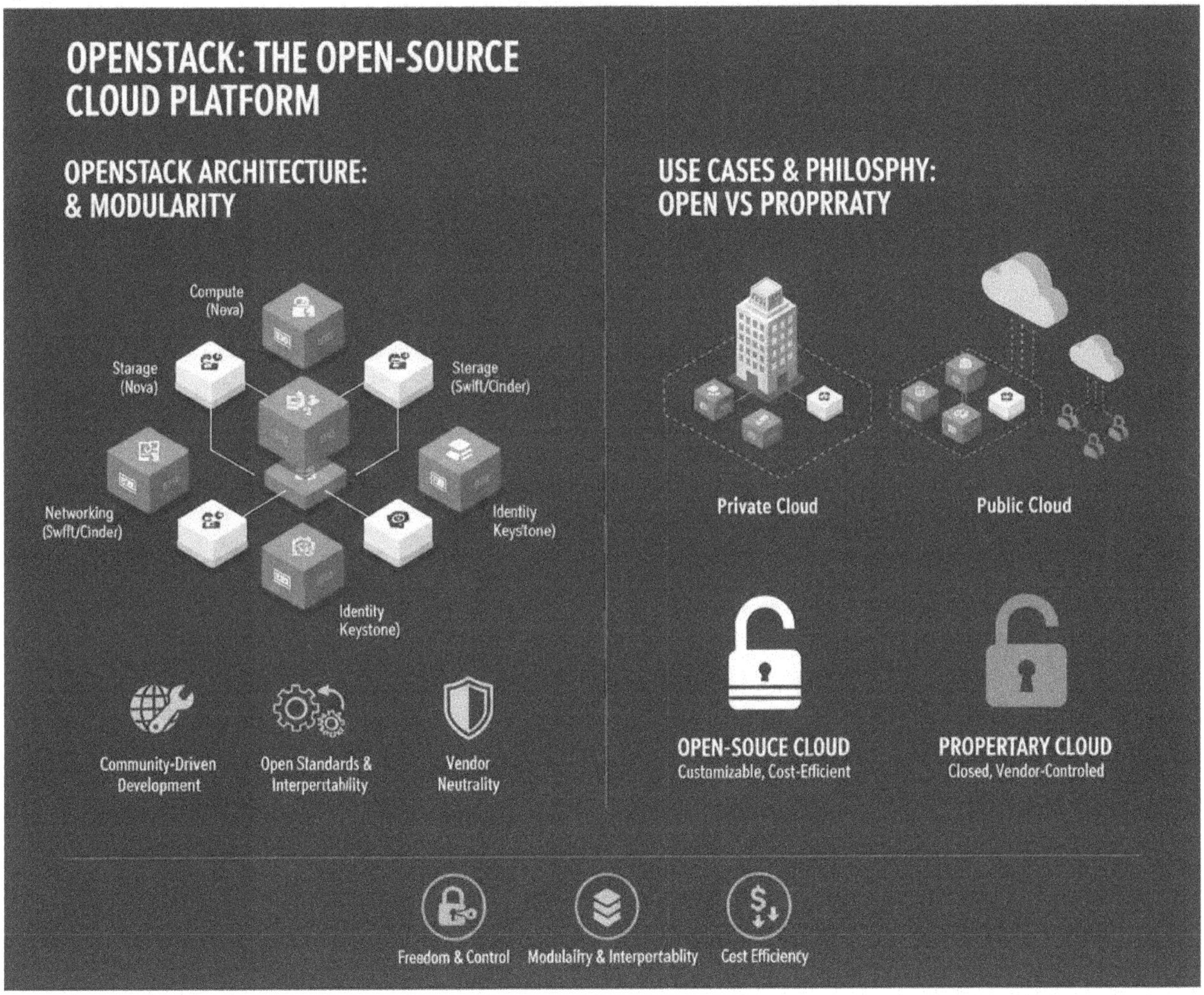

While AWS and GCP are proprietary, the open-source community created **OpenStack** to provide a free, open-source platform for building private and public clouds.

5.1 The Architecture of OpenStack

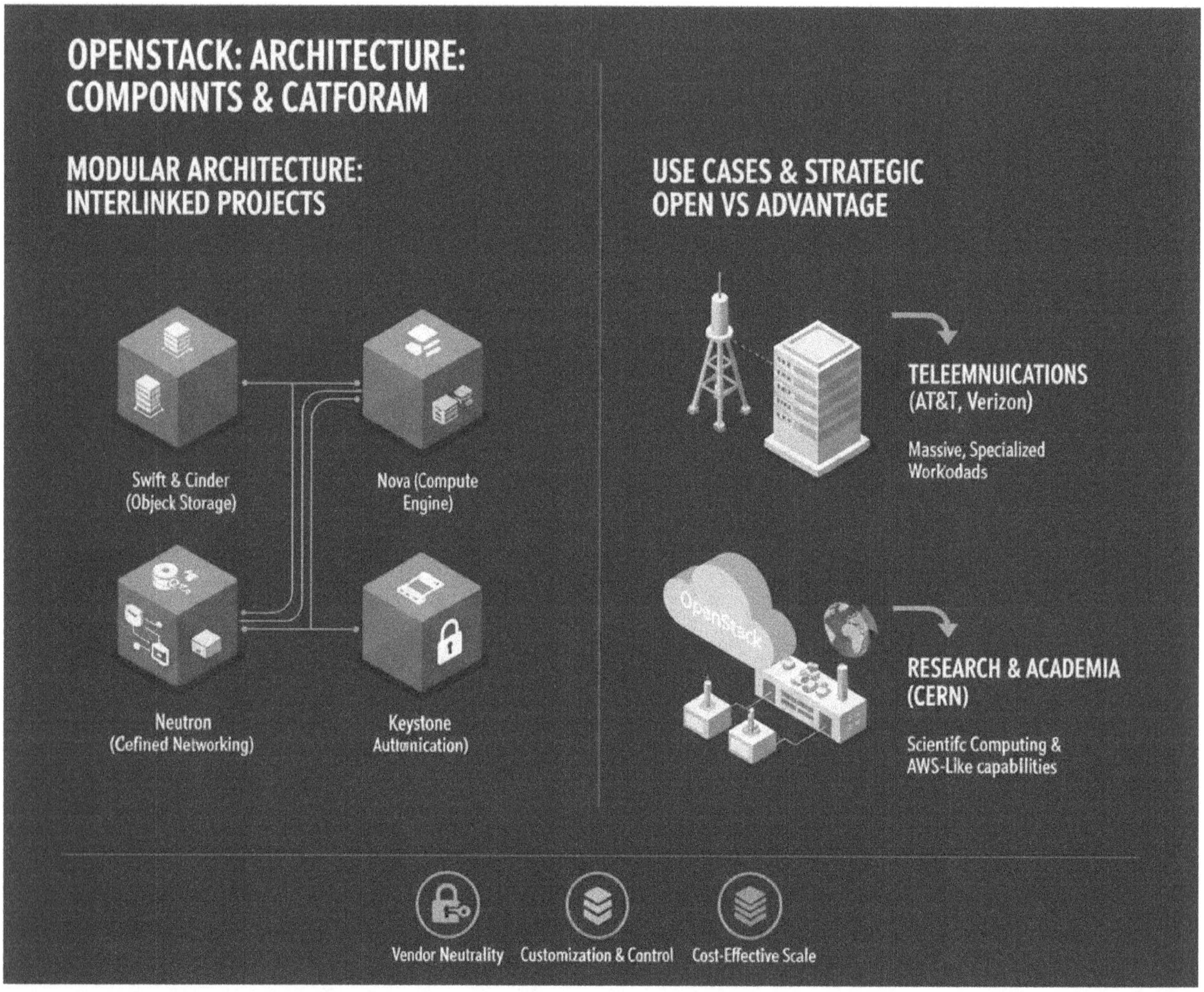

OpenStack is not a single program but a collection of interlinked projects:

- **Nova**: The compute engine (managing VMs).
- **Swift and Crate**: Object and Block storage.
- **Neutron**: Software-defined networking.
- **Keystone**: Identity and authentication.

OpenStack allows organizations to build "AWS-like" capabilities within their own data centers. It is widely used by telecommunications companies (like AT&T and Verizon) and research organizations (like CERN) to manage massive, specialized workloads without being tied to a single commercial vendor.

6. The Symbiosis of AI and Cloud Platforms

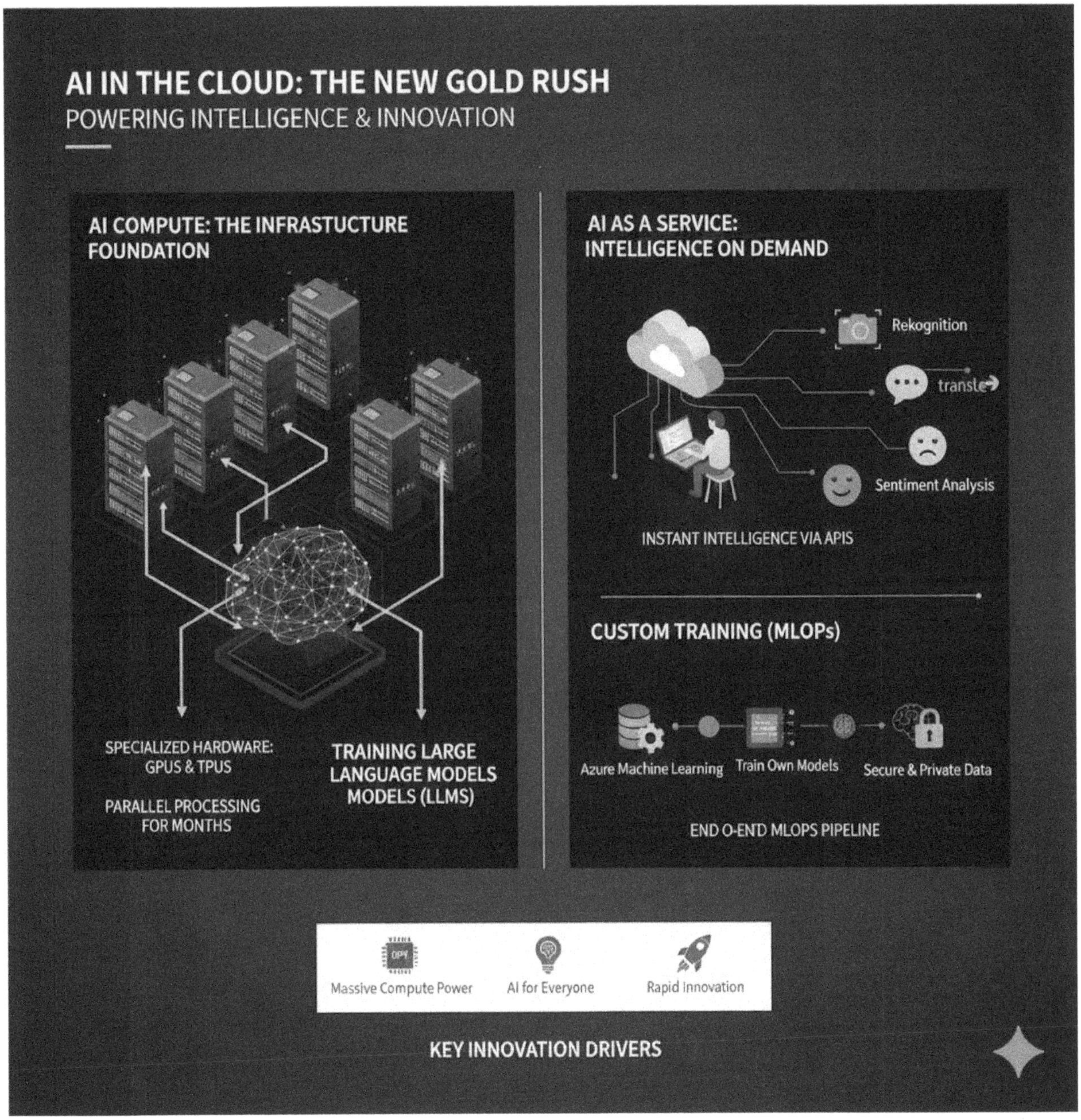

The current "Gold Rush" in Artificial Intelligence (AI) is only possible because of cloud platforms. Training Large Language Models (LLMs) requires thousands of specialized GPUs (Graphics Processing Units) or TPUs (Tensor Processing Units) working in parallel for months.

The Big Three have moved beyond providing raw GPUs to offering "AI as a Service."

- **Pre-trained Models**: Developers can use APIs to access Google's "Vertex AI" or AWS's "Rekognition" to add image recognition, translation, or sentiment analysis to their apps without knowing anything about neural networks.
- **Custom Training**: Platforms like **Azure Machine Learning** provide the entire "M LOps" (Machine Learning Operations) pipeline, allowing companies to train their own models on their own private data securely.

7. Comparative Analysis: Choosing Your Platform

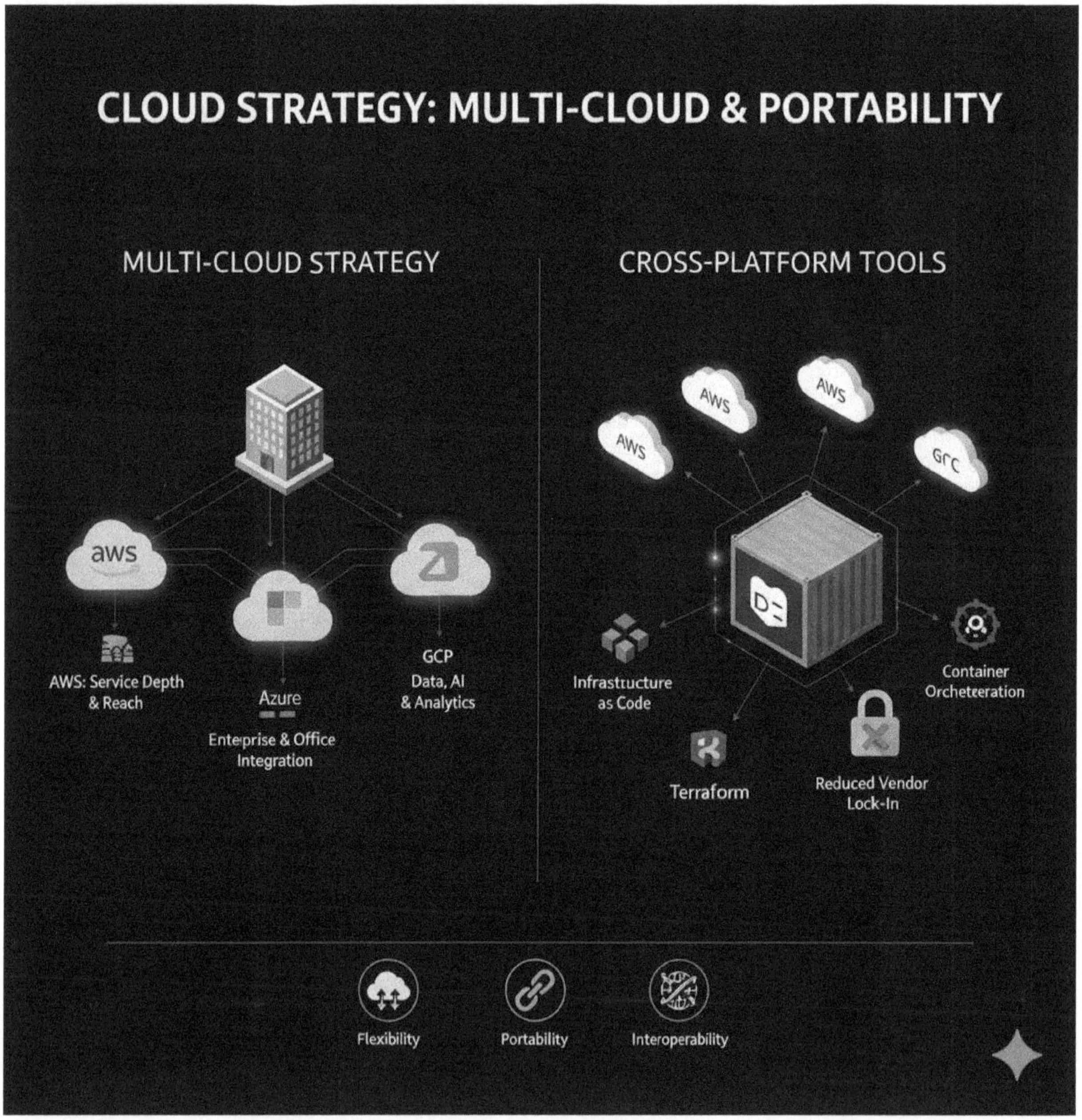

The decision to choose a platform is often a mix of technical requirement and business strategy:

- **Multi-Cloud Strategy**: Many large enterprises use a mix of platforms—AWS for its massive service depth, Azure for its Office integration, and GCP for its specialized AI and data analytics.
- **The Rise of Cross-Platform Tools**: Technologies like **Terraform** (for infrastructure as code) and **Docker/Kubernetes** (for containerization) allow organizations to move between platforms more easily, reducing the risk of vendor lock-in that plagued the early cloud era.

8. Summary: The Platform as the New Computer

Chapter 7 has explored the massive, complex platforms that have turned the "Cloud" from a theory into a reality. We have seen how AWS, Azure, and GCP have specialized into distinct roles, how Google AppEngine paved the way for serverless computing, and how the open-source Hadoop ecosystem democratized Big Data.

The "Platform" is now the computer. When we write code today, we aren't writing for a specific CPU or a specific OS; we are writing for the Cloud Platform. As we move into **Chapter 8: Cloud Security, Privacy, and Trust**, we will examine the immense challenges of keeping this global, multi-platform ecosystem safe. The cloud has given us infinite power, but it has also created a new world of risk that requires a fundamental rethinking of security in the digital age.

Chapter – 8

The Road Ahead: Challenges and Opportunities

The concluding chapter addresses the frontiers of the cloud. It covers Zero Trust security, the legal complexities of Data Sovereignty, and the emerging technologies of Serverless, Edge Computing, and Quantum Cloud.

1. Introduction: The Double-Edged Sword of Cloud Dominance

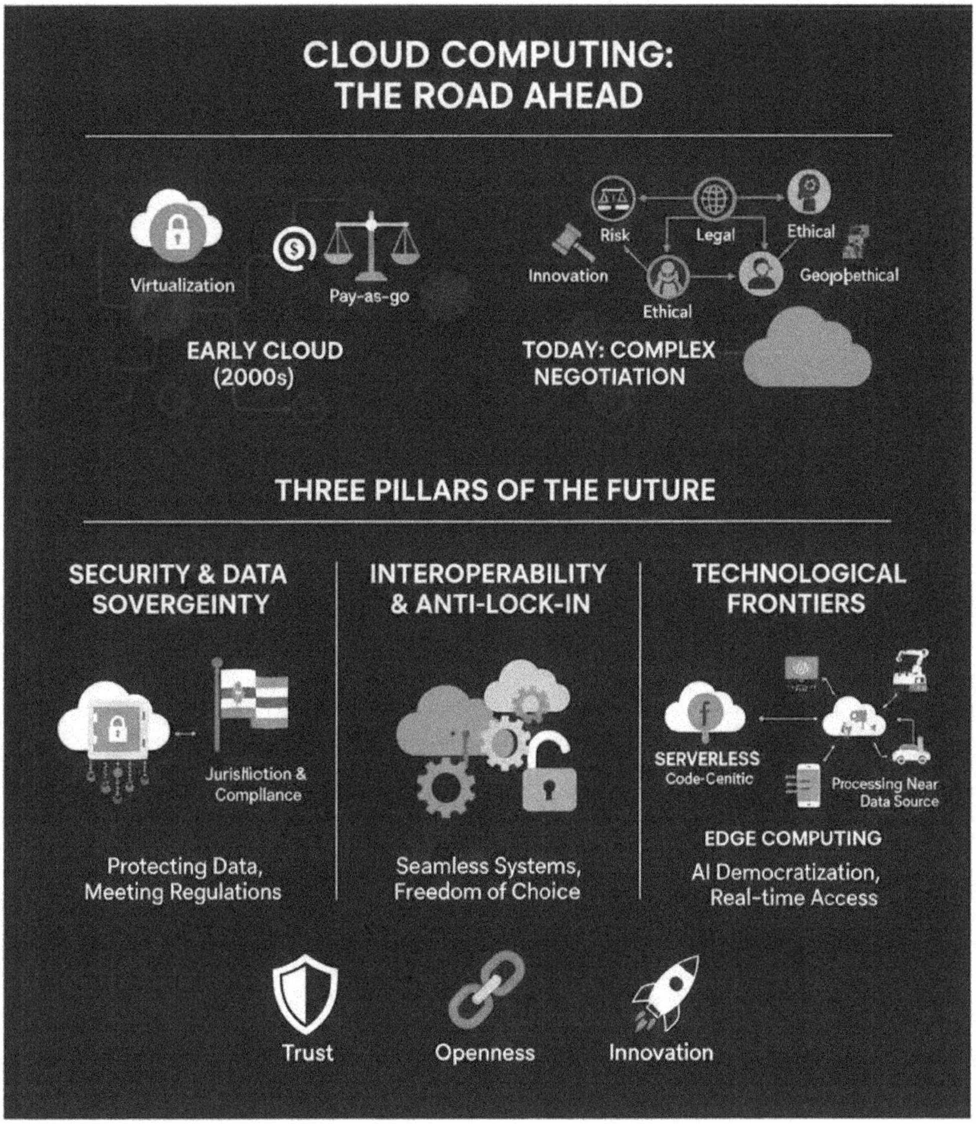

As cloud computing transitions from an emerging paradigm to the default operating system of the global economy, the focus of industry leaders and researchers has shifted. In the early days, the conversation was dominated by the technical feasibility of virtualization and the economic allure of the "Pay-as-you-go" model. Today, as massive proportions of human knowledge, financial transactions, and critical infrastructure reside in the cloud, the dialogue has matured into a complex negotiation between innovation and risk.

The "Road Ahead" is paved with both immense opportunities—such as the democratization of Artificial Intelligence and the rise of Edge Computing—and existential challenges. These challenges are no longer just technical; they are legal, ethical, and geopolitical. This chapter provides a 5000-word exhaustive analysis of the three pillars of the cloud's future: Security and

Data Sovereignty, Interoperability and the war against Vendor Lock-in, and the technological frontiers of Serverless and Edge computing.

2. Security, Privacy, and the Battle for Data Sovereignty

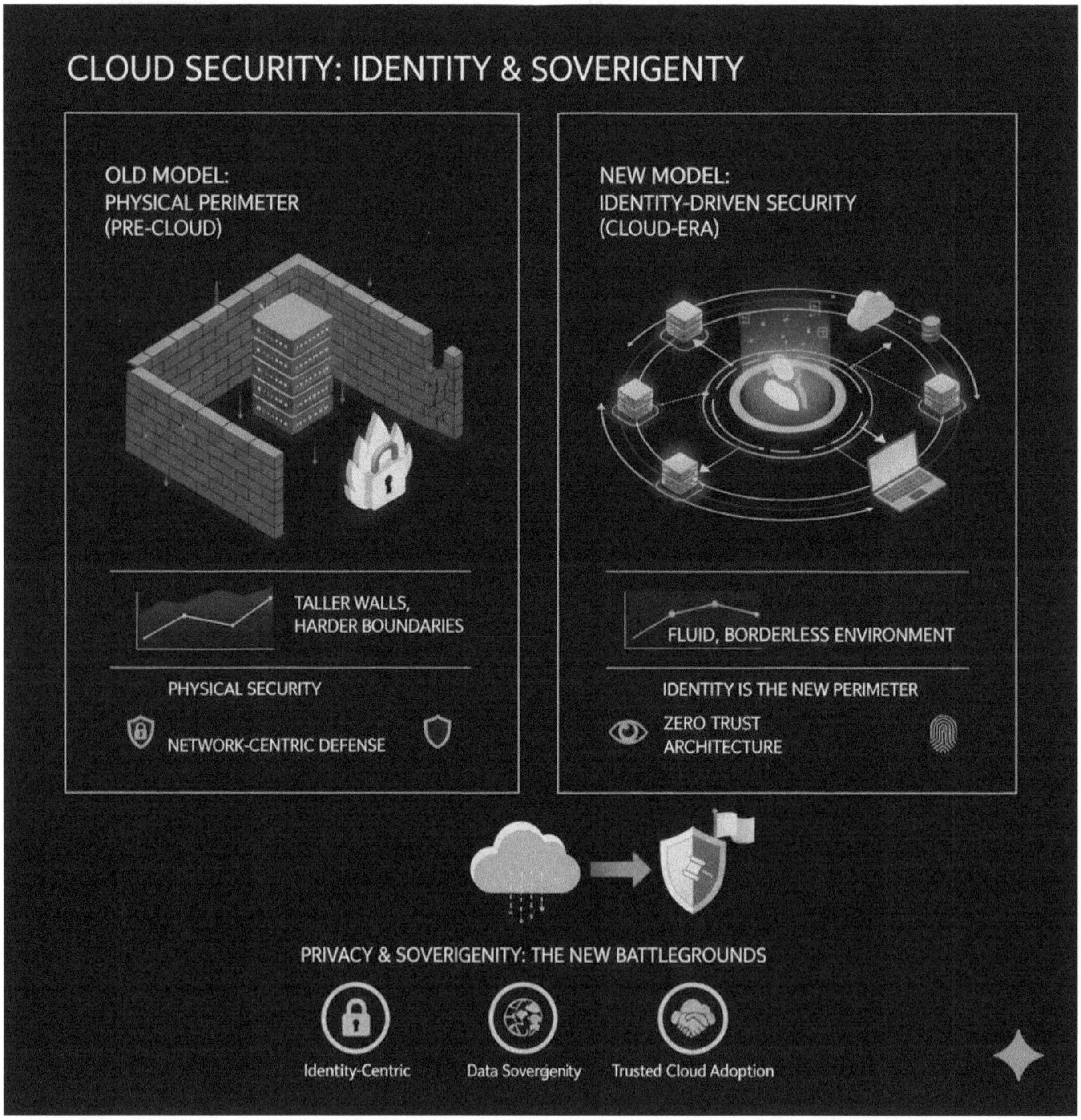

In the cloud, security is no longer about building a taller wall around a physical server; it is about managing a fluid, borderless environment where identity is the new perimeter. As we entrust more of our digital lives to third-party providers, the concepts of privacy and sovereignty have become the primary battlegrounds for cloud adoption.

2.1 The Zero Trust Architecture

The traditional "Castle and Moat" security model—where everything inside the corporate network is trusted and everything outside is suspicious—is dead. In its place, the cloud has birthed the **Zero Trust Architecture (ZTA)**. The fundamental tenet of Zero Trust is "Never Trust, Always Verify."

In a cloud-native world, every request for access to a resource (whether it is a database, an API, or a file) must be authenticated, authorized, and encrypted, regardless of where the request originates. This is achieved through **Identity and Access Management (IAM)**. Modern IAM systems use "Least Privilege" principles, ensuring that a user or service has only the absolute minimum access required to perform its task. The future of cloud security lies in the automation of these policies, using Machine Learning to detect anomalous behavior—such as a user logging in from a new country and immediately trying to download a terabyte of data—and automatically revoking access in real-time.

2.2 Data Sovereignty and the Geopolitics of the Cloud

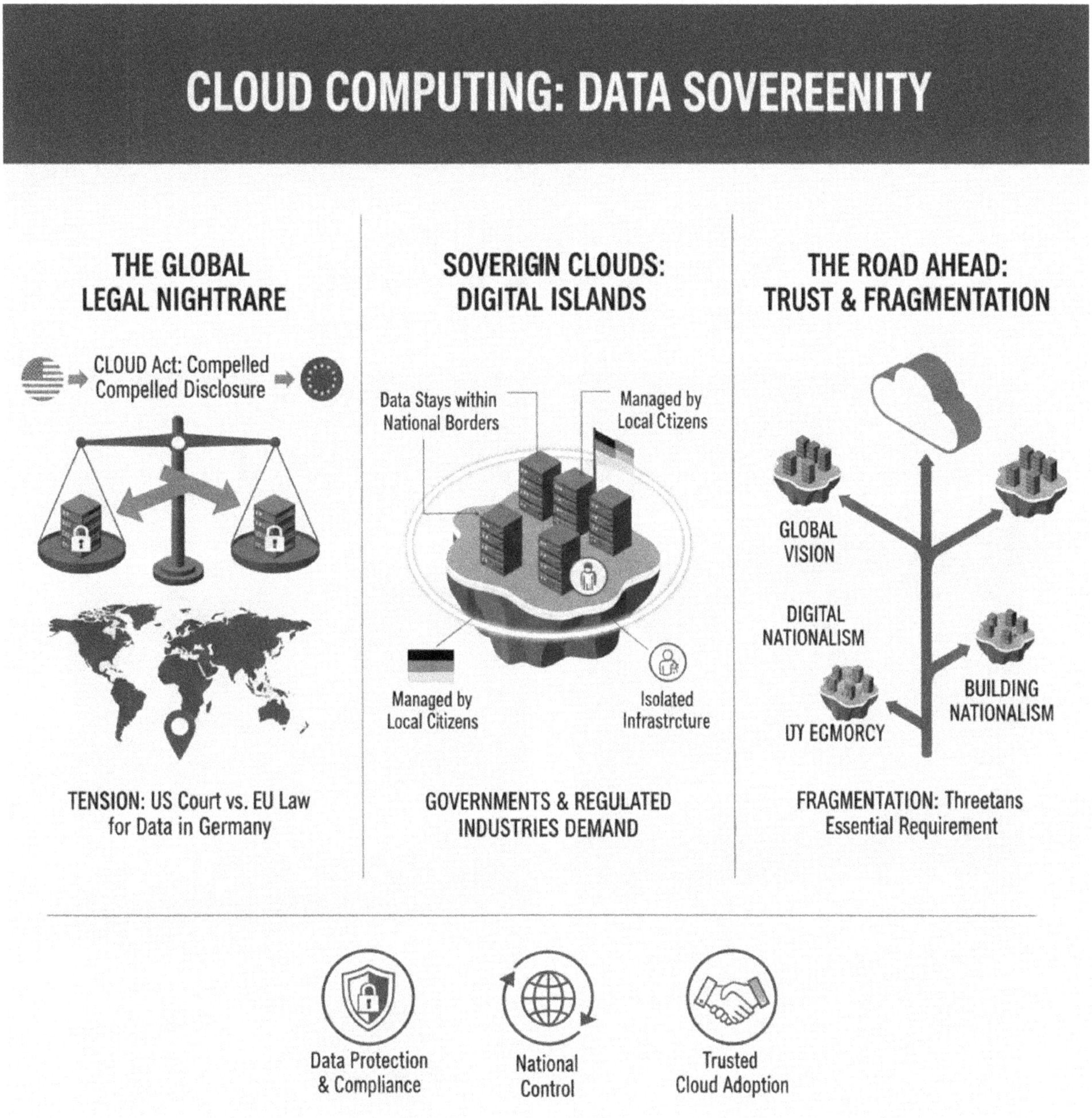

Perhaps the most complex challenge facing the cloud is **Data Sovereignty**—the concept that data is subject to the laws and governance structures of the nation where it is physically located. For a global cloud provider, this is a legal nightmare.

Consider the "Cloud Act" in the United States versus the "GDPR" (General Data Protection Regulation) in Europe. A provider might be legally compelled by a U.S. court to hand over data stored in a German data center, while simultaneously being prohibited by EU law from doing so. This tension has led to the rise of **Sovereign Clouds**. Governments and highly regulated industries are now demanding that cloud providers build isolated "Digital Islands" where data stays within national borders and is managed by local citizens. This fragmentation threatens the "Global Cloud" vision but is an essential requirement for building trust in an age of digital nationalism.

2.3 Confidential Computing: The Final Frontier of Privacy

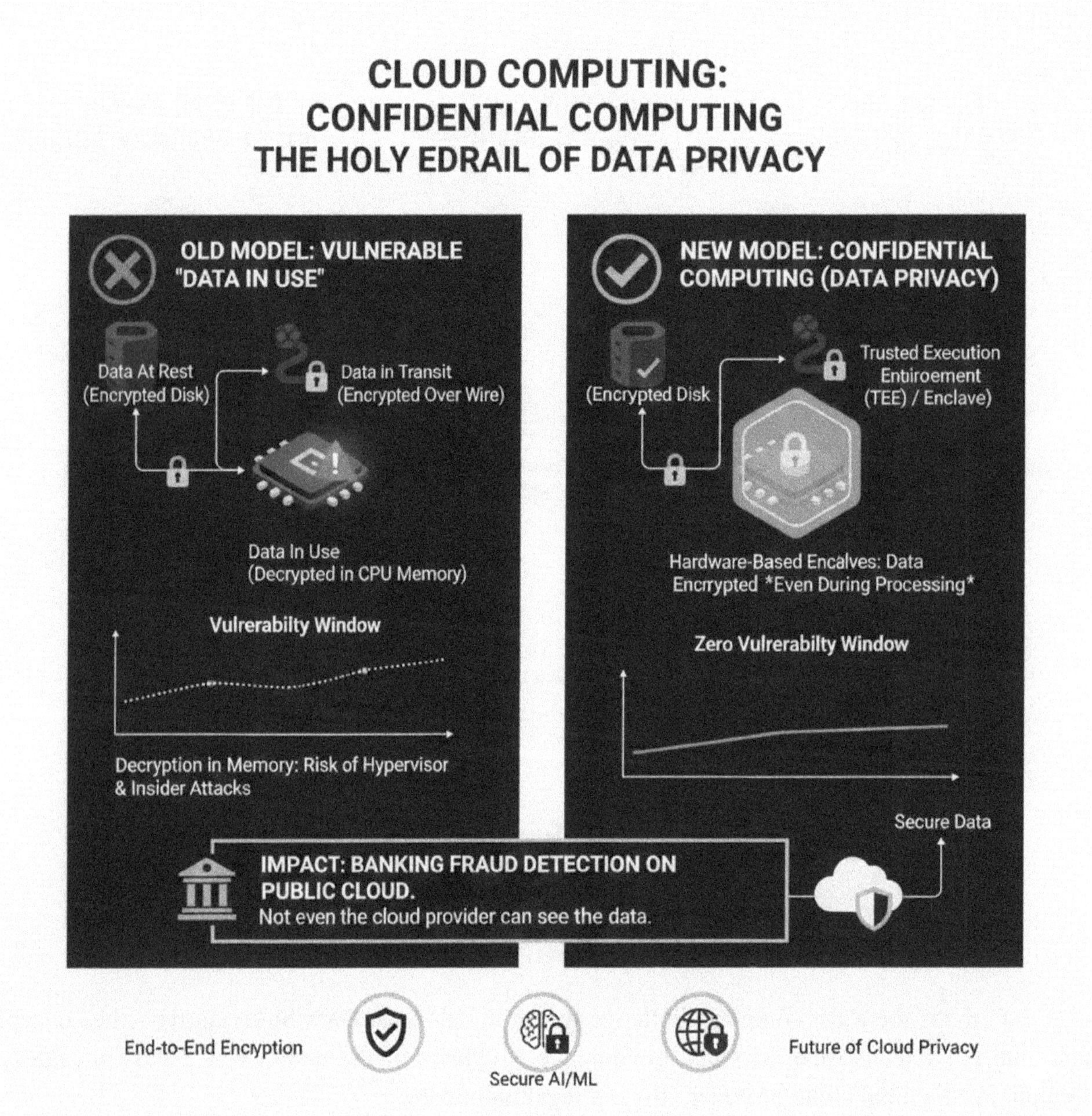

Until recently, data in the cloud was only protected "at rest" (encrypted on the disk) and "in transit" (encrypted while moving over the wire). However, to process data, it had to be decrypted in the CPU's memory, leaving it vulnerable to hypervisor attacks or malicious insiders.

Confidential Computing is the solution to this "data in use" problem. It uses hardware-based **Trusted Execution Environments (TEEs)**—often called enclaves—to encrypt data even while it is being processed by the processor. This allows a bank, for example, to run its most sensitive fraud-detection algorithms on a public cloud with the mathematical certainty that not even the cloud provider's employees can see the data. This technology is the "Holy Grail" of cloud privacy and will be the key to moving the world's most sensitive workloads (defense, healthcare, and high finance) into the public cloud.

3. Interoperability and the War Against Vendor Lock-in

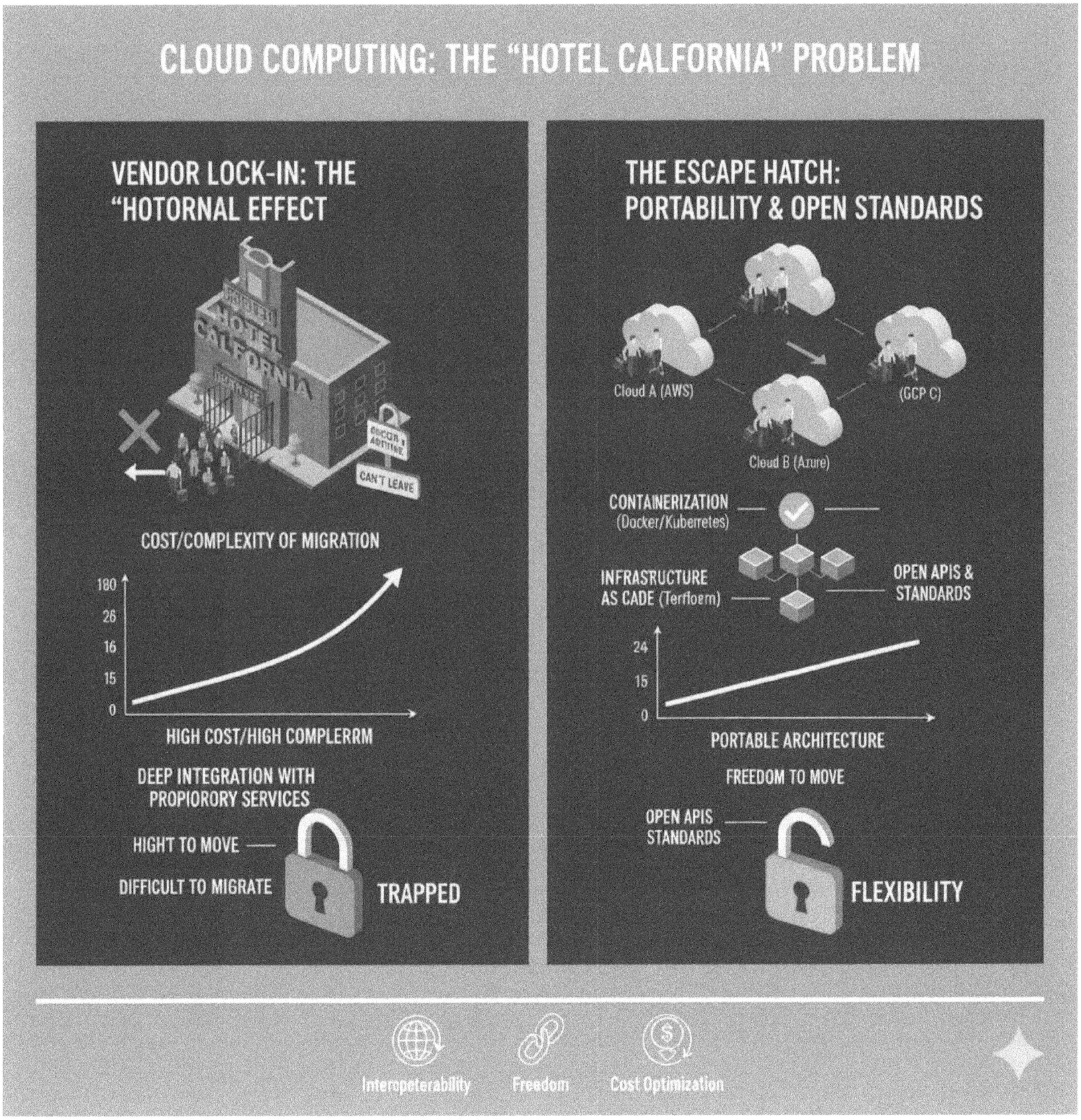

As organizations move deeper into the cloud, they face the "Hotel California" problem: they can check in any time they like, but they can never leave. **Vendor Lock-in** occurs when the cost or technical complexity of moving an application from one provider (e.g., AWS) to another (e.g., Azure) is so high that the organization is effectively trapped.

3.1 The Architecture of Lock-in

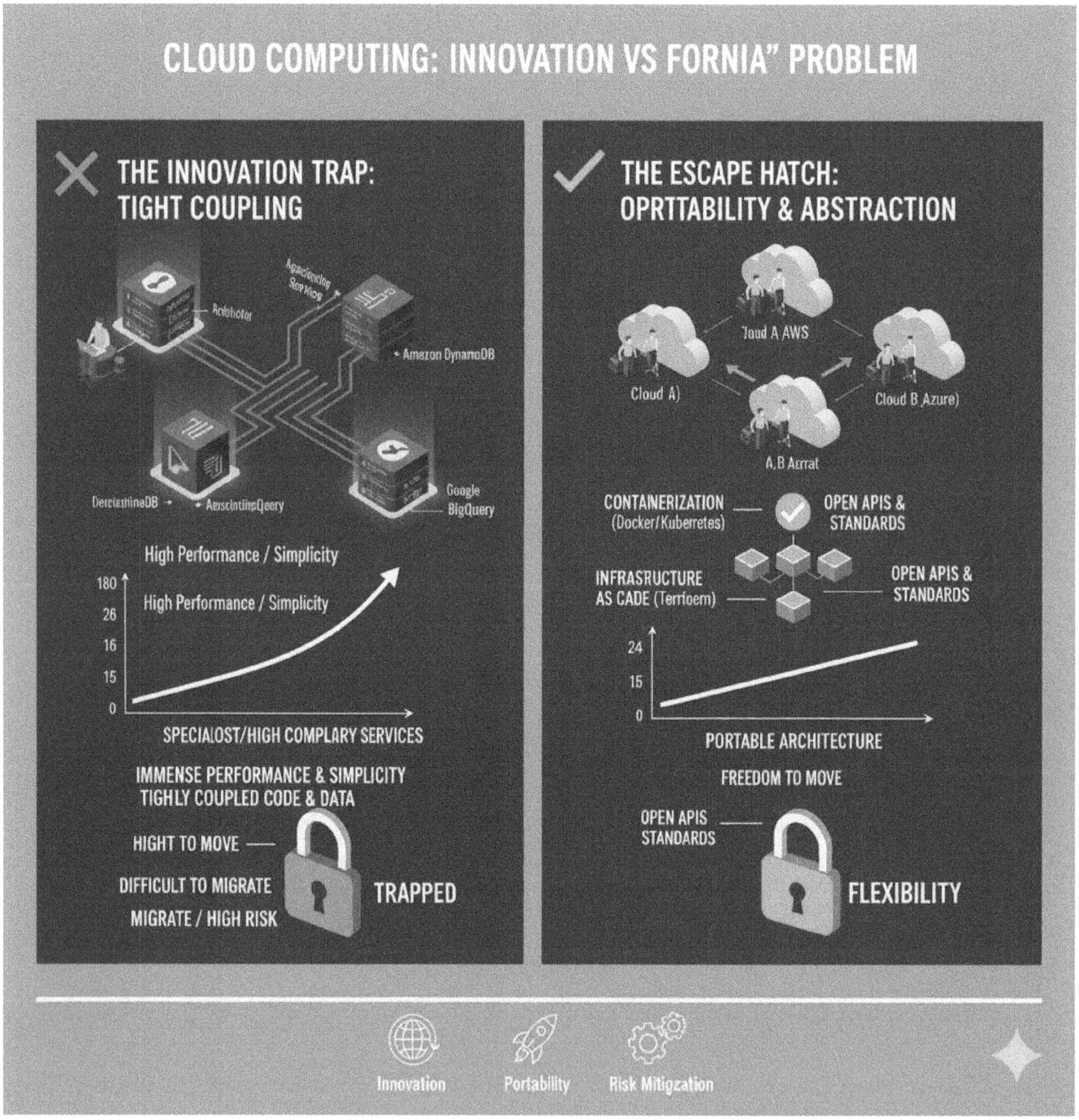

Lock-in is rarely a result of a malicious "trap"; rather, it is a byproduct of innovation. When a developer uses a highly specialized, proprietary service like Amazon DynamoDB or Google BigQuery, they are gaining immense performance and simplicity. However, their application's code becomes tightly coupled to that specific provider's API. If the provider raises prices or suffers a major outage, the customer cannot easily move.

3.2 Interoperability and the "Open Cloud" Movement

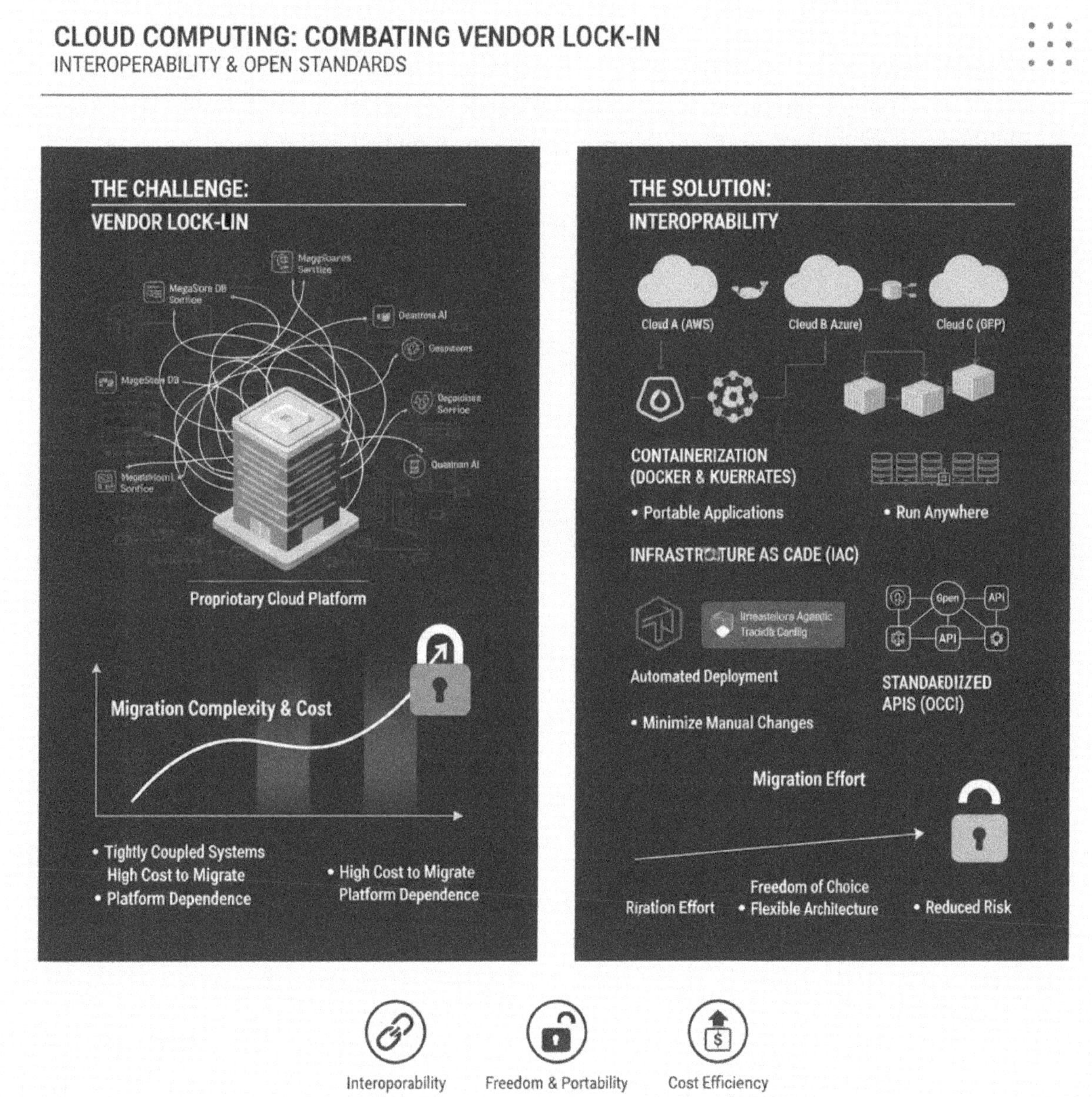

To combat lock-in, the industry is moving toward **Interoperability** through the use of open standards and abstraction layers.

- **Containerization (Docker & Kubernetes)**: This is the most significant weapon against lock-in. By packaging an application into a container, it becomes portable. A Kubernetes cluster looks the same whether it is running on a laptop, a private data center, or any of the Big Three clouds.
- **Infrastructure as Code (IaC)**: Tools like **Terraform** allow architects to define their infrastructure in a provider-agnostic language. This makes it possible to "re-deploy" an entire data center onto a different provider with minimal manual changes.
- **Standardized APIs**: Initiatives like the "Open Cloud Computing Interface" (OCCI) aim to create a common language for managing cloud resources, though adoption remains a challenge as providers continue to differentiate through proprietary features.

3.3 The Multi-Cloud and Poly-Cloud Reality

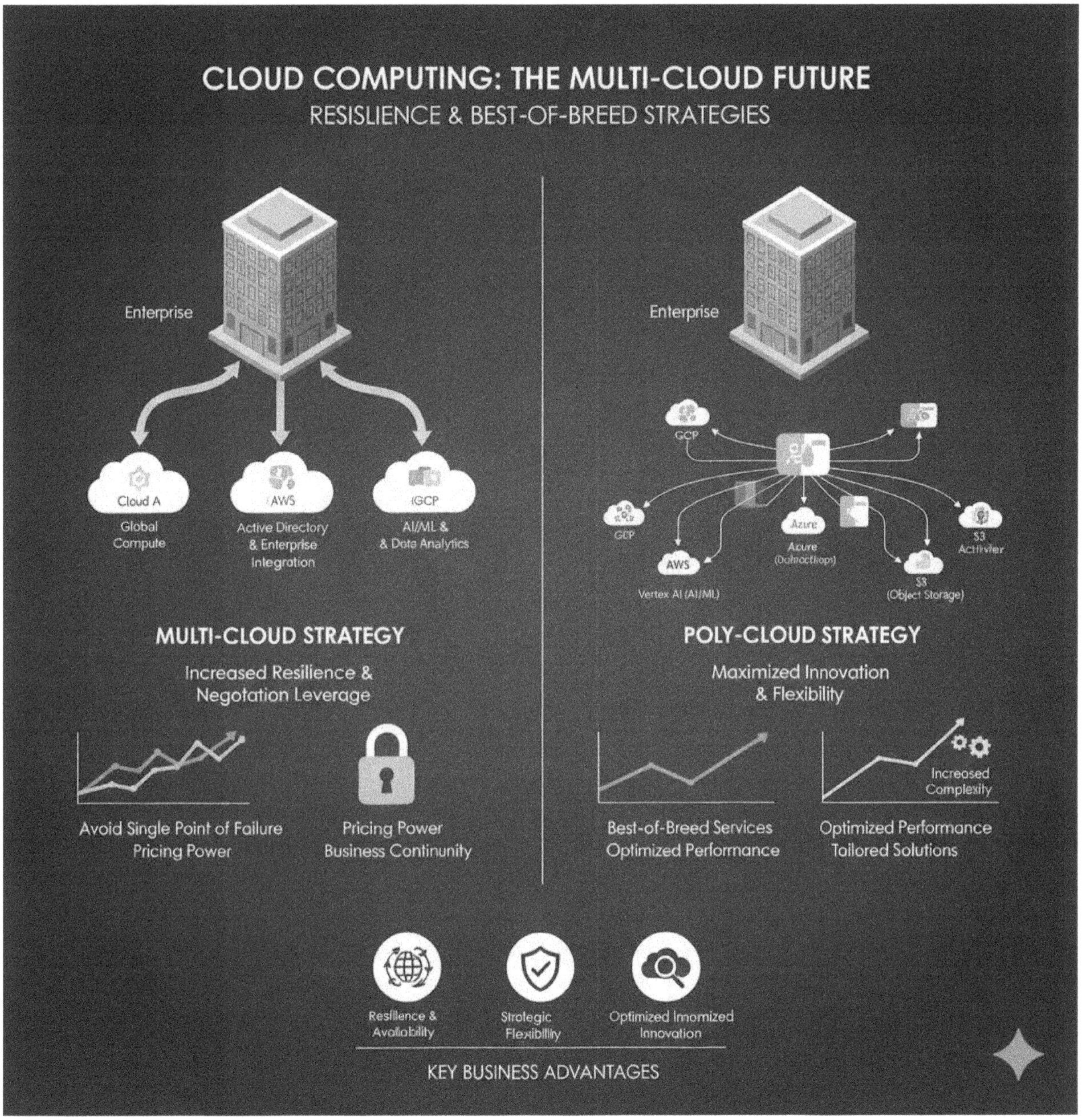

The future is not a single cloud, but a **Multi-Cloud** environment. Large enterprises are increasingly spreading their workloads across multiple providers to avoid a "Single Point of Failure" and to gain leverage during price negotiations. Some organizations are even adopting a **"Poly-Cloud"** strategy, where they pick the "Best of Breed" services from each provider—using GCP for AI, Azure for Active Directory, and AWS for global compute. While this increases complexity, it provides the ultimate level of resilience and flexibility.

4. The Future of Cloud: Serverless, Edge Computing, and Beyond

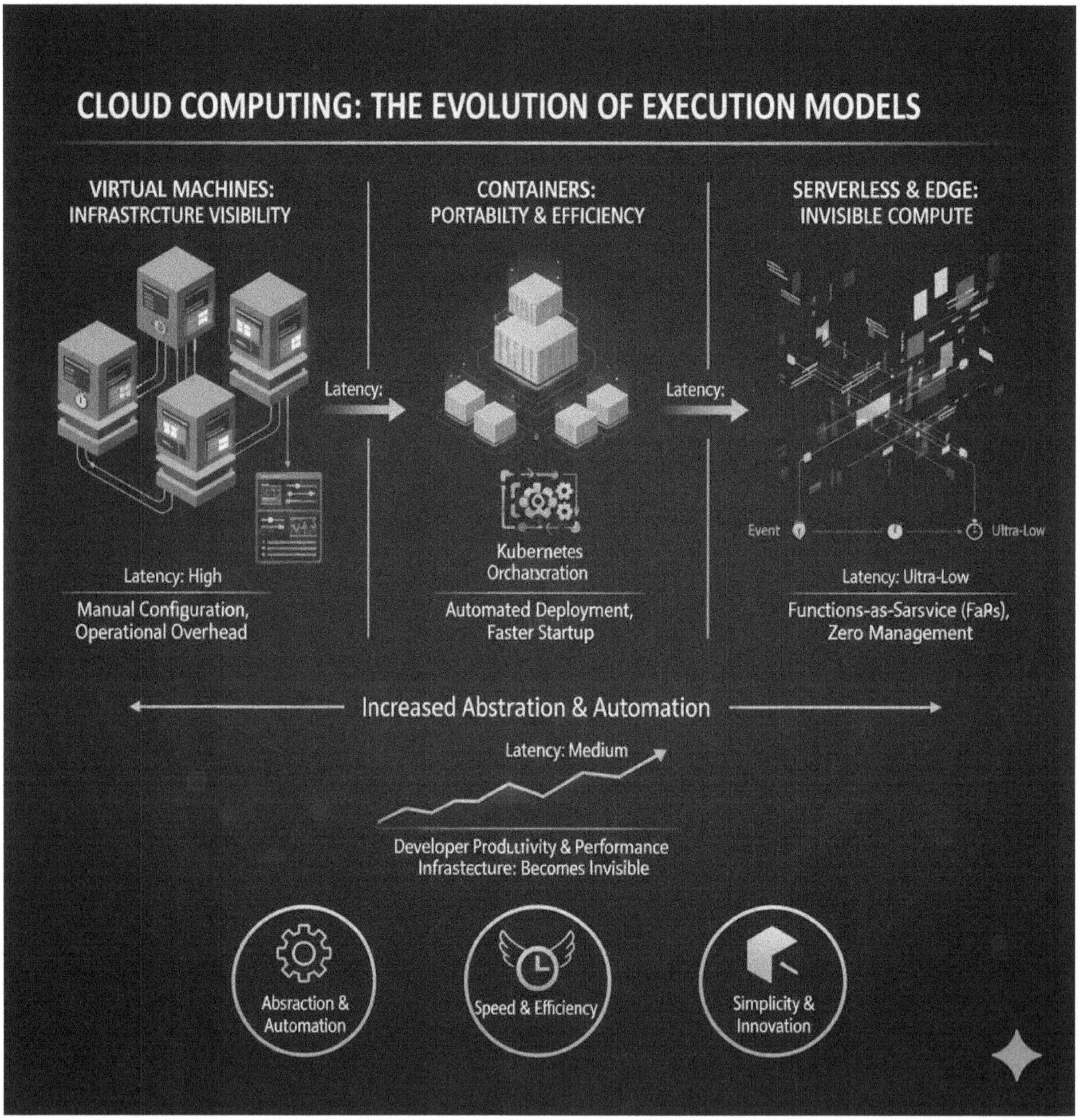

The cloud is moving away from the "Virtual Machine" and toward more granular, invisible forms of computing. This evolution is driven by the need for lower latency and the desire for "Zero Management."

4.1 Serverless Computing: The End of Infrastructure

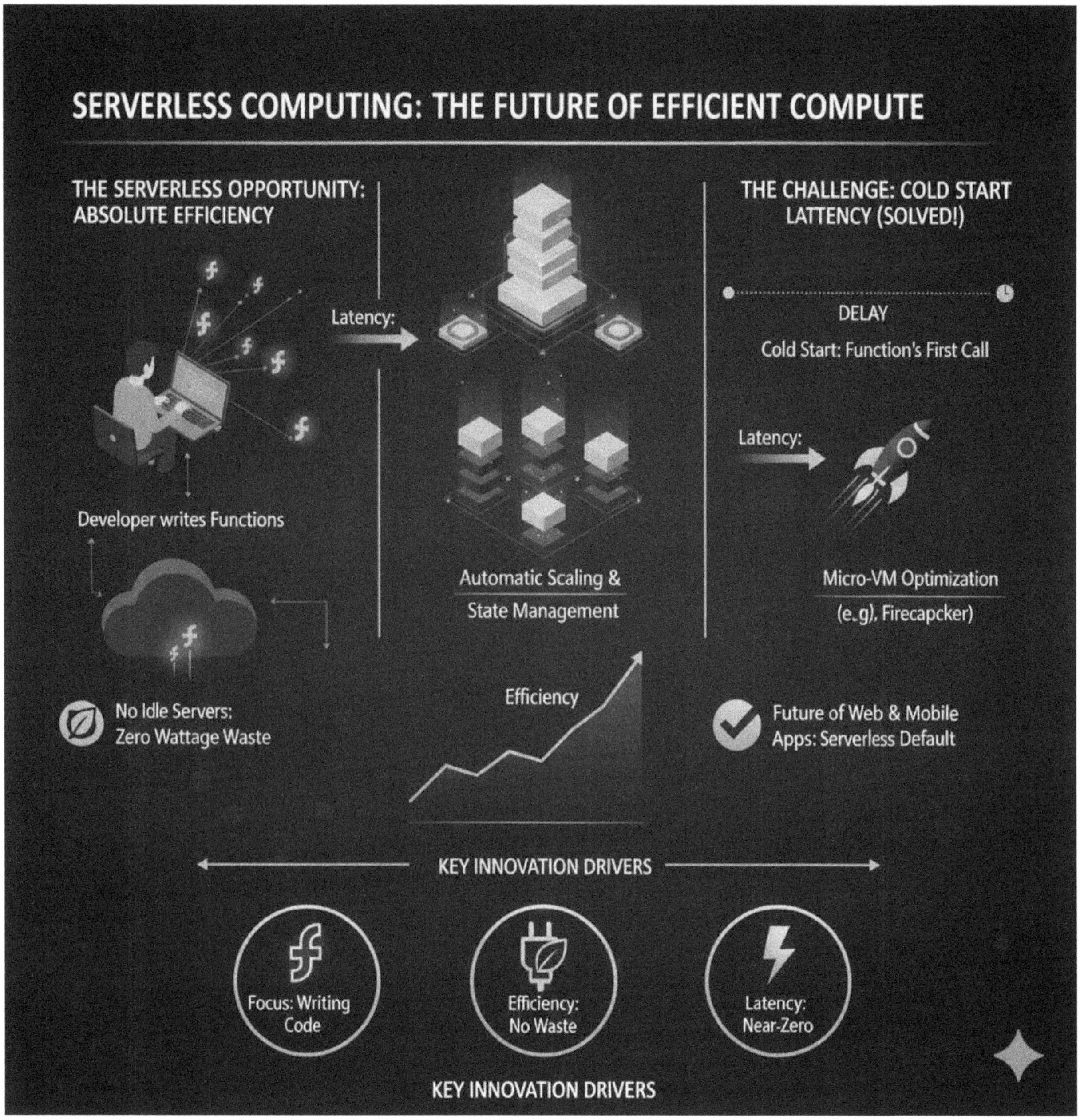

As discussed in Chapter 5, **Serverless (or FaaS)** is the logical conclusion of the cloud's abstraction journey. In the future, developers will not "provision" anything. They will simply write functions. The cloud will handle the "Cold Starts," the scaling, and the state management.

The opportunity of serverless is **Absolute Efficiency**. In a world concerned with the environmental impact of data centers, serverless ensures that not a single watt of electricity is wasted on an idle server. However, the challenge remains the "Cold Start" latency—the delay when a function is called for the first time in a while. As providers optimize their micro-VM technologies (like AWS

Firecracker), this latency is disappearing, paving the way for serverless to become the default for all web and mobile applications.

4.2 Edge Computing: Bringing the Cloud to the User

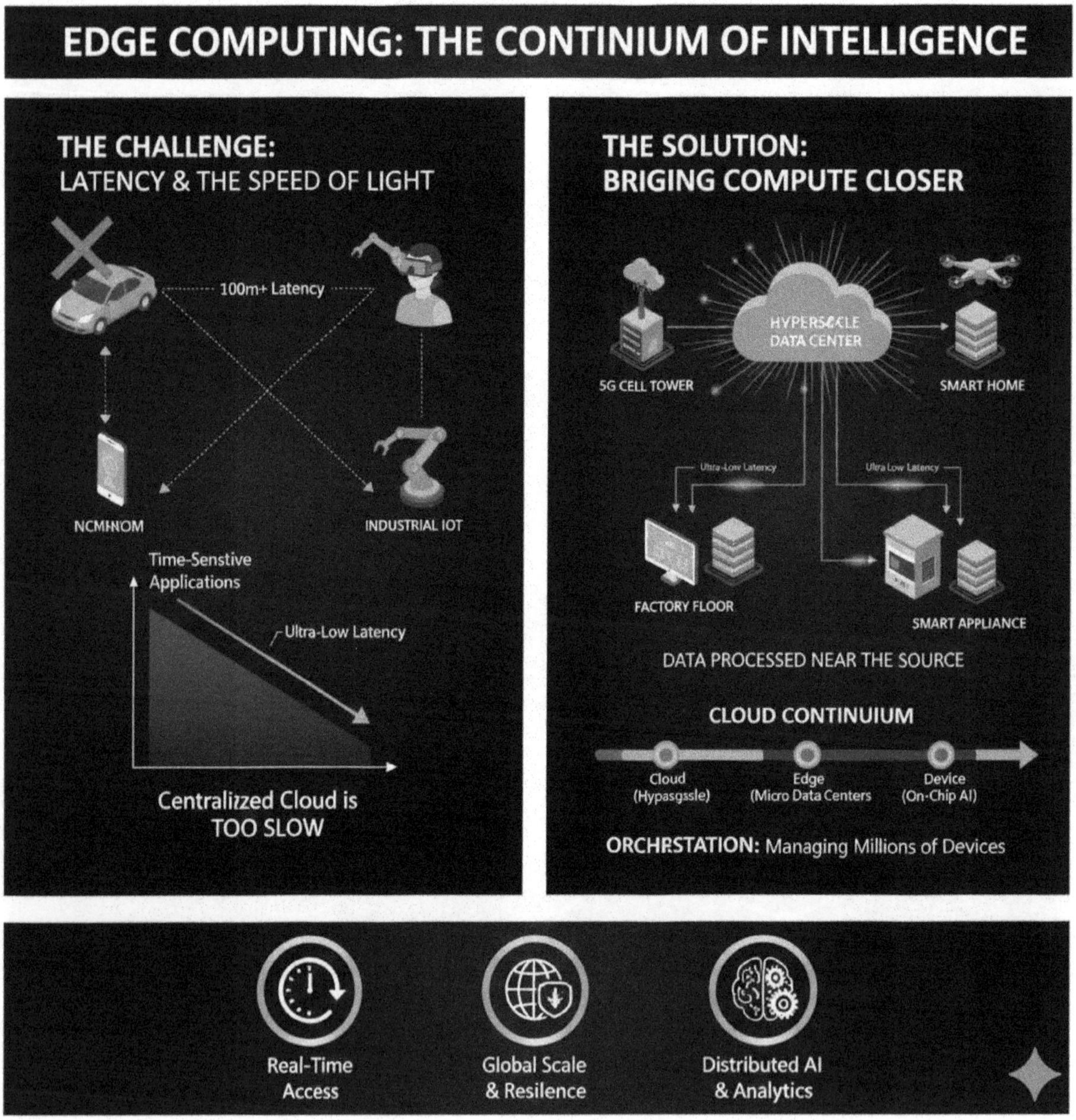

While the "Centralized Cloud" is efficient, it is limited by the speed of light. For applications like self-driving cars, remote robotic surgery, or augmented reality (AR), a 100-millisecond round-trip to a centralized data center is too slow.

Edge Computing solves this by moving the "Cloud" closer to the source of the data. This means placing small, powerful micro-data centers at the base of 5G cell towers, inside factory floors, or even within smart appliances. The "Future Cloud" will be a **Continuum**—a seamless web of compute power that ranges from the massive "Hyper-scale" data center in the middle to the "Edge" device in your pocket. The challenge here is **Orchestration**: how do you manage, secure, and update millions of disparate devices scattered across the globe as if they were a single system?

4.3 Quantum Computing in the Cloud

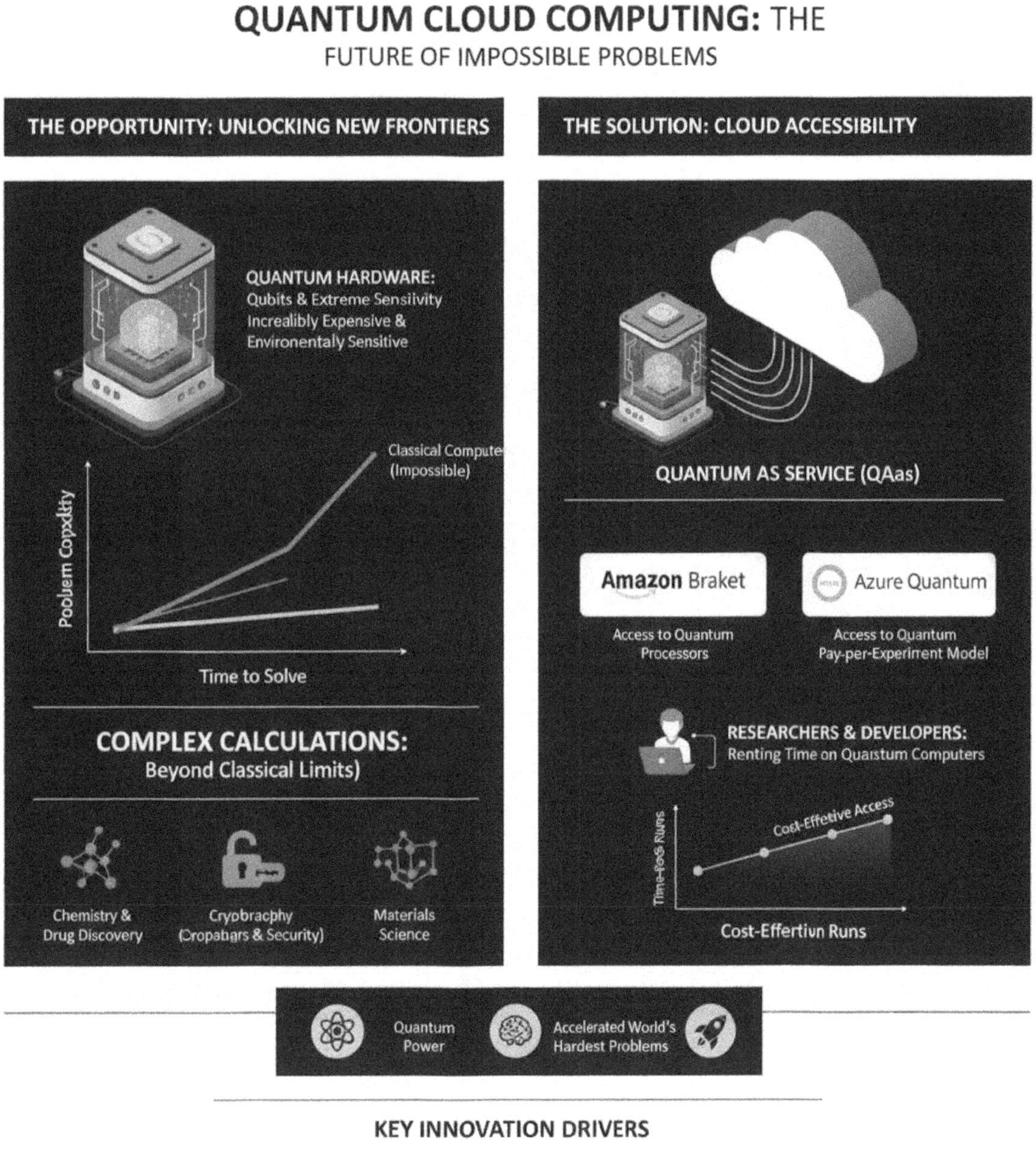

The most speculative but potentially transformative opportunity is **Quantum Cloud Computing**. Quantum computers, which use qubits to perform calculations that are impossible for classical computers, are incredibly expensive and sensitive to their environment. They will likely never be "personal" computers. Instead, they will be accessible as specialized resources in the cloud. We are already seeing the beginning of this with "Amazon Braket" and "Azure Quantum," where researchers can rent time on a quantum processor to solve complex problems in chemistry, cryptography, and materials science.

5. Sustainability and the "Green Cloud"

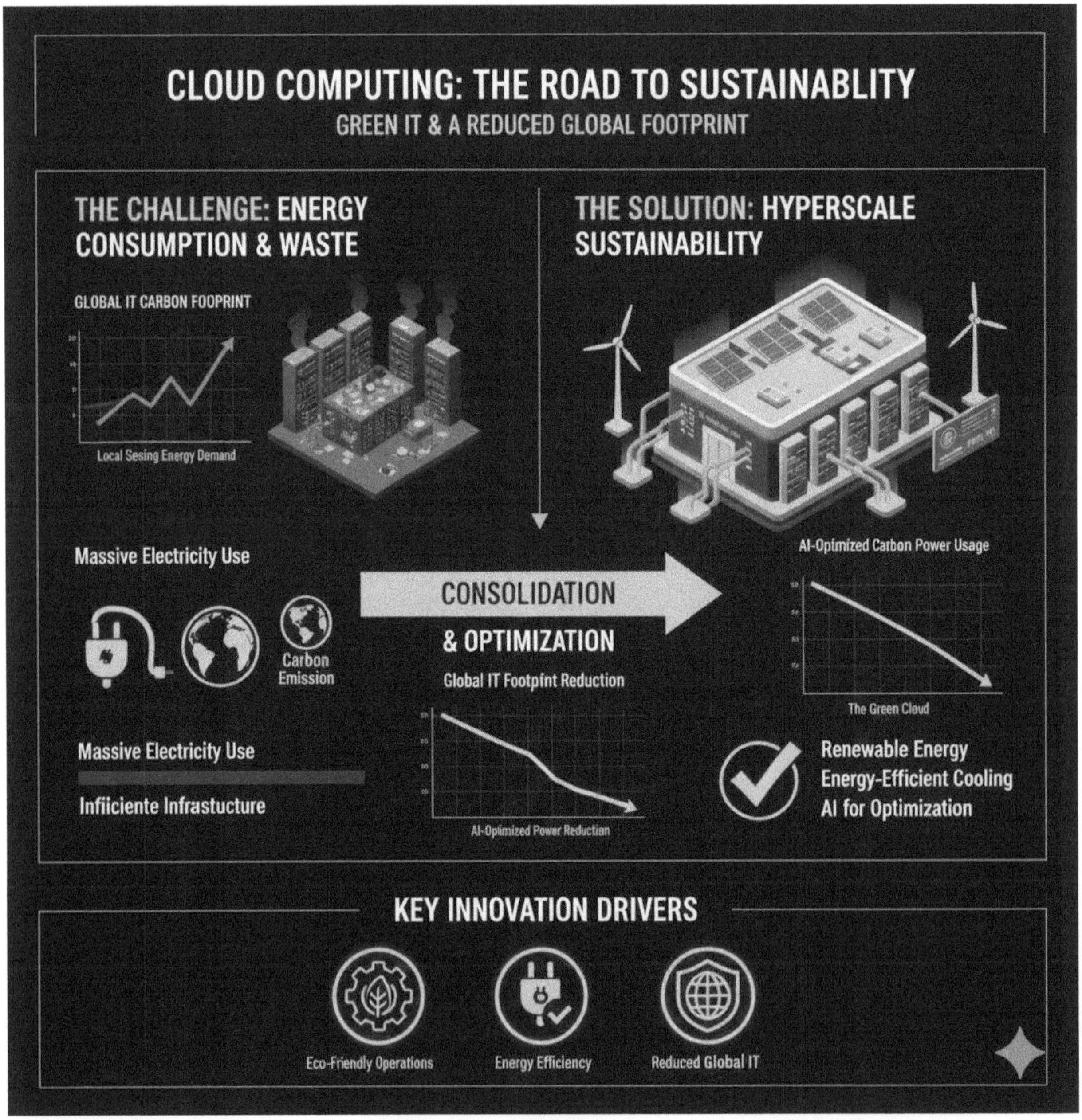

As the cloud consumes an ever-increasing percentage of the world's electricity, **Sustainability** has become a core challenge and a massive opportunity for innovation. The "Road Ahead" for the cloud is green.

Major providers are now competing not just on price, but on their "Carbon Footprint." They are investing billions in renewable energy, designing more efficient "Liquid Cooling" systems, and even using AI to optimize data center power usage in real-time. The cloud has the potential to be a major force for environmental good; by consolidating the world's messy, inefficient local servers into highly optimized "Hyper-scale" facilities, the global IT footprint can be significantly reduced.

6. Conclusion: The Invisible Utility

Over the course of these eight chapters, we have tracked the journey of the cloud from the early days of the mainframe and the theoretical breakthrough of the hypervisor to the global, multi-platform ecosystem of today. We have seen how the SPI model (Software, Platform, Infrastructure) has redefined the boundaries of responsibility, and how the "Big Three" have turned the world's data into a liquid resource.

The "Road Ahead" is one where the cloud becomes invisible. Just as we do not think about the power lines or the water pipes in our walls, the next generation of users will not think about "The Cloud." It will be the background radiation of our digital lives—omnipresent, elastic, and infinitely powerful.

However, this invisibility comes with a caveat. The challenges of security, sovereignty, and lock-in require constant vigilance. As the cloud becomes more integrated into the physical world through Edge computing and AI, the "Opportunities" for human progress are matched only by the "Challenges" of maintaining a safe, open, and equitable digital society. The cloud is no longer a technology; it is the infrastructure of modern civilization, and the road ahead is ours to build.

www.ingramcontent.com/pod-product-compliance
Ingram Content Group UK Ltd.
Pitfield, Milton Keynes, MK11 3LW, UK
UKHW061541190726
13845UKWH00031B/1153

9 789355 252890